Dalits, Tribals and Human Rights

Savita Bhatt

ADHYAYAN

ADHYAYAN PUBLISHERS & DISTRIBUTORS

NEW DELHI (INDIA)

Published by
ADHYAYAN PUBLISHERS & DISTRIBUTORS
4378/4B, 105, J.M.D. House, Murari Lal Street
Ansari Road, Darya Ganj, New Delhi - 110002
Ph.: 011-23263018, 011-23277156, Fax: 011-23280028
Email: adhyayanpublishers@yahoo.com

Dalits, Tribals and Human Rights

Edition 2011
ISBN 978-81-8435-293-1

Printed in India

Published by Harish Chandra Yadav for Adhyayan Publishers & Distributors, Laser Typeseting at A.V. Rao and Printed at Tarun Offset Printers, Delhi

Preface

Human rights is one crucial aspects being prominently discussed these days. It is more critically conversed in the wake of growing atrocities against the historically deprived groups like dalits and tribals. Although the practice of "untouchability" was abolished in 1950, it remains and is very much alive in India. The caste still operates as a defining condition in establishing marriages, social relations and access to employment, millions of Dalits and other former low-caste people remain behind in education, employment and access to wealth. Caste-based discrimination is widely practiced, and statistics draws the logical conclusion that there is a broad correlation between one's economic state and one's position within the caste hierarchy.

The government may boast of economic progress and grand new development schemes, such as highways joining major cities or plans to interlink major rivers, but it has failed to address issues like education, caste and gender discrimination and the rural-urban gap. The result is continued upper-caste dominance in professions, business, and culture. Dalits continue to face the wrath of the caste lords and are denied of human dignity and their rights including a just share in the resources like land, water, mines, aqua resources, etc. The indigenous people continue to fight for their identity and dignity. Their right to a decent dignified life is under severe threat.

For the most part, the international community, particularly the general public residing outside of India, is unaware that untouchability and daily/routine forms of caste discrimination are still practised in India. However, in recent years an increasing number of human rights organisations and bodies are coming to recognise untouchability and caste discrimination as a gross human rights violation. Dalit human rights has become an international issue and organisations like Human Rights Watch, Amnesty International, Minority Rights Group and Anti-Slavery International are making Dalit Human Rights a priority issue and are concerned to raise the issue internationally in UN bodies, governments and the public-at-large.

This book covers the varied issues of human rights faced by dalits and tribals of India. It will prove useful for academics as well as for policy planners, administrators and social activists in the field.

Savita Bhatt

Contents

1

Introduction

The word "dalit" is understood to have one or more of the following meanings—means "burst, split, scattered, dispersed, broken, torn as under, destroyed, crushed". It is a word much preferred over "harijan", the term coined by Gandhi, which is viewed as condescending and having religious connotation. It has a political connotation which the legal term scheduled caste does not have. The widespread adaptation of the word dalit symbolizes the change in the ideology of the dalit movement—from a passive acceptance of amelioration handed out by others to a struggle carried on from within for empowerment—by fighting for their rights and against injustice. The movement emphasizes asserting a separate identity and inculcating pride in dalit cultural traditions.

Dalits are at the lowest rung in the caste hierarchy based on ritual purity and occupation, and outside the varna system, which gives them the traditional name panchamas. They have been oppressed throughout the recorded history of India, relegated to doing toiling and 'polluting' tasks like agricultural labour, disposing dead bodies, working with leather, cleaning toilets and sewage etc. They have been stripped of their dignity and denied basic human rights. They were "untouchaes" —others would be polluted by their touch, even by their shadows. To avoid such "pollution" dalits were segregated and denied access to many other community facilities—schools, temples, water tanks, etc. To this day thousands of villages have a separate area for dalit houses (including houses built for them by the government), separate wells for dalits, class rooms where dalit children sit separately, tea shops with separate glasses for dalits. Such discrimination occurs despite laws against such practices.

Centuries of such oppression has resulted in severe poverty and its associated problems amongst dalits. The statistics are illuminating—an illiterate person is far more likely to be a dalit than a non-dalit (the literacy gap between dalits and non-dalits is 14.8% and growing, even though the literacy rate of dalit in absolute terms has increased), a poor person is more likely to be a dalit than a non-dalit. Today they majority of dalits work as farm labourers, leather workers, sewage cleaners and their struggle to get out of the cycle of poverty continues, in spite of reservation of jobs in the public sector and seats in educational institutions.

There are several safeguards in the Indian constitution and laws enacted in the parliament including the SC and ST Prevention of Atrocities Act. But these legal safeguards have not proved very effective in eradicating the oppression of dalits within the caste system. According to a recent report, of the 1.47 lakh cases to date under this Act, only 1.14% have resulted in convictions (19.90% resulted in acquittals the rest are pending due to speedy Indian justice system!). The power structure of law-enforcement agencies and the prejudice of the general public make it almost impossible for dalits to get legal redress from discrimination and violence. The laws against injustice are necessary but are not sufficient. For the real redress the existing power structure must be dismantled.

Status of Dalits in India

To this day, most Indians still believe, and this includes a majority of Dalits, that Dalits are being punished by God for sins in a previous life. Under the religious codes of Hinduism, a Dalits only hope is to be a good servant of the high castes and upon death and rebirth they will be reincarnated a high caste. The original Aryans who imposed Hinduism on India beginning some 3,500 years ago The Dalit status has often been historically associated with occupations regarded as ritually impure, such as any involving leatherwork, butchering, or removal of rubbish, animal carcasses, and waste. Dalits work as manual labourers cleaning streets, latrines, and sewers engaging in these activities were considered to be polluting to the individual, and this pollution was considered contagious. As a result, Dalits were commonly segregated, and banned from full participation in Hindu social life. For example, they could not enter a temple or a school, and were required to stay outside the village.

Discrimination against Dalits still exists in rural areas in the private sphere, in everyday matters such as access to eating places, schools, temples and water sources. It has largely disappeared in urban areas and in the public sphere. Some Dalits have successfully integrated into urban Indian society, where caste origins are less obvious and less important in public life. In rural India, however, caste origins are more readily apparent and Dalits often remain excluded from local religious life, though some qualitative evidence suggests that its severity is fast diminishing.

The term Dalit means 'oppressed', 'broken' or 'crushed' to the extent of losing original identity. The word "Dalit" comes from the Marathi language, and means "ground", "suppressed", "crushed", or "broken to pieces However, this name has been adopted by the people otherwise referred to as Harijans, untouchables, and has come to symbolize for them a movement for change and for the eradication of the centuries-old oppression under the caste system. In legal and constitutional terms, Dalits are known in India as scheduled castes. The constitution requires the government to define a list or schedule of the lowest castes in need of compensatory programmes. These scheduled castes include untouchable converts to Sikhism but exclude converts to Christianity and Buddhism; the groups that are excluded and continue to be treated as untouchables probably constitute another 2 per cent of the population.

During the struggle for Indian independence two different approaches emerged for the improvement of the situation of the people now known as Dalits. The first was led by Mahatma Gandhi, who believed in raising the status of Dalit people (or, as he preferred to call them, Harijans) while retaining elements of the traditional caste system but removing the degrading stigma and manifestations of 'untouchability'. The other approach was led by Dr. Ambedkar, a lawyer and himself an 'untouchable', who believed that only by destroying the caste system could 'untouchability' be destroyed. Ambedkar became the chief spokesperson for those 'untouchables' who demanded separate legal and constitutional recognition similar in status to that accorded to Muslims, Sikhs and Christians. However, this was opposed by Gandhi and Ambedkar eventually gave up the demand. After rejecting Hindu values, in 1956 he converted to Buddhism and was later followed by a large number of converts.

After independence the Indian constitution abolished untouchability in law. Today Dalit politics largely centres around the just dispensation of the affirmative action benefits in employment, education and electoral representation granted to them under the constitution. However, the Protection of Civil Rights Act 1955/1976 and the Scheduled Caste and Scheduled tribes (Prevention of Atrocities) Act 1989, both derived from the constitution, remain largely ineffective in their implementation. Many reasons lie behind this, including a lack of political will on the part of both central and state governments, a lack of commitment of upper-caste and class bureaucrats to social justice, the absence of vigilance committees of citizens to monitor the implementation process.

Dalit women have been particularly badly affected in recent times. They are discriminated against not only because of their sex but also because of religious, social and cultural structures which have given them the lowest position in the social hierarchy. The stigma of untouchability makes them especially vulnerable victims of all kinds of discriminations and atrocities. Almost 90 per cent of Dalits live in rural areas. Economic exploitation remains their most acute problem. They are almost all marginal farmers or landless labourers. Large numbers migrate to cities or to labour-scarce rural areas in different parts of India. Many are in debt and are obliged to work off their debts as bonded labour, despite the fact that this practice was abolished by law in 1976. In these cases a labourer takes a loan from a landlord or moneylender and in return agrees to work for that person until the debt has been repaid. In practice such debts are difficult to repay as interest rates are high and poverty forces the labourer into deeper debt. The debt can then be passed on to the next generation and it is almost impossible to escape the cycle of bondage. In some areas many high-caste landlords pay their Dalit labourers minimum wages in cash or food, or nothing at all; resistance is frequently met by violence, sometimes resulting in the death or injury of the victim. Mob violence against Dalit communities is frequently reported, sometimes led by landlords, and has been especially noticeable in situations where Dalit workers have joined labour unions or made progress in gaining education and economic mobility. Many Dalit families have left rural areas to live in slums and on the pavements.

ORIGIN OF CASTE SYSTEM

Origin of this caste system in the Indian society dates back to thousands of years. The fair skinned Aryans arrived in India a.ound 1500 B,C. from South Europe and North Asia. When the fair-skinned Aryans invaded India, about two thousand years before Jesus Christ they defeated the dark-skinned indigenous people, Dravidians, who were the founder of the Indian Civilization. The Aryans subjugated them, learnt many things from them and built up another civilization, which came to be known as the Ganges Valley or Hindu Civilization.

To perpetuate the enslavement of the original inhabitants of India, the Aryans created the caste system, and thereby excluded them from their own society.These people were left as 'outcastes' who were even denied of human status. In order to secure their status the Aryans resolved some social and religious rules, which allowed only them to be the priests, warriors and the businessmen of the society. History of the Aryan intrusion into India and their dominance over the original inhabitants, Dravidians and the prominence given to the scriptures of the former were the root cause for this caste discrimination, what cannot be denied is the place in Hindu Vedas.

According to their tradition and scripture the high class people the Brahmins belong to the priestly class. The next is Kshatryas who are the warriors,. Vaishyas—traders, Shudras—labourers The Dalits belong no caste. They were degraded as castles people

LIVING CONDITIONS OF SCHEDULED CASTES

The "Scheduled Castes" is the legal and constitutional name collectively given to the groups which have traditionally occupied the lowest status in Indian society and the Hindu religion which provides the religious and ideological basis for an "untouchable" group, which was outside the caste system and inferior to all other castes. Today, untouchability is outlawed, and these groups are recognized by the Indian Constitution to be especially disadvantaged because of their past history of inferior treatment, and are therefore entitled to certain rights and preferential treatment.

The Scheduled Castes are not an homogenous group and are divided into many castes and sub-castes, as well as by language and geography. Collectively they are best known outside India as "Untouchables" but this term is not used in official Indian terminology where the word harijan is more likely to be favoured. Politically-aware members of the Scheduled Castes are likely to use the term dalit. At an everyday level specific caste names are more likely to be used. Some derogatory names have been banned by law; in practice they are commonly used. Members of the Scheduled Castes are found all over India in some areas rising to over 25% of the population. With total numbers of over 100 million, they are the largest minority group in the world — indeed one person in 40 is born "untouchable".

There is controversy on the origin of untouchability with some accounts stating that it was a feature of ancient Indian society and others that it was introduced with the Aryan invaders in the third century BC. The philosophy of caste is contained in the Manusmiriti, a sacred Hindu text dating from the second century BC and is related to the theory of transmigration of the soul and of karma (rebirth) and dharma (duty). "Untouchable" outcast communities were forbidden to join in the religious and social life of the community and were confined to menial "polluting" tasks such as slaughtering animals and leatherworking. The introduction of Islam from the thirteenth century AD led to widespread conversions by many low caste and "untouchable" groups and by the mid-nineteenth century about one quarter of the population was Muslim.

The period of British rule from the late eighteenth century brought little change and attempts to ensure that public facilities, such as government schools, would be open to all castes had little impact. During the first half of the twentieth century the British Indian government began to take an interest in the condition of "untouchable groups" and "depressed classes" and their special position was recognized under the term "Scheduled Castes". Among Indian politicians two main approaches emerged, typified by two political and religious leaders who have by their ideas and actions made most impact on "Untouchable" advancement.

M. K. (Mahatma) Gandhi, whose chief aim was liberation from colonial rule within a distinctive philosophical system based upon amhinsa (non-violence), believed in raising the status of "Untouchables" while retaining elements of the traditional caste system but removing the degrading stigma and manifestations of untouchability, and coined the term harijan (Children of God) to describe them. This term is still used widely today by the non-Scheduled Caste communities although many Scheduled Caste members have now rejected it. The other approach came from Dr B. R. Ambedkar, a brilliant "Untouchable" lawyer, who believed that only by destroying the caste system could untouchability be destroyed. Ambedkar became the chief spokesperson for Scheduled Castes who demanded recognition as a separate entity similar in status to Muslims, Sikhs and Christians. Ambedkar was forced to drop this demand after Gandhi threatened a hunger strike, but as a consequence Scheduled Castes were granted increased electoral representation and a guarantee of special protection and rights for them. Ambedkar also rejected Hindu values and in 1956 converted to Buddhism, later followed by about three million converts.

Constitution and Law

After Independence for a partitioned India in 1947, Ambedkar became Law Minister in the government of Jawaharlal Nehru and the drafter of the Indian Constitution of 1950. The Constitution states that no citizen should be discriminated against because of religion, race, or caste among other attributes, and should not be denied access to and the use of public services. Article 341 authorizes the President of India to specify "castes, races or tribes which shall for the purposes of this constitution be deemed to be Scheduled Castes". The First Amendment to the Constitution passed in 1951 allowed the state to make special provision for advancement of socially and educationally backward classes of citizens of the Scheduled Castes and Scheduled Tribes.

The Untouchability Offences Act of 1955 outlaws discrimination on "the ground of untouchability" in regard to public facilities, eating places, temples, residential choice etc. and provides for fines and imprisonment of offenders. However, relatively small numbers of convictions were made under the Act. In 1976 the Act was strengthened by the Protection of Civil Rights Act which increases punishment and allows for collective fines to be imposed on the offending community and for punishment of civil servants who neglect to investigate the offence. State governments were directed to introduce new measures such as providing officers, police stations and special courts to deal with offenders, to provide legal aid to victims and to identify special areas where there is a high incidence of untouchability. The central government has a special Commission for Scheduled Castes and Tribes which issues an Annual Report outlining processes, problems and violations of the law as regards the Scheduled Castes. However, despite these measures, there is still evidence that the law is often ignored and that untouchability continues, especially in rural areas.

The central and state governments have from time to time appointed Commissions of Enquiry to investigate the situation of the Scheduled Castes, especially after riots and violent incidents. After a series of attacks against Scheduled Caste communities which resulted in many deaths in Tamil Nadu in 1968, Scheduled Caste MPs compiled the Elaperumal Report, which detailed continuing untouchability in villages across India. Incidents of violence and discrimination, especially from the states of Bihar, Uttar Pradesh, Madhya Pradesh and Andhra Pradesh, continue to be regularly reported in the national press.

In Bihar during the 1980s many Scheduled Caste landless labourers in the central plains supported left-wing trade union and peasant groups, some of which used armed opposition to the state government and advocated land reform and standard wages. (Most of these demands were actually already on the Statute Book but had never been enforced.) As a result, landlord armies or senas have organized and used counter-violence against the lal senas or "red armies". Some estimates give a total of 2,000 deaths each year in land disputes in Bihar, most of the victims being landless labourers or small farmers. Landlord senas have been responsible for violent attacks on Scheduled Caste communities and there have been allegations that these attacks have been implicitly supported by police and leading politicians in the state government. After the most publicized of these incidents, politicians descend upon the village and many promises are made of compensation and justice. Yet few of the perpetrators of violence against Scheduled Caste communities are prosecuted by the government, and even fewer are convicted or sentenced.

Political Life

The Congress Party has dominated Indian politics from before independence and has been out of office at the centre only once — from 1977 to the beginning of 1980. However, from the mid-1980s, it has lost power in many of the states to regionally-based parties, while the Communist Party (Marxist) is the dominant party in the states of West Bengal and Kerala. Almost all political parties actively pursue their Scheduled Caste voters, and in some states there is reported to be widespread ballot-rigging. There is no one Scheduled Caste "vote bank", as was once thought to have existed in relation to the Congress Party, and there are Scheduled Caste voters for all parties, with probably the largest number of votes going to the Congress Party. Congress was reported to have lost much of its traditional Scheduled Caste support during the Emergency of 1975-77. Almost all parties have had Scheduled Caste politicians among their leading figures although few have gained real power. To date there have been no Scheduled Caste Prime Ministers, but the late Jagivan Ram served as Deputy Prime Minister in the brief Janata government of 1977-79 and at least three Chief Ministers in northern India have been from the Scheduled Castes.

There are also reservations for the Scheduled Castes in legislatures in the centre and the states. In the two houses of Parliament, the Lok Sabha and the Raiya Sabha, 15% of the seats are reserved for Scheduled Caste members and similar representation occurs in the state assemblies in proportion to the percentage of Scheduled Castes in the state's population. However, since the Scheduled Caste voters are always a minority in the reserved constituencies and in the assemblies as a whole, favourable legislation has been often blocked by vested interests. Furthermore, the system does not encourage Scheduled Caste organization by separate parties but facilitates organization and representation of Scheduled Castes by the major parties, especially the Congress Party, which has been in a dominant position since independence. On some occasions, however, Scheduled Caste legislators have been able to act and influence policies across party lines.

There have been several attempts to found distinctive Scheduled Caste political parties, among them the Republican Party of Ambedkar, which still exists but which has little political significance. In the early 1970s a new radical political movement in Maharashtra took the form of the Dalit Panther Party, which was inspired by the American civil rights movement and "black power". Dalit means the "oppressed ones" and the movement embraces not only Scheduled Castes but also Adivasis (Tribal peoples), low caste groups, Muslims, workers and women. The party later splintered and has since had only sporadic success. More durable was the accompanying literary and cultural movement which has spanned poetry, theatre, music and film, and the sense of pride and identity brought about by the Dalit movement. The Dalit movement has been concentrated in the Western states of Maharashtra and Gujarat and some of the larger Indian cities. Buddhism has also been a major influence in forming a new sense of identity, once again mainly in the western states. In the southern states there have recently been attempts by Christian groups, who have come from traditionally untouchable communities but who are not recognized as Scheduled Castes by the government, to organize within and outside the Christian community.

Economic Problems

Almost 90% of the Scheduled Castes still live in rural areas and economic exploitation remains their most acute problem. They are overwhelmingly marginal farmers or landless labourers. Large numbers migrate to cities or labour-scarce rural areas such as Punjab. Many are in debt and are obliged to work off their debts through debt-bonded labour despite the fact that this practice was abolished by law in 1976. In these cases a labourer takes a loan from a landlord or moneylender and in return agrees to work for that person until the debt is repaid. In practice it is difficult to repay the debt as interest payments are high and cumulative, and poverty forces the labourer deeper into debt. The debt can be passed onto the next generation and thus it is impossible to escape the cycle. In some areas many high-caste landlords pay their Scheduled Caste labourers minimum wages in cash or food, or nothing at all, and any resistance is frequently met by violence, sometimes resulting in the death or injury of the victim. Sexual harassment against Scheduled Caste women is frequent. Mob violence against Scheduled Caste communities is frequently reported, sometimes led by landlords or community leaders, and has been especially noticeable in situations where Scheduled Caste workers have joined labour unions or made progress in gaining education and economic mobility.

Many Scheduled Caste families have left rural areas and come to live in slums and on the pavements in the rapidly growing cities. Here also they tend to do the worst jobs for the lowest wages. However in some cities, traditional occupations such as sweepers have been organized in municipal unions and have the advantage of regular work and wages. Most Scheduled Caste workers are casual day labourers, in small factories, quarries and brick kilns or on construction sites, or work as cycle rickshaw drivers or in petty trade. Women and children as well as men work in such jobs but at lower wages. In the large textile mills of Bombay, Scheduled Caste workers have been generally confined to less skilled and less well-paid work. There are, however, growing numbers of Scheduled Castes in relatively secure areas such as the public service, banking and railways and sometimes in private industry. Those resident in the cities have greater access to secondary and higher education and a growing middle class has evolved within the Scheduled Caste community. Discrimination is less evident in the urban areas but residential patterns, particularly in poorer areas, are often on a caste basis.

As a result of the official policy of "positive discrimination" in favour of the Scheduled Castes in the civil service there have been growing numbers of Scheduled Caste public servants. To date there has been some improvement in the levels of Scheduled Caste recruitment in the central civil service. From 1949 to 1979 this rose from 0.71% to 4.5% in Class I posts, from 2.01% to 7.3% in Class II posts, and from 7.03% to 12.35% in Class III posts. There has been a similar slow process in public-sector and nationalized industry posts, where positive discrimination did not begin until the 1970s. In private business and industry, however, there are no positive discrimination provisions and, therefore, progress has been limited. Members of the Scheduled Castes, however, are frequently over-represented in the lower Class IV posts and occupy almost all Class V posts (i.e sweepers — a traditional "Untouchable" occupation).

There has also been positive discrimination in education, but the poverty of many Scheduled Caste families often prevents utilization of education facilities. In 1977-78 only 75% of Scheduled Caste children in the age group six to eleven attended school, compared to 88% for other children, and the disparity becomes greater at older ages with the respective figures for the 11 to 14 age group as 26% to 42%. Places for Scheduled Castes in higher education, and especially for post-graduate posts, are sometimes not filled, either because of lack of qualified candidates or prejudice against qualified candidates. In 1981 there were riots in the state of Gujarat by high-caste students protesting against the system of reservation in education institutions, in which 42 people died.

However, despite the overwhelming odds against them, former "Untouchables" are gaining increasing access to education and their expectations and aspirations are rising. Increasingly they are refusing to accept their former degraded and subservient position and, if they are able to organize across barriers of language and sub-caste, should present a formidable challenge to government.

Living Conditions of Scheduled Tribes

The tribal people (Adivasis or original inhabitants) is the collective name used for the many tribal peoples of India. Officially they are termed "Scheduled Tribes" but this is a legal and constitutional term which differs from state to state and area to area and therefore excludes some groups who might be considered tribal. Adivasis are not an homogenous group — with over 200 tribes speaking over 100 languages, which vary greatly in ethnicity, culture and language; however there are similarities in their way of life and generally perceived inferior position within Indian society. There are over 50 million Adivasis constituting 7.5% of the Indian population, thus making it the largest tribal population in the world.

Adivasis are found throughout India but are primarily based in the mountain and hill areas, away from the fertile plains. The greatest concentration is in the central states of India, notably Madhya Pradesh, Orissa, southern Bihar, the western ghats (hills) of Gujarat and

Maharastra and northern Andhra Pradesh; where over 85% of the Tribal population is to be found. However in no peninsula state does the Tribal population reach more than one quarter of the population. There are smaller groups in the mountain areas of the south, notably in Kerala, Tamil Nadu and Karnataka. The other concentration is found in the north-eastern states, the "seven sisters" (Assam, Manipur, Nagaland, Mizoram, Tripura, Megalaya and Arunchal Pradesh) but here the situation is significantly different as in most of these states (the exceptions are Assam and Tripura) Adivasis are a majority and are likely to remain so since regulations restrict settlement by outsiders.

The Indian government has a special programme for the welfare of tribes it classes as "primitive" tribes. These are Adivasis engaged in pre-agricultural technology and shifting cultivation with either a static or declining population. In 1988 there were 73 such tribes totalling over one million people.

Adivasis are some of the earliest inhabitants of the sub-continent and once inhabited much greater areas than at present. However little is known of their history although it appears that many were pushed into the hill areas after the invasions of the Indo-Aryan tribes 3,000 years ago. Tribals were not integrated into Hindu caste society; they stood outside it but nevertheless there were many points of contact. Tribal religious beliefs contain many aspects of Hinduism (and vice-versa); Tribals traded with settled villages on the plains and sometimes paid tribute to Hindu rulers. In turn some Tribal rulers conquered and ruled over non-tribals and some Tribals permanently settled and entered caste society.

It was not until the unifying political rule of the British from the late eighteenth century that government made substantial inroads into Adivasi society. British rule brought money, government officials and moneylenders into tribal areas, beginning the process of encroachment of Adivasi land by outsiders. As a result there were tribal revolts from the mid-nineteenth century in several parts of eastern India and this forced the administration to recognize the vulnerable position of Tribals and pass laws to protect their lands from outsiders. These laws (some of which are still on the Statute Book) completely barred the sale of Tribal lands to non-Tribals and made provisions to restore alienated land. However in practice most of these laws were widely disregarded and unscrupulous merchants and money-lenders found ways to circumvent them. These problems still face Adivasis today although their opponents are as likely to be large companies and state corporations as small traders and moneylenders. Christian missions began to proselytize in some tribal areas where (in contrast to Hindu and Muslim areas) they achieved a degree of success and also, most notably in the north-east, began the process of education and political awareness. Tribal peoples played little role in the run-up to independence and it was only in the north-east that they had enough political consciousness to make demands for separation or autonomy.

Constitution and Law

Under the constitution of the Republic of India of 1950, Tribal peoples along with so-called "Untouchables" became subject to special protective provisions. The vast majority of tribes were classified as "Scheduled Tribes". Article 341 authorizes the President of India to specify "castes, races or tribes which shall for the purposes of this constitution be deemed to be Scheduled Tribes". The first amendment to the Constitution passed in 1951 allowed the state to make special provision for the advancement of socially and educationally backward classes of citizens of the Scheduled Castes and Scheduled Tribes. The central Government has a special Commission for Scheduled Castes and Scheduled Tribes which issues an Annual Report. These reports give accounts of illegal actions against Adivasis and makes recommendations to improve their position.

There are reservations for the Scheduled Tribes in legislatures in the central and the state governments. In the two houses of Parliament, the Lok Sabha and the Raiya Sabha, 7% of the seats are reserved for Scheduled Tribe members and similar representation occurs in the state assemblies in proportion to the percentage of Scheduled Tribes in the state's population. However since the "Scheduled Tribe" voters are always a minority in the reserved constituencies and in the assemblies as a whole, favourable legislation can be blocked by vested interests. Furthermore the system does not encourage Scheduled Tribe organization by separate parties but facilitates organization and representation by the major parties, especially the Congress Party which has been in a dominant position since independence.

Governments normally have Scheduled Tribe Ministers and sometimes Cabinet Ministers but to date in peninsula India there has been only one Chief Minister from a Scheduled Tribe (in Gujarat) although in the five predominantly Tribal north-eastern states the Chief Minister invariably comes from a Scheduled Tribe.

There have been very few attempts to found distinctive Scheduled Tribe political parties, apart from those in the north-eastern states. Perhaps the most notable example in peninsula India has been that in eastern and southern Bihar, where a tribal regionalist movement known as the Jharkhand movement has been a factor since independence. The roots of this movement lie in the Santhal peoples of eastern Bihar and western Bengal, the scene of one of the early tribal revolts against land alienation under British rule. Some of this area also contains India's richest mineral deposits and mining, and subsequent industrialization and deforestation has added to Tribal grievances.

The Jharkhand Party was first formed in 1950 and had as its main demands the formation of a separate state or territory in the traditional Adivasi areas of Santhal Paganas and Chotanagpur and areas in West Bengal, Orissa and Madhya Pradesh. The party went into decline after its leader joined the Congress Party but was revived in 1973 when a new party the Jharkhand Mukti Mocha (JMM) was formed, led by a charismatic Santhal leader, who, despite his arrest during the Emergency, later worked closely with and eventually joined the Congress Party. This factionalized the JMM into several smaller groups but in 1987 a new co-ordinating organization the Jharkhand Co-ordinating Committee (JCC) was formed, with over 50 constituent organizations. This group has led a number of bandhs (strikes) and mass demonstrations in support of its demands and also tried to set up a parallel government although with little success, and both the central and state governments have consistently refused to consider a Jharkhand state. Were such a state to be granted it would not have a majority of Adivasis although they would probably be the largest single group if the different tribes were totalled together.

Land and Economic Factors

Over 95% of Scheduled Tribes still live in rural areas and economic exploitation remains their most acute problem. Less than 10% are shifting hunter-gatherers but more than half depend on forest produce for their livelihood, many in the form of the tendu leaf, used for the production of bidis (local cigarettes). From the time of the British administration there have been laws regulating the ownership and use of the forests and today most forest land is effectively nationalized or in the hands of state governments, and large areas are contracted to outside commercial interests. This has progressively deprived Adivasi communities of rights in the land and they can be fined or imprisoned for taking forest produce which has traditionally been theirs. The ostensible reason for state intervention has been to stop the destruction of forest land which has continued throughout this century. There are a number of reasons for deforestation which is often blamed on Adivasi shifting cultivation practices; one has been the increase in demand for firewood as fuel; another is the impact of commercial, sometimes illegal, cutting down of forests.

Although many Adivasis already have a similar lifestyle to small peasant farmers, farming marginal plots of land, they are even less likely to have the traditional agricultural skills to exploit such land, or the knowledge of government to enable them to get the loans and grants to which they may be entitled.

Another threat to Adivasis is large-scale dam building, for irrigation and hydro-electricity. A number of such schemes have been carried out since independence but the largest is the giant World Bank-financed Narmada Valley project which involves 30 major, 135 medium and 3,000 minor dams and which will flood 350,000 hectares of land, including 11% of the forests of the Narmada Valley. Up to 300,000 people, the majority of them Tribals, may be forced to relocate to make way for the dam. Furthermore compensation is limited to landowners (which is difficult for many Adivasis to prove) and is normally given in money rather than land. There have been campaigns by organizations within India and internationally to at least give compensation in the form of an equal amount of land to the displaced but, although these schemes have achieved a limited amount of success in delaying the project and gaining better compensation terms, the dams will still go ahead. Furthermore it is doubtful whether sufficient land for resettlement is available in such a densely populated country, where pressures on land are already high.

Social Developments

As with the Scheduled Castes, members of Scheduled Tribes are beneficiaries of "positive discrimination" provisions laid down in the constitution, reserving places in education, the civil service and nationalized industries. Problems of remoteness, poverty and prejudice mitigate against Adivasis exploiting these provisions however. For example, in Andhra Pradesh the Tribal literacy rate is only 11% against an all-India level of 29% (in the north-east, however, Tribal literacy is considerably higher). Because few Adivasis finish their schooling, few are able to use the reserved places in higher education or the civil service. Nevertheless some Adivasis do manage to achieve positions of responsibility in government and education, although they continue to be under-represented in almost every field.

Some Adivasis have been organized by left-wing groups, known commonly in India as "Naxalites", to press for higher wages and payments for forest produce. As a result Adivasis may become victims of both Naxalite pressures and government counter-insurgency campaigns. More commonly police, forest guards and officials frequently cheat, bully and intimidate Adivasis and large numbers are routinely arrested and jailed, often for petty offences. In such circumstances many Adivasis prefer to bribe officials to escape harassment or flee into the jungles when they appear.

Although Adivasis are not, as a general rule, regarded as "unclean" by caste-Hindus in the same way as Untouchables are, they continue to face prejudice and often violence from society. They are at the lowest point of almost every socio-economic indicator. The majority of the population regards them as primitive and government programmes aim to "integrate" them with the majority society, rather than to emphasize their distinctiveness. While the larger tribal groups and languages will survive as a result of numbers, the destruction of their economic base and environment poses grave threats to those who are still able to follow the basis of a traditional way of life and may result in the cultural extinction of many of the smaller Adivasi peoples.

Dalits and Human Rights

Over one-sixth of India's population, some 170 million people, live a precarious existence, shunned by much of Indian society because of their rank as "untouchables" or Dalits—literally meaning "broken" people—at the bottom of India's caste system. Dalits are discriminated against, denied access to land and basic resources, forced to work in degrading conditions, and routinely abused at the hands of police and dominant-caste groups that enjoy the state's protection.

Historically, the caste system has formed the social and economic framework for the life of the people of India. In its essential form, this caste system involves the division of people into a hierarchy of unequal social groups where basic rights and duties are assigned based on birth and are not subject to change. Dalits are 'outcastes' falling outside the traditional four classes of Brahmin, Kshatriya, Vaishya, & Shudra. Dalits are typically considered low, impure & polluting based on their birth and traditional occupation, thus they face multiple forms of discrimination, violence, and exclusion from the rest of society.

Beginning in the 1920s, various social, religious and political movements rose up in India against the caste system and in support of the human rights of the Dalit community. In 1950, the Constitution of India was adopted, and largely due to the influence of Dr. B.R. Ambedkar (chairman of the constitutional drafting committee), it departed from the norms and traditions of the caste system in favour of Justice, Equality, Liberty, and Fraternity, guaranteeing all citizens basic human rights regardless of caste, creed, gender, or ethnicity. The implementation and enforcement of these principles has, unfortunately, been an abysmal failure.

Despite the fact that "untouchability" was abolished under India's constitution in 1950, the practice of "untouchability"—the imposition of social disabilities on persons by reason of their birth in certain castes— remains very much a part of rural India. "Untouchables" may not use the same wells, visit the same temples, drink from the same cups in tea stalls, or lay claim to land that is legally theirs. Dalit children are frequently made to sit in the back of classrooms, and communities as a whole are made to perform degrading rituals in the name of caste. Most Dalits continue to live in extreme poverty, without land or opportunities for better employment or education. With the exception of a small minority who have benefited from India's policy of quotas in education and government jobs, Dalits are relegated to the most menial of tasks, as manual scavengers, removers of human waste and dead animals, leather workers, street sweepers, and cobblers. Dalit children make up the majority of those sold into bondage to pay off debts to dominant-caste creditors.

Dalit women face the triple burden of caste, class, and gender. Dalit girls have been forced to become prostitutes for dominant-caste patrons and village priests. Sexual abuse and other forms of violence against women are used by landlords and the police to inflict political "lessons" and crush dissent within the community. Less than 1% of the perpetrators of crimes against Dalit women are ever convicted.

The plight of India's "untouchables" elicits only sporadic attention within the country. Public outrage over large-scale incidents of violence or particularly egregious examples of discrimination fades quickly, and the state is under little pressure to undertake more meaningful reforms. Laws granting Dalits special consideration for government jobs and education reach only a small percentage of those they are meant to benefit. Laws designed to ensure that Dalits enjoy equal rights and protections have seldom been enforced. Instead, police refuse to register complaints about violations of the law and rarely prosecute those responsible for abuses that range from murder and rape to exploitative labour practices and forced displacement from Dalit lands and homes. Laws and government policies on land reform and budget allocations for the economic empowerment of the Dalit community remain largely unimplemented.

Dalits who dare to challenge the social order have often been subject to abuses by their dominant-caste neighbuors. Dalit villages are collectively penalized for individual "transgressions" through social boycotts, including loss of employment and access to water, grazing lands, and ration shops. For most Dalits in rural India who earn less than a subsistence living as agricultural labourers, a social boycott may mean destitution and starvation.

The present time is an historic moment, not only for Dalits, but for all those committed to basic human rights and principles of justice, equality, liberty, fraternity. India, a rising star and increasingly important player on the world stage, must not be allowed to ignore the injustice and oppression within its own borders any longer. Together, we must unite, nationally and internationally, to force the Indian government to rise above an entrenched caste-mentality and to properly enforce its laws, implement its policies, and fulfil its responsibility to protect the basic human rights of ALL of its citizens.

Dalit Movements

Today the Dalit movement is trying to gain political force. There is increasing intolerance of the situation that has not changed for the majority of the dalits in the fifty five years after independence. The educated Dalits, who can articulate about the exploitation the dalits are subjected to, try to use intellectual organizational means to fight it. Some visible efforts are: using conferences and media (some examples are the recent campaign to include caste in the UN World Conference on Racism, International Dalit Human Rights Conference, First World Dalit Convention: Towards a Casteless Society, Dalit Solidarity Programme), publication of books and journals (International Journal of Dalit Studies, The Dalit Magazine (a U.S. based publication), Bahujan Youth Times, forming discussion groups (Dalit and Bahujan egroups), action groups (Dalit Liberation Education Trust, DalitIndia) and building websites to create awareness. They educate themselves on the constitutional and legal rights of the Dalits and fight for their implementation and extension using national and international forums. Dalit intellectuals and activists seek to educate and unite Dalits to strength their power base. They internationalize Dalit issues to get world attention and support.

Some recent publications give an idea of the force of the Dalit intellectual movement and they exhibit an intolerance for the continuation of the oppressive system. The provocative tone of the book "Why I am not a Hindu" by Kanchan Illiah is an illustration of the radical thoughts of some Dalit activists. "The caste system that subjugated more than one fifth of the population to levels worse than animals' for more than two millennia and which represented institutionalization of the most heinous inequality ..." reads an article by Anand Telutumbde ("'Ambedkar' In and For the Post-Dalit Movement"). Many of the educated Dalits look at their historical conditions and their contemporary solutions differently from the mainstream India. They find shared grievance with oppressed people outside India. They challenge Hinduism. They take pride in their culture and frown on adopting the cultural habits of the upper castes. To give one example, where lower caste people were once denied the use of their caste names or forced to conceal their caste names while their status improved by the adoption of upper caste names, some Dalit leaders now openly add their caste name to their name. This is to announce their identity publicly and to demand their acceptance in that form. Some Dalit meetings make it a point to serve beef and toddy as a celebration of their customs. There is a developing genre of Dalit literature where Dalit cultural words are used, that are taboo in the main stream literature. All this is to break the norms accepted in the main stream society. And to highlight the dignity of an oppressed people. The Dalit International Organization has on its logo "Dalit means Dignity".

The Dalit movement also argues for the need to break away from Hinduism for liberation, which gave religious sanction to oppression and inhuman treatment by the concept of ritual pollution and legitimized it through the concept of karma. The movement's breaking of norms of the main stream society is an expression of this view of liberation. The Dalit movement today can be compared with the feminist movement in the world and the black movement in the U.S. in such an ideology and strategies of liberation. It strives to move beyond gaining sympathy of the upper castes and welfare from them and to organize politically and intellectually to fight their own battles.

References

Barbara R. Joshi, (1986), *Untouchable!: Voices of the Dalit Liberation Movement*, Zed Books.

Fernando Franco, Jyotsna Macwan, Suguna Ramanathan. (2004), *Journeys to Freedom: Dalit Narratives*, Popular Prakashan.

Michael, S M (2007), *Dalits in Modern India - Vision and Values*, , Sage Publications, New Delhi.

Oliver Mendelsohn, Marika Vicziany, (1998), *The Untouchables: Subordination, Poverty and the State in Modern India*, Cambridge University Press.

Rajshekhar, V.T. (2003), *Dalit: The Black Untouchables of India*, 2nd print, Clarity Press, Inc.

2

Social Exclusion of Dalits

Social exclusion is a process in which one section of society looks down upon the other, and alienates and excludes the latter from all opportunities of development on an arbitrary basis. The dominant section uses not only religion, tradition and culture but also political and bureaucratic powers and if nothing works also indulges in violence to perpetuate its dominant position.

Social exclusion reflects the multiple and overlapping nature of the disadvantages experienced by certain groups and categories of the population, with social identity as the central axis of their exclusion. The value-addedness of the social exclusion approach is its emphasis on the role of relational features in deprivation. Social exclusion can therefore be explained in terms of group interactions aimed at maximizing value and minimizing costs. Individuals are most vulnerable when they have fewest personal capacities and material resources but none of these threatens their survival so long as they enjoy the protections afforded by membership of an inclusive group that cooperates productively and redistributes its product.

Reviewing the effectiveness of policies and programmes in addressing social exclusion relates to the discussion on human development and human rights. Put simply, development approaches from the 1950s to the 1980s primarily focused on social and economic development as an outcome of the development process and were less concerned with civil and political rights. During this period, government policy and the development community were also less concerned with the quality of the process by which the outcomes were achieved. In contrast, the human rights-based approach to development recognizes both the achievement of a desirable outcome and the establishment of an adequate process to achieve and sustain that outcome. "Participation, local ownership, empowerment, and sustainability are essential characteristics of a high-quality process. A rights perspective is based on principles that emphasize accountability of those with obligations to realize the rights of children; the universality of rights; the indivisibility and interdependence of rights; and also the principle of the best interests of the child and taking into account the views of the child. The state and the other 'duty-bearers' (eg. parents and teachers) have obligations to fulfil these rights. As rights-holders, children are entitled to demand that the duty-bearers meet their respective obligation to respect, protect and fulfil their rights.

Extent of Social Exclusion

As per the Census 2001, the total population of the Scheduled Castes (SC) in India is 166,635,700, which is 16.3 per cent of the total population. The population of SCs is unevenly distributed among the states in India, with nearly 60 per cent of all SC children of primary school-going age (6-10 years) residing in the following six states: Andhra Pradesh, Bihar, Madhya Pradesh, Orissa, Rajasthan and Uttar Pradesh. The latter five states are among the most disadvantaged states in India across most social indicators.

Historically, the caste system classified people by their occupation and status. "Each caste had a specific place in the hierarchy of social status. Although in "scriptural terms" social and economic status were supposed to be separated, the economic and social status of the various castes tended to coincide. However, since the 19th century, the link between caste and occupation has become less rigid as it became easier for people to change occupations. This change has accelerated with the economic boom, which has taken place in India since the early 1990s. There has not, however, been a corresponding fluidity in caste, as intermarriage is very rare. Privileged sections of society tend to be from "upper castes" while the disadvantaged sections by the so-called "lower castes". Caste "can be seen as the institution that has been structuring and maintaining for centuries relations of power among different communities, and seeks to legitimize these power relations through systematically dispensing mixes of economic and cultural assets/opportunities and deprivations to different communities. Many have commented on the robustness of the caste system, "which has survived in the South Asian societies in one form or the other, despite the fundamental ideological and structural changes that have occurred through the spread of religions like Islam and Christianity as well as of model secular and egalitarian ideologues, all opposed to the very idea of hierarchy based on inherited statuses."

The specific structure and hierarchy related to castes is specific to various states and regions in India, with only the highest caste, the Brahmins, consistently faring better throughout the country. Not only are there differences in the names of the various castes, but also the hierarchy between them may also be different between regions. However, castes who traditionally suffered discrimination based on untouchability, which was an element of the caste system throughout India, have been identified, enumerated and incorporated in the "schedule" of the Constitution. "The implicit criterion for inclusion in the SC list is the social and religious disability suffered by a caste on account of untouchability i.e. being at the pollution end of the social hierarchy".

In defining who would be included in the Schedules, the government originally used the 1931 census report, and to a large extent duplicated a list created in 1936. Currently, the National Commissions for Scheduled Caste (SC) and Scheduled Tribe (ST) are vested with the responsibility of considering castes for inclusion or exclusion from the Schedule, which then needs to be ratified in Parliament. The discriminated communities are then officially designated as Scheduled Castes (SCs). Included in the SC category are communities from three different religions, Hinduism, Sikhism and Buddhism, all having within them communities traditionally suffering from untouchability. The term Dalit (meaning downtrodden or oppressed) is the generally accepted term for the "ex-untouchables", which corresponds to Scheduled Castes, which as mentioned above denotes the legal states as coined in the Constitution.

The Government of India's approach to historically marginalised groups draws on provisions made in the Indian

Constitution, which contains explicit state obligation towards protecting and promoting social, economic, political and cultural rights. "The State shall promote with special care the educational and economic interests of the weaker sections of the people and, in particular, of the Scheduled Castes and the Scheduled Tribes, and shall protect them from social injustice and all forms of exploitation". The Constitution mandates positive discrimination in government services, state-run, and sponsored educational institutions. Amendments to the Constitution also enabled representation of SC men and women in local governance structures.

Some of the constitutional provisions which aimed at positive discrimination are:

- *Article 17*: Abolition of "untouchability" and making its practice in any form a punishable offence
- *Article 46*: Promotion of educational and economic interests
- *Article 16 and 335*: Preferential treatment in matters of employment in public services
- *Article 330 and 332*: Reservation of seats in the Lok Sabha (lower house of Parliament) and State Assemblies

Scheduled caste (SC) children remain disadvantaged across many social indicators. Estimates from the 2000 National Sample Survey suggest that SC "constituted 20 per cent of the rural population, but 38 per cent of the poor". Table 1 shows that as an average for India, 27.09% of the population live below the poverty line in rural areas, compared to 36.25% of the SC population and 23.62% in urban areas compared to 38.47% of the SC population. Furthermore, after holding a variety of individual and household characteristics constant, Kabeer notes that the SCs were still 19 percent more likely to be poor than the rest of the population.

Table 1. Population below poverty line in India, SC and ST (NSSO, 1999/00)

Population below poverty line (%)	India	SCs	STs
Rural Areas	27.09	36.25	45.86
Urban areas	23.62	38.47	34.75

There has been political and social mobilization of SCs in India, particularly in certain poor states such as Uttar Pradesh, which is one of the poorest states in India. However, this mobilization has failed to translate into positive change in the social sector for this excluded population. As Mehrotra wrote, "while UP's immobilisers of the dalits (SCs) have focused exclusively on capturing power, the gains to the lowest castes have been entirely of a symbolic nature."

Social exclusion of Dalit Caste Children

There has been a significant increase in overall literacy rates and school participation rates across the country since the early 1990s. Gender and social disparities have also declined with an overall increase in school attendance. This is confirmed by the data from various sources including the National Family Health Survey–II (1998/99), Reproductive and Child Health Survey 2002-2004, the 2001 Census and routine monitoring information from the Department of Education. The country is approaching near universalisation of enrolment at the primary stage. The Gross Enrolment Rate has increased from 90% in 2003-2004 to 98% in 2004-2005. Similarly, the net enrolment rate has risen from 72% to 82% during the same period. A number of factors have contributed to the rising enrolment rate including the introduction of mid-days meals, opening of alternate schools, promoting the participation of Parent Teacher Associations (PTAs) and massive enrolment drives.

A constitutional amendment was passed in 2002 making free and compulsory education a fundamental right for children aged 6-14 years. The national and state governments continue to deliver the programme *Sarva Shiksha Abhiyan* (SSA), which aims to achieve universal elementary education by 2010.

While enrolment and attendance in primary school has increased, the quality of education remains a major concern. Little emphasis has been placed on making education more relevant or in encouraging learning by doing and learning by observation. Activity-based and child-centred learning arrangements are still very weak. There are many situations where children mechanically go through five years of primary education and emerge barely literate, leading to community apathy towards schooling. The poor quality of education is reflected in the continuing low level of completion rates of primary school. The National Sample Survey Organisation (NSSO) and National Family Health Survey (NFHS) collected data on the 'level of education completed', whereas the Reproductive Child Health Survey (RCHS) provided data on the years of education completed. The length of primary education is also defined differently in different states of India with some states having 5 years of primary education and others having 4 years. Hence in some states the completion rate is calculated for 9-11 years age group while in others it is with the 10-12 years of age. Table 2 indicates that, based on the RCHS-II (2002-2004), 37.8% of children in 10-12 years age group have completed at least 5 years of schooling.

Table 2. Percentage of Children Completing Primary School (various sources)

Survey	% Completed
NSS 52 (1995-96)	32.8
NSS 55 (1999-00)	36.8
NFHS-II (1998-99)	37.7
RCHS-II (2002-04)	37.8

Disparities in primary education can be seen between children from different castes, economic group, sex, rural and urban, certain characteristics of households and between the different regions in India. These different forms of deprivation do not work in isolation. The most disadvantaged children would suffer from multiple forms of exclusion and disadvantages, including for example being SC, girls, poor, living in a poor and/or remote location, etc. It is therefore important to acknowledge the multiplicity of deprivations and the interrelationship between them.

Using completion rates of five years of schooling as a key indicator of education status, Table 3 shows that SC population are disadvantaged when compared to Other Backward Classes (OBCs) others. It should also be noted that ST children are in some ways even more disadvantaged than SCs in terms of education status. Regarding the accessibility of the education system for ST children, issues such as the language of instruction, remoteness of their habitations, poverty and other factors are barriers to access for this disadvantaged group. The tables below show ST children as a reference.

Table 3. Completion Rate of 10-12 years by caste (RCH 2002-2004)

Social Group	SC	ST	Others
Male	36.3	32.6	44.8
Female	32.3	26.6	44.1

Based on the National Family Health Survey of 1998/99, Table 4 shows that only 65.7% of SC children age 7-17 are currently attending school compared to 81.3% of higher caste groups. Furthermore, 20.8% of SC children never attended school compared to 7.6% of children from high caste.

Table 4. Percent of children age 7-17 by schooling outcomes

		Ever attended	
Caste/Religion of the household head	Never Attended	Dropped out	Currently Attending
Hindu SC	20.8	13.0	65.7
Hindu ST	29.7	13.9	56.3
Hindu other	7.6	10.6	81.3
Other	7.8	10.7	81.1

Table 5 indicates the disparities in rural areas between children from SC castes and also between the poorest 20% compared to the richest 20% of households using data from RCHS-II for boys and girls. This survey defined economic status based on household's ownership of assets such as electric fan; radio/transistor, pressure cooker, telephone, bicycle, car, tractor and water pump among others. The table indicates that SC children are disadvantaged compared to children from other castes in each of the economic groups, but also that the economic status of the household is a very important discriminating factor in accessing education. The table also indicates that girls are disadvantaged compared to boys in the lower economic group, but less so in the higher economic group.

The literacy rates of women, SC and ST continue to be below average. Table 6 shows the percentage of the ever-married women by caste who are illiterate in India, and in two selected states: Uttar Pradesh, which is one of the most disadvantaged and Tamil Nadu, which is among the most advantaged states in India.

Table 5. % children in 10-12 years age group who have completed at least 5 years of schooling across economic groups and gender in rural areas

	Male			
Rural	SC	ST	Other	Total
Poorest 20%	23.5	22.9	22.2	22.5
Richest 20%	50.0	56.9	54.2	52.9
	Female			
Poorest 20%	17.4	15.5	18.5	16.5
Richest 20%	52.5	45.4	55.1	53.0

One can see that there is a significant difference in the level of illiteracy in the two states among all the castes, therefore confirming the significance of disparities between regions in India. However, SC ever-married women were disadvantaged in both states, with 85% of SC women illiterate compared to 57.2% of other higher castes in Uttar Pradesh, and 64.1% of SC women in Tamil Nadu compared to 5.0% of higher castes.

Table 6. Distribution of ever-married women 15-49 who are illiterate: UP, Tamil Nadu and India

	Tamil Nadu	Uttar Pradesh	India
SC	64.1	85.0	73.0
Others	5.0	57.2	43.8

According to a UNICEF supported Baseline Survey which was undertaken in 2005 by the National Sample Survey Organization in 43 districts in the country, there are significant disparities in attendance rates and also learning achievements between children from scheduled caste and other castes. Graph 1 indicates the percentage of children (6-14 years) attending school, which is 72.5% for SC compared to 83.6% for children from other castes.

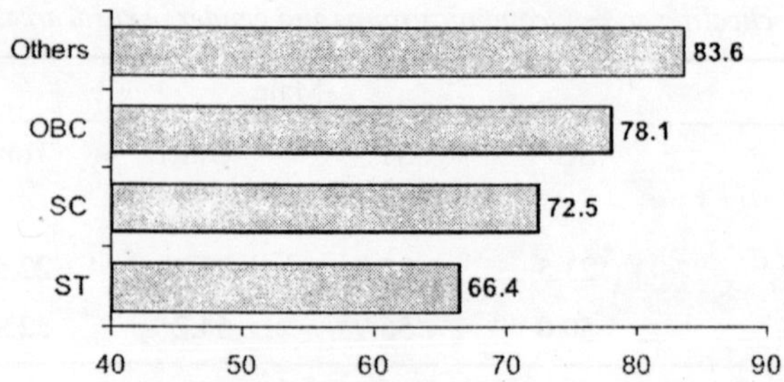

Graph 1. Percentage of Children Attending School

Graph 2 indicates the percentage of children who can read and write, disaggregated by caste (and also included the tribal children as reference). There is a difference between SC children and children from other castes in the percentage who can read and write, which is 58.2% compared to 72.0% respectively.

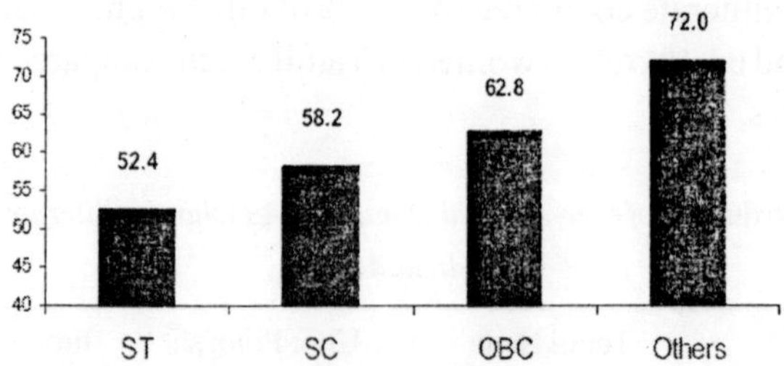

Graph 2. Percentage of Children 6-14yrs) who can read and write

Disadvantages of Dalit Children in Education

The physical distance to school is often cited as a barrier for children in India particularly at the higher levels of middle and secondary school, and is of particular importance for SC children as they often live in hamlets, which are on the outer edge of the village. However, in addition to the physical distance, the 'social distance' to the school also needs to be considered. As the Public Report on Basic Education (PROBE) report concluded, "In many areas, villages are divided into separate hamlets, and children from one hamlet may be reluctant or unable to go to school in another hamlet due to caste tensions." Only half of all hamlets (the sub-unit of a village) in rural India have a primary school, and in states like Uttar Pradesh, the proportion of such hamlets is a low as 30 percent. In rural villages particularly in disadvantaged states such as Bihar and Uttar Pradesh, SC tend to be clustered in particular habitations within villages. If the school is then located in the central part of the village (or where higher castes reside), then this presents another challenge for SC children in accessing the school. According to a study conducted in 1995, "SC/ST families tend to live in colonies removed by a kilometre or more from the main village. A school in the village within walking distance for the families in the main village would still be at a distance to these children." Additional analysis based on village level data on the location of the school and caste composition of the habitations within a village are necessary in order to draw conclusions related to this issue.

Another element of social exclusion of SC children from primary education in India is the extent to which discrimination is practised by teachers. While reliable quantitative data are not available related to the perception or levels of sensitivity of teachers to caste-based discrimination, anecdotal evidence and certain smaller scale qualitative studies suggest that teaching practices in the classroom negatively affect SC children and result in another 'push' factor from primary school. "Teachers in India are predominantly upper caste and bring their own understandings of the legitimacy of caste relations into the classroom. Dalit children are expected to run errands and are assigned menial tasks such as sweeping and cleaning the classrooms. Higher rates of teacher absenteeism were reported when children were mainly from dalit and tribal communities."

Recruiting teachers from marginalised communities is an important means of signalling state commitment to making services more accessible to excluded groups. However, not only their background and caste are important, their empathy with children from scheduled caste will affect their behaviour in the classroom, and the resulting education experience of children from scheduled caste. Jha and Jhingran however noted that "teachers' educational qualifications and their pre-service training are not discriminating factors in teacher performance" in relating to children from disadvantaged backgrounds. The Joint Review Mission of SSA highlighted the importance of training teachers to "address issues of attitude and classroom practice in order to improve the academic performance of SC children." Teachers' empathy with children from diverse or disadvantaged backgrounds is important in providing an education service which is attractive to marginalised groups. More data and analysis are required on the background of teachers including their caste and also their level of sensitivity and skills related to promoting social exclusion and the impact of these characteristics on the education experience of SC children.

The perception of the quality of the education system (which it is reasonable to expect to be somewhat correlated with the actual quality of the system including the curriculum, pedagogy, etc.), by the parents and students, and their assessment on the benefits of education (will their child get a better job etc.), and the accessibility of the education system (distance, cost etc.) will influence the decision of whether parents decide to send their children to school (and children themselves). As mentioned above, the social status of the child, which is predominantly determined by caste, also influences this assessment. "In a socially and economically stratified society like India, decision-making at the individual level is closely linked with collective or group behaviour. Individual preferences and collective or social norms may not move in the same direction." The above analysis of the additional challenges to accessing education by scheduled caste is a example of the individual aspirations of these children and their parents not matching the social norms of the wider community.

Table 7 indicates the reasons for children never attending or dropping out of school based on the National Family Health Survey (NFHS) -II. Unfortunately, this information is not available for different social groups. The table indicates that cost is a significant barrier to accessing education, which is consistent with other studies including the PROBE study. The high cost of providing education and the lack of interest in studies are given as reasons for nearly 50 per cent of boys in both rural and urban areas for having never attended school. For girls, along with the cost of education, the opportunity cost of attending school was cited as too high; that is, the loss of their contribution to the work at home. While the National Family Health Survey (NFHS) did not collect data related to the specific issues of social exclusion of SC mentioned above, recognizing that children from Scheduled Castes also tend to be poorer than children from other castes, they will be disproportionately affected by this barrier.

Table 7. Reasons for never attending or dropping out of school, children aged 6-17 years.

	Males		Females	
Reasons	Urban	Rural	Urban	Rural
Never attended School (%)	6.4	13.6	9.0	25.7
- School far away	1.5	4.4	3.4	5.2
- Education not necessary	6.1	7.8	12.9	13.1
- Required for work at home or outside for cash/kind	12.6	17.1	15.4	24.5
- Costs too much	28.5	25.8	30.1	23.8
- Not interested in studies	26.5	25.7	15.7	15.9
- Other	26.5	17.0	19.7	15.4
- Don't know	3.0	2.0	2.8	2.1
Total	*100.0*	*100.0*	*100.0*	*100.0*
Dropped out of school (%)	10.6	10.6	11.0	12.6
- School far away	0.3	1.4	1.2	7.5
- Education not necessary	2.4	2.3	5.4	4.3
- Required for work at home or outside for cash/kind	21.9	28.4	20.8	26.2
- Costs too much	5.2	13.3	17.0	11.4
- Not interested in studies	42.5	40.0	30.2	24.8
- Repeated failures	6.0	5.3	6.1 3	.7
- Other	5.9	5.5	14.3	18.2
- Don't know	5.7	3.8	5.1	4.0
Total	*100.0*	*100.0*	*100.0*	*100.0*

In order to try and discern the extent to which social exclusion based on caste is a barrier to education, multilevel regression analysis was undertaken based on the data from the National Family Health Survey 2 (1998/99). Based on this regression, Table 8 shows that for children aged 7-17 years of age, children from other castes are 1.35 times more likely to have ever been to school than SC children. Similarly, children 11-17 years old from higher castes (i.e. neither SC nor OBC), are 1.33 times more likely to complete grade 5 than SC children after controlling for working status, number of children in the family, adult female and male education levels, urban/rural and also the standard of living index.

The following table clearly indicates that caste has a significant influence in the educational status of children.

Table 8. Multilevel model regression for 1) ever been to school 7-17 years of age and 2) completing grade 5 among children age 11-17 years in India

Caste	Odds Ratio between castes	
	Ever been to school 7-17 years of age	Completing Grade 5 among children age 11-17 years of age
Scheduled caste	1.0	1.0
Other backward classes	1.07	1.1
Other Hindu castes	1.35	1.33

Recent years in India have seen a proliferation of private schools, both aided and unaided, and alternative and education guarantee schemes. Data are limited on the actual number of private schools and also the numbers of children attending these schools. At the primary level, 6 per cent of rural children and 19 per cent of urban children are studying in private unaided schools; this proportion goes up when we include the 31 per cent of children who are studying in private aided schools. Among the reasons for the growth of private schools is the reported decline in government-school quality (poor infrastructure, shortage of teachers, lack of accountability of government schools leading to teacher absenteeism and negligence). This gives way to a positive preference for private schools, even though they may have a relatively poor infrastructure, less qualified teachers and are definitely more expensive. The proliferation of private schools in rural and urban areas has the potential of further widening the divide between castes, as children from Scheduled Castes cannot afford (nor may be welcome) at private schools to the same extent as children from other castes, although this is an area which requires further study. From the little information which is available, one can conclude that the SC children predominantly attend the poorly functioning government schools or alternative schools. This situation has however resulted in one district education official commenting that the public school system in slowly turning into a system for SC children only.

Addressing the Issues of Social Exclusion in Education

With the significant increase in public resources to primary education, and the increased attention more generally both of senior decision-makers and the public, there is now a unique opportunity to transform the education system in India, with the potential of inducing fundamental changes in the opportunities to socially disadvantaged populations in the country. An improved education system may be one of the key ingredients to breaking the cycle of poverty and deprivation to scheduled caste children in India.

During the 1990s, the focus on improving access and quality of education was on increasing public resources to education and addressing the poor quality of teaching. It is however now widely recognized that finances alone will not ensure regular attendance of the most disadvantaged. Explanations of educational disadvantage, particularly in the context of gender and social attributes often focus on the supply dimensions of the problem, which again often emphasize the necessity of providing additional resources. A broader approach however is needed for education policy and resulting programmes to effectively address social exclusion of SC children from primary school. A more comprehensive approach is therefore proposed which highlights the various interrelated processes which influence decision-making at various levels related to a child's education.

In order to better understand social exclusion of scheduled caste from education, it is important to develop a framework which would help to categorize the factors which influence the decision to attend (or not attend) school and to understand who takes this decision. Diagram 1 illustrates the proposed framework which includes:

— characteristics and processes within the school (i.e. teaching processes, school environment, background of teachers, discriminatory practices etc.),

— processes within the community (i.e. social dynamics, inclusive decision-making, social norms within the community related to education etc.), and

— household characteristics and related processes (i.e. caste, poverty, gender, numbers of children, nutrition, educational level and occupation of parents, value places on education etc.).

Each of these elements affect a child's chances of accessing school, regularly attending, completing and ultimately, achieving a certain level of learning.

The processes within each of these components are not independent of each other, and therefore the relationship and interplay between them also influences the education status of SC children (illustrated by the arrows between the circles). The relationship and interplay between the school, community and household is important in understanding the decision-making processes related to a child's attendance. That is, there is an interplay between life situations, school functioning, classroom processes, community norms, parental aspirations and other factors which have an influence on educational outcomes of disadvantaged groups. For example, recognizing that teachers are a part of the community and therefore are influenced by societal norms, it is clear that prejudices within the community would have an influence on teachers' attitude and possibly their teaching practice towards SC children.

Another example of the interplay is the perception of the quality and accessibility of education by the parents, which correlates with the actual quality of the school system but is also formed based on the expectations of parents and the societal norm or "lens" they apply when assessing the education experience of their children. The extent the community is involved in the management of the school, and the level of diversity and inclusiveness of this process, is also an important factor and relates to the interplay between households and the school. Similarly, the nature of the relationship between parents and teachers, and how that relationship is influenced by caste, is another example of the interplay between households and schools. Unfortunately, very little is known about how the influence of various characteristics of households, schools and communities, and their interplay, influences social exclusion of SC children from primary school. Further study on the various interrelationships between these elements and their influence on children's education status is necessary in order to better understand and therefore be able to address the main determinants of the social exclusion of SC children.

Jha and Jhingran make the distinction between the individual decision-making (children and their parents) regarding sending children to school, and the institutional decision-making process, including deciding on the level of resources, which are provided to the education system. To realize a policy objective of ensuring all children are in school, including those who are socially excluded, it is necessary that policies and programmes are built on a comprehensive understanding of the decision-making processes at the various levels, and when necessary influence these in a desired direction. They wrote "it was clear that the voicelessness and powerlessness of poor people also affects the relationship between poor parents and schools".

Policy Implications

The Government of India has repeatedly acknowledged the disadvantaged status of the SC population in education and recognized the need to address it. The National Policy on Education (1986) declared "The central focus in the SC's educational development is their equalization with the non-SC population in all stages and levels of education". The policy focused on incentives, scholarships, reservations, recruitment of teachers, location of school buildings and 'constant micro-planning and verification to ensure that the enrolment, retention and successful completion of SC students". However, the situation of SC children has continued to lag significantly behind the national average, indicating either a failure in the implementation of national policies and programmes to address the situation, or a problem in the model or approach to addressing the issue.

In the recently finalized Approach Paper to the 11th Five Year Plan of the Government of India, which will provide the overall framework for the Government's work from 2007-2011, the Government reiterated its commitment to addressing disparities in education between castes. The Approach Paper states the following:

> "Development and empowerment of socially disadvantaged groups is a commitment enshrined in the Constitution, and education is the

> most effective instrument of social empowerment. Schemes for the educational uplift of the SCs and STs have borne fruit although the gap between the general population and SCs and STs are still at unacceptable levels....Some minorities have fallen far behind the national average in education. It will be necessary to go to the root of the problem and examine the reasons for the decline so that remedial measures can be taken during the 11th Plan."

In India, there have been various schemes and programmes which have been introduced to bridge the divide between SC children and other children in primary school. Regarding supply side interventions, there are two basic approaches to addressing social exclusion in education, targeting excluded groups with supplementary service or focusing on universal improvements of the system. "Universalist approaches are essential to building a sense of social solidarity and citizenship." Targeted programmes have generally served as a means of compensating for government weakness in delivering on universal services, and may actually be marginalising those they are intending to reach if they result in labelling of particular groups and don't act as a bridge to mainstream education services. Kabeer concludes that such approaches "need to go beyond 'ameliorative' approaches that address the symptoms of the problem to 'transformative' approaches that address its causes."

During the 1990s, the focus of the large-scale District Primary Education Programme and more recently the Sarva Shiksha Abhiyan (SSA) ("Universal Primary Education Campaign") was on addressing the inadequate budgetary resources and the poor quality of teaching, which were regarded as two key constraints to achieving universal participation. However, while it is obvious that universal elementary education demands a significant increase in financial allocation, it is also evident both from the experience in India but also based on global experience that finances alone will not ensure attendance of disadvantaged populations. One of the development objectives of the SSA is "enrolment of children of SC and ST will be near parity with that of other groups", which in itself is a relatively modest objective as it focuses on enrolment, rather than completion of learning achievements, and also mentions "near parity" rather than parity. However, the approach the programme has adopted is not sufficiently comprehensive in addressing the above mentioned constraints and will therefore fail to influence the relevant decision-making processes which relates to a child's education status, particularly related to the issues faced by SC children.

Addressing social exclusion requires a holistic approach which promotes involvement of excluded populations in community life; ensures access to all basic services; promotes behaviour change; increases income and addresses other key elements of exclusion. Similarly in education, a holistic approach is necessary based on an analysis of the various components of the decision-making process related to regularly attending school for an SC child and, from the supply side, all elements of the education experience must be addressed. This obviously entails a *multi-sectorial response* which is broader than education alone, as the challenge of social exclusion does not only exist in the education sector (as mentioned above), and factors outside the education sector will relate to the education opportunities available to SC children. A comprehensive response will also need to be context-specific, with the need for innovative programmes to bring and keep children into the mainstream school system by making schooling attractive to them and also worthwhile for the parents. A *comprehensive and context specific strategy* must be adopted, which is often not the case with existing programmes and policies in India. For example, many of the schemes which focus on increasing demand for education, such as providing text books and uniforms and/or a conditional cash transfer for SC children, do not address other factors within the household related to the decision-making process or to the other factors related to the school or the community. The above conclusion is consistent with the outcome of the Joint Review Mission of the SSA in 2006, which stated that "in certain groups like SC, ST and minority children, the number of out-of-school children is still high. It is necessary to identify specific contextual aspects including sociocultural reasons that inhibit the enrolment and retention of these groups. The requires building of appropriate capacity and resource support at the subdistrict level to develop relevant strategies and interventions."

While the global literature on conditional cash transfers highlights the importance of addressing supply-side constraints (i.e. the education system) at the same time or as a prerequisite to influencing the demand-side with a conditional cash transfer (CCT), the other determinants discussed above must also be addressed if a CCT is to be effective. A CCT implemented as a vertical, isolated intervention, without a more comprehensive response may actually result in negative consequences if children increase their attendance in schools or communities that do not meet at least a minimum level of acceptability for SC children from a social exclusion perspective. For example, if SC children are faced with discriminatory practices within the classroom, or within the community more generally on the way to school, negative results may be realized as a result of a programme which focuses only on stimulating demand.

In order to address all of the determinants of social exclusion, it is important for any intervention designed to reduce disparities to include *strengthening local capacity to manage a comprehensive response*. This will ensure that approach is context-specific and addresses the local particular determinants and dynamics of exclusion, which exist within a community. This is of particular relevant to caste issues in India and the forms of exclusion, recognizing that the nature of the caste relationship varies greatly between regions and communities. It is therefore necessary for any strategy to include the facilitation of a process in which communities undertake an analysis of causes and factors which lead to social exclusion of children from primary school and develop a comprehensive response. Consistent with a human rights based approach, both the nature of the process of addressing this issue, as well as the results itself, are factors which should be prioritised. The 73rd Amendment of the Constitution, which was enacted in 1992, delegated various powers and responsibilities to the locally elected bodies called the Panchayats, which provides a platform for strengthening a broader process to address social exclusion. One of the main recommendations from the review of SSA in 2006 was "Greater use of Innovation Funds should be encouraged for interventions to boost the performance of first generation learners, especially SC and ST children and older girls". The innovation funds should be managed locally and based on an analysis of the barriers faced by SC children within the household, the community and in the school (and the interplays between these).

Encouraging the enrolment of SC children in the problem-solving and solution process, and also the care-givers in a community level process may in itself contribute to positive change at community level. Similarly, encouraging *children themselves to participate in the management of the school,* and also reaching children who are not attending, and promoting the diversity of this participation by ensuring that SC children participate in the process, could be a significant step towards making schools more inclusive. The "Child Cabinet" initiative supported as part of the UNICEF Quality Education Package is one such opportunity and while not yet evaluated, is showing some positive signs of contributing to children's involvement in the management of the school. It however does not include the stipulation of ensuring that the cabinet is made up of children from various castes (and other characteristics), and therefore will not necessarily address issues related to social exclusion.

Another element in a comprehensive response to addressing social exclusion in primary education is the *importance of reaching children at a very young age*, as issues related to social exclusion summarized above are more difficult to address as children become older. The literature on the importance of early childhood development is well developed, and is particularly relevant to the issue of social exclusion in primary education for two reasons. First, in order for children to perform effectively in primary school, they must have an enabling environment and be adequately prepared, which includes having access to early childhood development opportunities either within or outside the home. This can be one of the most effective means of "levelling the playing field" for excluded children. Secondly, social discrimination is a learned behaviour, as evidenced by the fact that young children do not hold prejudices which exist in the society as a whole. Therefore, intervening at the household, community and school level as early as possible, preferably before the time a child learns discriminatory norms held in the community, would be more effective than attempting to have children "unlearn" these processes later. One way this could be achieved in India is by broadening the mandate of the Department of Education (DoE) to include providing educational opportunities and other forms of support to 3-6 year olds. This is currently the mandate of the Department of Women and Child Development (DWCD), which manages the Integrated Child Development Scheme which is intended to reach children from 3-6 years old with learning opportunities (and also younger children with other services). By shifting this responsibility from DWCD to DoE, the educational continuum beginning with the young child would be more integrated, pro-active system of addressing social exclusion by reaching younger children with educational service.

Information regarding the level of exclusion of SC children from education is necessary to enable an effective management process at local level. The attendance of socially excluded children, such as the scheduled caste, tends to be more irregular than other children and therefore moving beyond enrolment data, to focus instead on retention, transition, average years of schooling data, and most importantly completion rates and assessment of basis learning competencies, disaggregated by caste (and gender, other social groupings) is necessary in order to assess and monitor the capacity of the education system to reach and provided a quality service to traditionally excluded groups. *Strengthening data management systems which provide disaggregated data by caste, gender and other characteristics at local level* is therefore necessary. This data must be complemented by data on dropouts and on those how have never attended school. However, this level of disaggregation is often not currently included in either routine government monitoring systems (such as the Education Management Information System (EMIS) of DPEP, or the District Information System for Education (DISE of SSA) or surveys which collect information on education indicators. Strengthening the generation and use of data, including placing it in the public domain, would complement the recent positive developments related to expanding the power and use of the "Right to Information" Act, which promotes the availability and use of information related to government services (and other information) to the public. It would also be important to include private schools in this equation, recognizing the trend discussed above regarding children (particularly boys belonging to higher caste) being sent to private school.

A comprehensive, context specific, participatory process which includes reaching young children would go a long way in addressing social exclusion of SC children from primary education in India. Programmes which improve only the supply-side or the demand-side, or even those which address both but are not based on a more comprehensive analysis of the factors which influence the various decision-making processes related to a child's education status, will not be comprehensive enough to address this multifaceted and long-standing issue which continues to exclude SC children from the education system.

References

Ajwad, Mohamed Ihsan (2006) "Anti-Poverty Programs in Uttar Pradesh", World Bank Staff Paper, World Bank, Washington.

Department of Education (2006) *Sarva Shiksha Abhiyan: Fourth joint Review Mission.* Aide Memoire, New Delhi.

Government of India (2003) *Tenth Five Year Plan 2003-2007,* Planning Commission, New Delhi.

IIPS (International Institute for Population Sciences), 1999a, National Family Health Survey II, 1998/9, National Report, Mumbai.

Jonsson, Urban (2003) *Human Rights Approach to Development Programming,* Eastern and Southern Africa Regional Office, UNICEF, Nairobi.

Sharankumar Limbale. (2004), *Towards an Aesthetic of Dalit Literature*, Orient Longman.

3

Economic Exclusion of Dalits

In India, exclusion revolves around the societal interrelations and institutions that exclude, discriminate, isolate and deprive some groups on the basis of group identities like caste and ethnicity. It is caste-based exclusion which forms the basis for various anti-discriminatory policies. Historically, the caste system has regulated the social and economic life of the people in India. The organisational scheme of the caste system is based on the division of people into social groups (or castes) in which the civil, cultural and economic rights of each individual caste are predetermined or ascribed by birth and made hereditary. The assignment of civil, cultural and economic rights is therefore unequal and hierarchical. The most important feature of the caste system, however, is that it provides for a regulatory mechanism to enforce social and economic organisation through the instruments of social ostracism, and reinforces it further with justification and support from philosophical elements in the Hindu religion.

The caste system's fundamental characteristics of fixed civil, cultural and economic rights for each caste, with restrictions on change, implies "forced exclusion" of one caste from the rights of the other caste, or from undertaking the occupations of other castes. Exclusion and discrimination in civil, cultural, and particularly in economic spheres such as occupation and labour employment, are therefore internal to the system and a necessary outcome of its governing principles.

In the market economy framework, occupational immobility operates through restrictions in various markets such as land, labour, credit, other inputs and services necessary for any economic activity. Labour, being an integral part of the production process of any economic activity, would obviously become part of market discrimination. This implies that the caste system involves the negation of not only equality and freedom, but also of basic human rights, particularly of low-caste untouchables, thus becoming an impediment in personal development.

The principles of equality and freedom are not the governing principles of the caste system. This is because the underlying principles of the caste system assume particular notions of 'human rights'. Unlike many other human societies, the caste system does not recognise the individual and his/her distinctiveness as the centre of the social purpose. In fact, for the purpose of rights and duties, the unit of Hindu society is not an individual. Even the family is not regarded as a unit in Hindu society, except for the purposes of marriage and inheritance. The primary unit in Hindu society is caste, and hence the rights and privileges (or lack of them) of an individual are on account of him/her being a member of a particular caste.

Due to differential ranking and the hierarchical nature of the caste system, the entitlements to various rights become narrower and narrower as one goes down the hierarchical ladder within the caste system. Various castes get artfully interlinked and coupled with each other in a manner such that the rights and privileges of the higher castes become the causative reasons for the disadvantage and disability of the lower castes, particularly the untouchables. As Ambedkar observed, a caste does not exist in a single number, only in plural. Castes exist as a system of endogenous groups that are interlinked with each other in an unequal measure of rights and relations in all walks of life. Castes at the top of the order enjoy more rights at the expense of those located at the bottom. Therefore, the untouchables located at the bottom of the caste hierarchy have much fewer economic and social rights.

Since the civil, cultural and economic rights (particularly with respect to occupation and property rights) of each caste are ascribed, and are compulsory, the institution of caste necessarily involves forced exclusion of one caste from the rights of another. The unequal and hierarchical assignment of economic and social rights by ascription obviously restricts freedom of occupation and human development.

In India, caste has become co-terminous with race in the definition and exclusion of distinct population groups because of their descent. For one hundred and sixty million Dalits or 'untouchables' at the bottom of India's caste system a population on par with that of Russia or Brazil the exclusion extends to the economic realms of wages, jobs, education, and land. Despite formal protections in law, discriminatory treatment remains endemic and discriminatory societal norms continue to be reinforced by government and private structures, often through violent means. Dalits are denied access to land, forced to work in degrading conditions, and routinely abused at the hands of the police and of higher-caste groups that enjoy the state's protection. In what has been called India's "hidden apartheid," entire villages in many Indian states remain completely segregated by caste. Untouchability endures as a cover for exploitative economic relationships and the caste system survives a cruel and efficient economic order.

Under constitutional provisions and various laws, the state grants Dalits a certain number of privileges, including reservations (quotas) in education, government jobs, and government bodies. National and state legislation also outlaw the practice of bonded labour and manual scavenging, set ceilings on a single landowner's holdings, allocate surplus government lands to Dalit and tribal populations, and criminalise the practice of 'untouchability' and other atrocities against low-caste communities.

The government has also attempted to increase the self-sufficiency of the scheduled-caste population through financial assistance for self-employment activities and through development programs designed to increase education and skills. Protective measures are monitored by the National Commission for Scheduled Castes and Scheduled Tribes. Development measures for the educational, social, and economic uplifting of scheduled castes are administered by the Department of Welfare.

Despite this large body of legislation and administrative agency mandates assigned exclusively to deal with the plight of scheduled castes, the laws have benefited few and, due to a lack of political will, development programs and welfare projects designed to improve economic conditions for Dalits have generally had little effect.

Although the constitutional abolition of 'untouchability' in 1950 meant that upper-caste Hindus could no longer segregate Dalits or force them to perform any 'polluting' occupation, caste prejudice and corruption within the police and judiciary have effectively ensured that atrocities against Dalits go unpunished, that land reforms remain unimplemented, and that prohibitions on bonded labour and manual scavenging remain unenforced. Upper-caste threats of physical abuse and social boycotts for refusing to perform demeaning tasks also ensure preservation of the economic status quo.

Forms of Caste Exclusion and Discrimination

The practice of caste-based exclusion and discrimination thus involves what has been described as "living mode exclusion", exclusion in political participation, and exclusion and disadvantage in social and economic opportunities. Caste/untouchability and ethnicity-based exclusion reflects in the inability of individuals and groups like former untouchables, adivasis and similar groups to interact freely and productively with others and to take part in the full economic, social and political life of a community. Incomplete citizenship or denial of civil rights (freedom of expression, rule of law, right to justice), political rights (right and means to participate in the exercise of political power), and socio-economic rights (economic security and equality of opportunities) are key dimensions of impoverished lives.

Caste and untouchability-based exclusion and discrimination can be categorised in the economic, civil, cultural, and political spheres as follows:

Firstly, economic exclusion can be practised in the labour market through denial of jobs; in the capital market through denial of access to capital; in the agricultural land market through denial of sale and purchase or leasing of land; in the input market through denial in sale and purchase of factor inputs; and in the consumer market through denial in the sale and purchase of commodities and consumer goods.

Secondly, discrimination can occur through what Amartya Sen describes as "unfavourable inclusion", through differential treatment in the terms and conditions of contract, one of them reflecting in discrimination in the prices charged and received by discriminated groups. Discriminated groups can get lower prices for the goods that they sell, and could pay higher prices for the goods that they buy, as compared with the market price or the price paid by other groups.

Thirdly, exclusion and discrimination can occur in access to social needs supplied by government or public institutions, or by private institutions in the fields of education, housing and health, including common property resources like waterbodies, grazing land and land for common use.

Fourthly, groups (particularly untouchables) may face exclusion and discrimination from participation in certain categories of jobs (the sweeper being excluded from household jobs) because of the notion of purity and pollution, and may be restricted to so-called "unclean" occupations.

In the civil and cultural spheres, untouchables may face discrimination and exclusion in the use of public services like roads, temples, waterbodies, and institutions delivering services like education, health and other public services.

In the political sphere, untouchables could face discrimination in the use of political rights, and in participation in the decision-making process. Due to physical (or residential) segregation, and social exclusion on account of the notion of untouchability, they may suffer from a general societal exclusion.

Since there is a societal mechanism to regulate and enforce the customary norms and rules of the caste system, untouchables generally face opposition in the form of social and economic boycott, violence, and such acts as a general deterrent to their right to development.

Caste and untouchability-based exclusion and discrimination are essentially "structural in nature" and comprehensive and multiple in coverage, involving the denial of equal opportunities.

Economic Exclusion: Empirical Evidences

Studies show that dalits suffer from limited access to capital assets like agricultural land and non-land assets (and/or low productivity of those assets), less urbanisation and employment diversification away from agriculture, exceptionally high dependence on casual wage labour, high underemployment, lower daily wages, particularly in non-farm activities, and low levels of literacy and education compared with non-dalit/adivasi groups in Indian society.

The question is why dalits and adivasis, categorised as scheduled castes (SCs) and scheduled tribes (STs), have poor access to resources that directly and indirectly determine the level of income. Why their ownership of agricultural land and non-land capital assets is low compared with non-SC/STs. Why unemployment rates are high compared with non-SC/STs. Why daily wage earnings of SC/STs in non-farm activities are lower compared with non-SC/STs. Why literacy rates and education levels are much lower when compared with non-SC/STs.

Let us look at the evidence on discrimination in civil, cultural and political spheres provided by official data, besides all-India and regional studies. These include an all-India 2000 ActionAid study ('Untouchability in Rural India' by Ghanshyam Saha, Satish Deshpande, Sukhadeo Thorat, Harsh Mander, Amita Baviskar and research and other regional staff, Delhi), a study on Karnataka (1973-74 and 1991), Andhra Pradesh (1977), Orissa (1987-88) and Gujarat (1996). The all-India study presents evidence from 11 states. The studies based on village surveys bring out the actual magnitude of the exclusion, discrimination and atrocities against dalits.

ActionAid's study — conducted in 555 villages across 11 Indian states — found that discrimination in labour markets operates through exclusion in hiring, and unfair or low wages. In about 36% of the villages, SCs were denied casual employment in agriculture. In about 25% of villages, SCs faced discrimination in wage payments. SCs received daily wages at a rate that was less than the market wage rate, or wages paid to non-SC workers. Belief in the concept of purity and pollution also impacted hiring of SC labourers — in about one-third of villages SCs were excluded from employment in the construction of houses.

In the case of other markets, the study observed discriminatory treatment of SCs in access to irrigation water and public and private services. In a little more than one-third of the villages, SCs were denied access to water for agriculture. In case of agricultural land, selective evidence from some states brings out the restrictions placed by the high castes on SCs in the purchase of private agricultural land, and use of public land for agriculture and housing. In the case of access to common property resources like grazing land, fishing ponds, and other resources, SCs faced exclusion in about one-fifth of the sample villages.

The notion of pollution and purity reflected in the exclusionary and discriminatory behaviour of higher castes in the consumer markets — in the sale and purchase of consumer goods, particularly milk, vegetables and other such goods. In 35% of the villages surveyed, SCs were not allowed to sell any kind of goods at village-level markets. In about 47% of villages, SCs were not allowed to sell milk to village cooperatives and private buyers. The survey data also reveals some isolated evidence of exclusion and discrimination in the sale and purchase of consumer goods like bakery products and vegetables. Such restrictions compelled SCs to go to small towns and other nearby marketplaces where their caste identity was not so obvious, or was hidden.

Micro-level studies such as those from Andhra Pradesh and Karnataka provide some evidence on economic discrimination in occupation, employment, wages, and the credit market as well as in other economic spheres. The Andhra Pradesh study observed that SCs faced restrictions in efforts to change their occupation. Similarly, the Karnataka study revealed that nearly 85% of SC respondents continue to be engaged in their traditional occupations, with only 15% able to make a switch-over. The Orissa study observed discrimination in land lease, credit and labour markets in rural areas. Nearly 96% of untouchable respondents in one village and all untouchable respondents in the second village were discriminated against in wage payment, with 28% in one village and 20% in another facing discrimination in payment of rent.

For urban areas, Banerjee and Knight observed that "there is indeed discrimination by caste, particularly job discrimination" and that "discrimination appears to operate at least in part through traditional mechanisms, with untouchables disproportionately represented in poorly-paid dead-end jobs... Even if discrimination is no longer practised, the effects of past discrimination could carry over to the present. This may help explain why discrimination is greatest in operative jobs in which contacts are more important for recruitment, and not in white-collar jobs in which recruitment involves formal methods."

Such economic discrimination had obvious impacts on the earnings of SC households, and reflected in the incidence of high poverty among them.

Caste Discrimination and the Right to Food

Empirical studies also show denial of access and differential treatment in food security programmes like the midday meal (MDM) scheme and fair price shops (FPS). The study on the midday meal scheme in Rajasthan reported the exclusion of scheduled caste persons from employment as cooks and helpers in almost 60% of the sample villages. Another study based on a sample of about 550 villages in five states — Uttar Pradesh, Bihar, Andhra Pradesh, Tamil Nadu and Rajasthan — reported exclusion and discriminatory treatment in the operation of midday meal schemes and fair price shops.

In terms of scale, caste discrimination afflicts more than one out of three fair price shops and more than one out of three government schools serving midday meals. In terms of geographical spread, it is unquestionably a nationwide problem — from 24% in Andhra Pradesh to 52% in Rajasthan, to a vast majority in Uttar Pradesh and Bihar, respondent villages from every state reported problems of caste discrimination and exclusion in the midday meal scheme. Likewise with the FPS, no state is free of discrimination — from 17% in Andhra Pradesh to 86% in Bihar. For instance, every state reports a substantial percentage of dominant caste public distribution system (PDS) dealers practising caste-based discrimination in the distribution of PDS goods, for example preferential order of service by caste, or hierarchically segregated timings for dominant caste and dalit customers.

While the problem is nationwide, its degree varies considerably from state to state. Where higher percentages of midday meal cooks and organisers are dalit, and where a higher percentage of midday meals are held in dalit colonies, a lower incidence of caste discrimination in the scheme is reported. In Andhra Pradesh, where indicators of dalit participatory empowerment and access are relatively high (49% of respondent villages have dalit cooks, 45% have dalit organisers, and 46% are held in dalit localities), reported caste discrimination in the midday meal scheme stands at 24%. In Tamil Nadu, where the same empowerment and access indicators are lower (31%, 27% and 19%, respectively), reported discrimination stands at 36%. And in Rajasthan, where the indicators are alarmingly low (8% dalit cooks, 0% dalit organisers, 12% held in dalit colonies), reported discrimination was extremely high at 52%.

A similar pattern emerges in access to fair price shops, where higher proportions of dalit dealers and FPS held in dalit colonies correspond with lower proportions of reported discrimination and 'untouchability' practices.

Exclusion from Civil and Political Spheres

During 1999-2001, an average of 28,016 cases per year were registered by untouchables in the country under the Anti-Untouchability Act of 1955 and the SC and ST Prevention of Atrocities Act. This comes to about three cases per 100,000 population and included restrictions on access to temples, wells, taps, tea stalls, restaurants, community baths, roads, and other services. The ratio of such cases was highest in Rajasthan (9.3), followed by Madhya Pradesh (7.7). The ratio was about three cases per 100,000 population in Orissa, Karnataka, Gujarat and Andhra Pradesh.

The break-up of crimes against untouchables for the year 2000 include 526 cases of murder, 3,497 of grievous hurt, 290 cases of arson, 1,000 cases of sexual assault, and 11,587 cases of other offences. During a nine-year period between 1992 and 2000, a total of 252,370 cases of crime, including cases of discrimination and atrocities, were registered by untouchables.

Access to Justice

A number of anti-discrimination statutes and other legal provisions exist as legal safeguards against caste and untouchability-based discrimination. As mentioned earlier, the primary piece of legislation designed to provide a measure of protection to people from scheduled castes and scheduled tribes and to enforce their rights are the Anti-Untouchability Act, 1955 (in 1979 it was re-named the Civil Rights Act) and the Scheduled Caste and Scheduled Tribes Prevention of Atrocities Act, 1989.

There are limited studies that examine the effectiveness of these legislations and access to institutions of justice. However, available evidence indicates that these legislative provisions are highly underutilised. SC/STs also suffer from discriminatory access to institutions of justice such as the police and the judiciary. Studies indicate that the scheduled castes/tribes face insurmountable obstacles at various levels from village-level functionaries like sarpanchs to the police, public prosecutors and other functionaries who are extremely non-cooperative and discriminatory. This is essentially reflected in denial of justice to SC/STs.

Official data on civil rights cases shows that of the total number of cases registered in 1991, only 1.56% were convicted. The conviction rate came down to .60% in 1999 and .85% in 2000. This shows that the conviction rate in cases relating to civil rights violations and atrocities was less than 1% and close to 0%.

Analysis of 100 documented cases of atrocity during 2000-2003 in Andhra Pradesh throws some light on the reasons for the low conviction rate. The case studies indicated "a disturbing trend of subversion of the rights of dalits to justice and compensation under the law once an atrocity takes place" The study observed negligence and collusion at the stages of registration, chargesheeting and investigation, at seeking justice before the law in the courts and in giving compensation. About the role of the judiciary, Dalit Human Rights Monitor 2003 observed: "If the low conviction rate under the Act is any indication, the judiciary has responded poorly to the Act. Judiciary delay and dilution of the scope, applicability and meaning of the SC/ST Act has resulted in denial of justice to the dalits".

Caste and Employment Discrimination

Allocation of labour on the basis of caste is one of the fundamental tenets of the caste system. In traditional Indian society, Hinduism's fourfold varna theory describes a broad functional division of labour. For those within the four principal caste categories, caste has not proved to be a completely rigid system. Just as the higher ritual status of Brahmins does not necessarily translate into economic or political supremacy, those lower in the ranks are able to move up in the local hierarchy through the capture of political power, the acquisition of land, and migration to other regions.

For Dalits, however, who occupy the fifth and lowest caste category, caste remains a determinative factor for the attainment of social, political, civil, and economic rights. Migration and the anonymity of the urban environment have in some cases resulted in upward occupational mobility, but the majority continues to perform their traditional or 'polluting' functions. A lack of training and education, as well as discrimination in seeking other forms of employment, have kept these traditions and their hereditary nature alive. Many 'untouchable' community members, for example, continue to work as leather workers, disposers of dead animals, and manual scavengers. As part of village custom, Dalits are made to render free services in times of death, marriage, or any village function. The cleaning of the whole village, the digging of graves, the carrying of firewood, and the disposal of dead animals are also tasks that Dalits are made to perform. A majority of the Dalit rural workforce subsists on the menial wages of landless agricultural labourers, earning less than US$1 a day. Those in urban areas, work mostly in the unorganised sector. India's much touted system of affirmative action or reservations for scheduled castes assists less than 1 percent of the Dalit population. In all forms of labour, women are consistently paid less than men, compounding the dual discrimination of caste and gender.

Manual Scavenging

According to government statistics, an estimated one million Dalits are manual scavengers (a majority of them women) who clear faeces from public and private latrines and dispose of dead animals; unofficial estimates are much higher. Manual scavenging is a caste-based occupation, deemed too polluting and filthy for anyone but Dalits. Manual scavengers exist under different caste names throughout the country, such as the Bhangis in Gujarat, the Pakhis in Andhra Pradesh, and the Sikkaliars in Tamil Nadu. Members of these communities are invariably placed at the very bottom of the caste hierarchy, and even the hierarchy of Dalit subcastes. Using little more than a broom, a tin plate, and a basket, they are made to clear faeces from public and private latrines and carry them to dumping grounds and disposal sites. Though long outlawed, the practice of manual scavenging continues in most states.

An activist in the southern state of Andhra Pradesh, who has been working for the rehabilitation of cleaning workers for the past sixteen years, describes the pay scale in his state:

> Private cleaners receive Rs.5 to ten a month for each house they clean [US$0.11 to $0.21]. They clean up to ten to fifteen houses a day, many of which have six or more family members. Those employed by urban municipalities are paid Rs.2,000 to Rs.2,500 [US$43—$53] a month but are only paid once every four to six months. Some are permanent, and some are casual. There are no health benefits, no gloves, no masks, and no utensils. The majority is made up of women.

Social discrimination against scavengers is rampant. Most scavengers live in segregated rural colonies and are unable to make use of common resources. According to the activist:

> In one toilet there can be as many as four hundred seats which all have to be manually cleaned. This is the lowest occupation in the world, and it is done by the community that occupies the lowest status in the caste system. Even other scheduled-caste people won't touch the safai karamcharis [cleaning workers]. It is 'untouchability' within the 'untouchables,' yet nobody questions it.

Poverty among Bhangis is so acute, that some have even been known to separate non-digested wheat from buffalo dung to make chappatis (flat bread). When interviewed in early 1998, thirty-year-old Parsotambhai, a mother of three in Ahmedabad district, Gujarat, earned Rs.10 (US$0.21) a month for each house she cleaned. She also received small amounts of food once a day and complained that there was too much work. Others voiced similar complaints:

> They give one person too much work so they have to take their family members, even their children, at night to finish the work; otherwise, they would be fired. It takes four people to do the work that they give one person. None of the children are really studying. Girls sometimes study up to fifth standard, boys up to seventh.

The Employment of Manual Scavengers and Construction of Dry Latrines (Prohibition) Act, 1993 prohibits the employment of scavengers or the construction of dry (non-flush) latrines with imprisonment for up to one year and/or a fine as high as Rs.2,000 (US$43). Offenders are also liable for prosecution under the Scheduled Castes and Scheduled Tribes (Prevention of Atrocities) Act, 1989.

In 1992, the government launched a national scheme that called for the identification, training, and rehabilitation of safai karamcharis (cleaning workers) throughout the country. Yet when confronted with the existence of manual scavenging and dry latrines within their jurisdiction, state governments often deny their existence altogether or claim that a lack of water supply prevents states from constructing flush latrines. This despite the fact that a sum of Rs.4,640,000,000 (US$992.3 million) was allocated to the scheme under the government's Eighth Five-Year Plan. Activists claim that the resources, including government funds, exist for construction and for the rehabilitation of scavengers; what is lacking is the political will to do so.

Landless Agricultural Labourers

Most Dalit victims of abuse are landless agricultural labourers who form the backbone of India's agrarian economy. Despite a host of land reform legislation, today over eighty-six per cent of Dalit households are landless or near landless. Those who own land often fall into the category of marginal landowners. Land is the prime asset in rural areas that determines an individual's standard of living and social status.

Lack of access to land makes Dalits economically vulnerable; their dependency is exploited by upper- and middle-caste landlords and allows for many abuses to go unpunished. Landless agricultural labourers throughout the country work for a few kilograms of rice or Rs.15 to Rs.35 (US$0.32 to $0.75) a day, well below the minimum wage prescribed in their state. Many labourers owe debts to their employers or other moneylenders.

Land reform and increased wages for rural labourers are the central demands of most leftist guerrilla organisations active in West Bengal, Bihar, and Andhra Pradesh. Private landlord militias and state security forces have targeted civilians thought to be guerrilla sympathisers. The failure of most state governments to implement land reform legislation has only added to the sense of economic vulnerability that fuels militant movements. In Bihar in particular, guerrillas enjoy Dalit support, as most of the Dalit community lives on the edge of starvation. Laws and regulations that prohibit alienation of Dalit lands, set ceilings on a single landowner's holdings, or allocate surplus government lands to scheduled castes and scheduled tribes have been largely ignored, or worse, manipulated by upper castes with the help of district administrations. In 1996, a door-to-door survey of two hundred and fifty villages in the state of Gujarat found that in almost all villages those who had title to land had no possession, and those who had possession had not had their land measured or faced illegal encroachments from upper castes. Many had no record of their holdings at all. Even those who had been offered land under agrarian reform legislation refused to accept it for fear of an upper-caste backlash. Efforts by Dalits to acquire land through the land reforms are met with social boycotts ostracising them from buying or selling anything in the village. These boycotts and other retaliatory acts are described further below.

Bonded Labour

Given the insignificant amounts of remuneration in manual scavenging, agricultural labour, and other fields of Dalit employment, it comes as little surprise that many families borrow money from their upper-caste neighbours and consequently go into bondage.

An estimated forty million people in India, among them fifteen million children, are bonded labourers working in slave-like conditions in order to pay off a debt. Bonded labour refers to work in slave-like conditions in order to pay off a debt. Due to the high interest rates charged and the abysmally low wages paid, the debts are seldom settled. Bonded labourers are frequently low-caste, illiterate, and extremely poor, while the creditors/employers are usually higher-caste, literate, comparatively wealthy, and relatively more powerful members of the community.

The Bonded Labour System (Abolition) Act, 1976 abolishes all agreements and obligations arising out of the bonded labour system. It aims to release all labourers from bondage, cancel any outstanding debt, prohibit the creation of new bondage agreements, and order the economic rehabilitation of freed bonded labourers by the state. It also punishes attempts to compel persons into bondage with a maximum of three years in prison and a Rs. 2,000 (US$43) fine. However, the extent to which bonded labourers have been identified, released, and rehabilitated in the country is negligible. A lack of political will, and outright abuse of the law has also sabotaged any meaningful implementation of protective criminal legislation, affirmative action quotas, or the constitutional promise of universal primary education.

Education and Reservations

The Indian Constitution mandates the state to provide free, compulsory and universal education for all children up to fourteen years, with special care and consideration given to promote the educational progress of scheduled castes. India's policy of reservations is an attempt by the central government to remedy past injustices related to low-caste status. To allow for proportional representation in certain state and federal institutions, the constitution reserves 22.5 per cent of seats in federal government jobs, state legislatures, the lower house of parliament, and educational institutions for scheduled castes and scheduled tribes.

Fifty years on, illiteracy still plagues almost two thirds of Dalits as compared to about one half of the general population. The literacy gap between Dalits and the rest of the population fell a scant.39 percent between 1961 and 1991. Ninety-nine per cent of Dalit students are enrolled in government schools that lack basic infrastructure, classrooms, teachers and teaching aids. A majority is also enrolled in vernacular schools whose students suffer serious disadvantages in the job market as compared to those who learn in English-speaking schools.

Despite state assistance in primary education, Dalits also face an alarming dropout rate. According to the National Commission for Scheduled Castes and Scheduled Tribes' 1996-97 and 1997-98 Report, the national dropout rate for Dalit children was a staggering 49.35 per cent at the primary level, 67.77 per cent for middle school, and 77.65 per cent for secondary school. Though these rates are partly attributable to the need for Dalit children to supplement their family wages through labour, more insidious and less well-documented are the loss of faith in education as an instrument for socioeconomic change, and the discriminatory and abusive treatment faced by Dalit children, who often sit in the back of classrooms, at the hands of their teachers and fellow students.

The reservation policy, too, has not been fully implemented. The National Commission for Scheduled Castes and Scheduled Tribes' report also indicates that of the total scheduled caste reservation quota in the Central Government, fifty-four per cent remains unfilled. More than eighty-eight per cent remains unfilled in the public sector and forty-five per cent in state banks. A closer examination of the caste composition of government services, institutions of education and other services, however, reveals an "unacknowledged reservation policy" for upper-castes, particularly Brahmins, insidiously built into the system. Though they represented only five per cent of the population in 1989, Brahmins comprised seventy per cent of the Class I officers in governmental services. At universities, upper-castes occupy ninety per cent of the teaching posts in the social sciences and ninety-four per cent in the sciences, while Dalit representation is a lowly 1.2 and 0.5 percent, respectively.

Physical and Economic Retaliation

A principal weapon in sustaining economic and racial discrimination against Dalits is the use of social and economic boycotts and acts of retaliatory violence. Dalits are physically abused and threatened with economic and social ostracism from the community for refusing to carry out various caste-based tasks. Any attempt to alter village customs, defy the social order, or to demand land, increased wages, or political rights leads to violence and economic retaliation on the part of those most threatened by changes in the status quo. Dalit communities as a whole are summarily punished for individual transgressions; Dalits are cut off from community land and employment during social boycotts, women bear the brunt of physical attacks, and the letter of the law is rarely enforced.

Large-scale clashes between caste communities in Tamil Nadu's southern districts in recent years, for example, have often been triggered by Dalits' efforts to draw water from a "forbidden" well or by their refusal to perform a delegated task. Describing a boycott in 1998, a village resident and social worker in the Marathwada region of the state of Maharashtra recalled:

> The upper caste got together and said that we touched their God so we shouldn't live here. They put a social boycott on all the Dalits. We could not enter their land, we could not work for them, we could not get wood, we could not buy goods from their stores, and we could not

> grind grain in the flourmill. We were not even allowed to go near the wells in upper-caste territory to fetch water.

The boycott is reinforced when the village council levies fines against caste Hindus who refuse to participate in it. In villages in Karnataka state, for example, upper castes have been known to fine Rs.501 (US$10.71) for giving employment to Dalits during a social boycott.

Despite their appalling work conditions, even manual scavengers are unable to demand higher wages or sanitary instruments for use in the collection of human excreta. According to one:

> "When we ask for our rights from the government, the municipality officials threaten to fire us. So we don't say anything. This is what happens to people who demand their rights."

Since the early 1990s, violence against Dalits has escalated dramatically in response to growing Dalit rights movements. Between 1995 and 1997, a total of 90,925 cases were registered with the police nationwide as crimes and atrocities against scheduled castes. Of these 1,617 were for murder, 12,591 for hurt, 2,824 for rape, and 31,376 for offences listed under the Prevention of Atrocities Act. Given that Dalits are both reluctant and unable (for lack of police cooperation) to report crimes against themselves, the actual number of abuses is presumably much higher.

India's National Commission for Scheduled Castes and Scheduled Tribes has reported that these cases typically fall into one of three categories: cases relating to the practice of 'untouchability' and attempts to defy the social order; cases relating to land disputes and demands for minimum wages; and cases of atrocities by police and forest officials. Most of the conflicts take place within very narrow segments of the caste hierarchy, between the poor and the not so poor, the landless labourer and the marginal landowner. The differences lie in the considerable amount of leverage that the higher-caste Hindus or non-Dalits are able to wield over local police, district administrations, and even the state government.

The state's failure to prosecute atrocities against Dalits is well illustrated by its manipulation of the Scheduled Castes and Scheduled Tribes (Prevention of Atrocities) Act. Enacted in 1989, the Act provides for stiffer punishments for abuses against members of scheduled castes and scheduled tribes. Its enactment represented an acknowledgement on the part of the government that abuses, in their most degrading and violent forms, were still perpetrated against Dalits decades after independence.

The potential of the Scheduled Castes and Scheduled Tribes (Prevention of Atrocities) Act, 1989, to bring about social change, however, has been hampered by police corruption and caste bias, with the result that many allegations are not entered in police books. Ignorance of procedures and a lack of knowledge of the act have also affected its implementation. Even when cases are registered, the absence of special courts to try them can delay prosecutions for up to three to four years. Some state governments dominated by higher castes have even attempted to repeal the legislation altogether.

Impact of Economic Reforms

The impact of India's aggressive shift from a state regulated economy to a market economy with the privatisation of industries and the liquidation of policies and controls in economic planning and regulation has been most acutely felt by Dalits. The now decade-old economic reforms cling faithfully to the flawed 'trickle down' theory a theory that holds even less relevance for Dalits for whom few benefits can permeate the caste ceiling.

Since 1991, the start of India's New Economic Policy, the country has made astounding progress in the areas of technology, infrastructure, machinery, science, space and even nuclear research. Much of this progress has meant little to Dalits; most continue to live without the very basic amenities of electricity, sanitation, and safe drinking water.

According to the Madras Institute for Development Studies, only thirty-one per cent of Dalit households are equipped with electricity, as compared to sixty-one per cent on non-Dalit households. Only ten per cent of Dalit households have sanitation facilities as compared to twenty-seven per cent of non-Dalit ones. Disparities in distribution are not accidental. 'Untouchability' is reinforced by state allocation of facilities; separate facilities are provided for separate colonies. Dalits often receive the poorer of the two, if they receive any at all. In many villages, the state administration installs electricity, sanitation facilities, and water pumps in the upper-caste section, but neglects to do the same in the neighbouring, segregated Dalit colony. Basic supplies such as water are also segregated, and medical facilities and the better, thatched-roof houses exist exclusively in the upper-caste colony.

Available statistics reveal that between 1987 and 1993, the percentage of Dalits living below the poverty line actually increased by five percent, reversing a declining trend of the previous fifteen years. Half of the Dalit population lived below the poverty line in 1993 compared to a third of the general population. The poverty gap has continued to widen since 1993, as have the trends toward economic "liberalisation" and the state's failure to equitably allocate and distribute resources.

As liberalisation leads to a capital-intensive mode of production requiring a greater proportion of highly skilled workers to manage automated production processes, a large migration of unskilled labour to the agricultural sector has led to lower wages for agricultural workers as a whole. Eighty-five percent of India's Dalit population lives in rural areas and is directly associated with agriculture and cultivation. In addition to a reduction in agricultural subsidies, Dalits are also affected by the increased acquisition of coastal lands by multinationals (via the central government) for aquaculture projects. Dalits are the main labourers and tenants of coastal land areas and are increasingly being forced to leave these areas to live as displaced people, for the most part as foreign investment rises.

A reduction in the budget and fiscal deficit, devaluation, privatisation, the elimination or reduction in subsidies, and export promotion have also all contributed to inflation. As is true the world over, inflation hits the poorest the hardest. With most of their earnings spent on food, shelter, and clothing, any rise in prices has had a direct negative effect on Dalits' level of consumption. A lack of purchasing power is compounded by the devaluation of currency. The devaluation, aimed at increasing exports and creating more markets for domestic industries, has also led to a rise in prices for general essential imports.

With the underlying economic philosophy of increased reliance on market forces, a dismantling of controls, and a drastically reduced role of the state, the public sector is shrinking. The reservations model is therefore affecting and able to assist fewer people, inasmuch as government-related jobs are being drastically reduced. Reservations in educational institutions and scholarships for Dalit students represent a critical component in Dalit socioeconomic development. Economic reforms have also led to a freezing in grants to many institutions. The privatisation of social services is also turning education and health services into commodities only affordable to the rich.

Strategies to Combat Discrimination

The exploitation of agricultural labourers and the rigid assignment of demeaning occupations on the basis of caste keep Dalits in a position of economic and physical vulnerability. The triple burden of caste, class, and gender effectively ensures that Dalit women are the furthest removed from legal protections. Only with the honest implementation of laws designed to protect agricultural labourers and abolish manual scavenging and bonded labour, and the systematic prosecution of those responsible for attacks on Dalit men and women, can the process of attaining economic and physical security begin.

Dalits' status as an excluded caste of landless labourers has also made them particularly vulnerable to the global economic forces unleashed by India's economic reforms. The impact of economic reforms on Dalits in India, to be meaningful to the majority of India's poor, any reform strategy must embody sustainable economic empowerment of rural masses; investments to enhance their capability and effective measures for accelerated development of the disadvantaged sections like Dalits. The prerequisite to reforms therefore could be the radical land reforms, massive investments in rural areas into agriculture-related infrastructural projects, universalisation of primary education, primary health care system and reinforcement of positive discrimination in favour of Dalits.

New steps are also required at the national and international level to give effect to international standards on racism in the areas of criminal justice and public administration. The International Convention on the Elimination of All Forms of Racial Discrimination requires remedial action whenever there is a racist effect from public policy, but many states interpret their obligations to combat racism as limited to addressing racist intent. In the absence of implementation data and constant monitoring, the racist effect of public policy in many countries can be expected to continue to comprehensively to block the enjoyment of social, economic, and cultural rights, through the denial of education, social services, and protection from economic exploitation.

In India's case, the government must make available to the public government studies on issues affecting Dalits. Specifically, the government should release the white paper on reservations and the white paper on land reform. The first outlines the extent to which constitutional reservations have been implemented at the state and central level since independence. In particular, attention should be given to implementation of reservations in all ministries, in the secretariats of the Prime Minister and President, and in the police and judiciary. The second outlines the extent to which tenancy acts and acts that establish ceilings on single landowners' holdings have been implemented in all states.

In upholding constitutional guarantees of equality, freedom, justice and human dignity, it must then commit to: land and wage reform and the realisation of primary education for all children; implement measures designed to ensure that states abolish the practice of 'untouchability,' in compliance with Article 17 of the Constitution; prevent further violence and prosecute both state and private actors responsible for caste-motivated attacks on Dalit communities; enforce the Scheduled Castes and Scheduled Tribes (Prevention of Atrocities) Act, 1989 and other relevant legislation; and educate state agents and the Indian population on the rights and constitutional freedoms of all citizens.

The government must also fill all vacant scheduled-caste reservation posts with Dalit candidates, and as recommended by the National Commission for Scheduled Castes and Scheduled Tribes, provide for reservations in the judiciary as well as the private sector, which continues to enjoy government patronage in terms of concessional land, financing, and excise and sales tax relief.

At the global level, a first and essential step is the recognition that caste-based discrimination bars hundreds of millions from the exercise of their civil and political, and their economic, social, and cultural rights a precondition for international programs to support the abolition of caste discrimination and to remedy abuses.

The World Bank and other international lending institutions operational in India should ensure that anti-discrimination measures are built into World Bank and Asian Development Bank-funded projects in areas where the problems of caste violence and caste discrimination are severe. As part of its commitment to good governance, the World Bank, as well as other international lending institutions, should establish ongoing dialogue with Dalit NGOs at all stages of the decision-making process—before a loan is released, while the project is being implemented, and in the course of any post-project evaluation. Of paramount importance is for the World Bank to ensure that its funds are not being routed by the government for the illegal employment of manual scavengers in their sanitation programs. Lending geared toward the promotion of privatisation must first evaluate and then counter the damage to social services resulting from an erosion of the public sector.

India's donors and trading partners must encourage India to implement its own laws and must use every opportunity to raise the problem of caste violence both publicly at international meetings, congressional or parliamentary hearings, and in press conferences and privately, at Consultative Group meetings and in meetings with relevant officials. They must also work to develop programs and strategies for bilateral and multilateral aid programs to India that would make funds available to promote legal literacy and economic rehabilitation programs. United Nations agencies active in India must also pay particular attention to the issue of caste violence and caste discrimination and develop programs and strategies designed to curb abuse and encourage accountability.

The approach of Indian policymakers to overcoming discrimination and addressing social exclusion include such policy interventions as legal enforcement of anti-discrimination laws, reservation and preferential and general empowering measures that form part of anti-poverty programmes. These polices have brought about positive changes, but the rate of improvement has not been fast enough to reduce the absolute level of deprivation and the gap between the excluded group of scheduled castes and tribes and other advanced sections. The continuing exclusion-induced deprivation of disadvantaged groups of SCs indicates that addressing social exclusion is often much more difficult than addressing poverty.Social and cultural sources of exclusion (in economic, civil and political spheres) are rooted in informal social structures and institutions of caste and untouchability covering not only the private but public domain governed by the State. In this context, the inclusion of excluded groups is different from the social inclusion of materially deprived people. Poverty, even when broadly defined as exclusion from the means necessary for full participation in the normal activities of society, is largely a question of access to resources and services. The social exclusion of groups or individuals within that group is foremost a denial of equal opportunity, respect and recognition of the right to development. Fighting discrimination therefore calls for additional policies complementing anti-poverty and economic development programmes. But there is also considerable overlap, and therefore the need to combine and complement, and not divide, programmes against poverty and economic deprivation and policies for equal rights and social inclusion of disadvantaged groups.

References

Eleanor Zilliot. (2005), *From Untouchable to Dalit - Essays on the Ambedkar Movement*, Manohar Publications, New Delhi.

Gail Omvedt. (1994), *Dalits and the Democratic Revolution - Dr. Ambedkar and the Dalit Movement in Colonial India*, Sage Publications, New Delhi.

Mulk Raj Anand, (1992), *An Anthology of Dalit Literature*, Gyan Books, New Delhi.

Pradeep K. Sharma, (2006), *Dalit Politics and Literature*, Shipra Publications, New Delhi.

Ranabira Samaddara, Ghanshyam Shah, (2001), *Dalit Identity and Politics*, Sage Publications, New Delhi.

4

Educational Status of Dalits

Untouchables are known by different names. Mahatma Gandhi called them *Harijan,* children of god. Religious books of the Hindus called them *Sudras;* Ambedkar called them "depressed classes". However since 1970 the term "dalit" has been widely used dalit is a Marathi word, first used by Mahatma Jotiba Phule, a 19th century social reformer who led a movement for the upliftment of untouchables, which means "broken people." In official documents they are designated as the scheduled Castes (SCs).

In no part of the world has so much injustice and systematic discrimination been done to a particular group of people for thousands of years as that in India with regard to the ex-untouchables/dalits. Curiously, the bases of this discrimination were not religion, language, sex or colour, which normally constitute the common grounds for discriminatory treatment in most parts of the world. Rather it was "caste" or "birth", which is unique.

No doubt India has a rich and glorious cultural legacy to feel proud of. But it should be noted that nowhere in the world we find the extent of discrimination that is perpetuated by one group of people against the other, as it is done in case of low caste untouchables by the high caste Hindus in India. Caste system is a unique feature of Indian life. It is believed that originally there were only four broad/main castes the Brahmins (the priestly class), the kshatriyas (the warrior class), the vaisyas (the merchant and peasant class), and the sudras (the untouchable class). But over the last two thousand years, these four castes have been astronomically subdivided into thousands of castes and subcastes. The 1901 census revealed that there were two thousand three hundred and seventy eight "main Castes" and tribes in India. The official list of "scheduled castes" prepared by the then British authorities of the government of India in 1935 contained four hundred twenty nine untouchable castes.

According to *Dhamasutras* (religious books), because sudras were born from the feet of the universal soul Brahma (god), *they were destined to serve the three upper castes/varnas* born from His mouth (Brahmins), arms (kshatriyas), and thighs (vaisyas). The hymns of Rigveda justified the hierarchical system of social orders saying that all these four orders represent the Creator, Brahma. It is believed that from the lord's "mouth" were born the Brahmins, so they became a priestly class; from His "arms" were born the kshatriyas, so they became warriors; from His "thighs" were born vaisayas, and they performed ordinary work, like business or agriculture; and from His "feet" the sudras were born and so they performed the dirty work of scavenging, disposing of dead animals or unknown human bodies. The untouchables were told by the rules of religious books that if they accept their position in life without questioning and by doing their assigned duties they become eligible to be born in the next life in a high caste. They were also told that because of the sins they committed in previous life, they were born in untouchable castes. In this way a system of hierarchical order was created which survives even today. In fact, it is the longest surviving apartheid-like system of exclusion in the world.

The old Hindu law prevented untouchables from reading/reciting the *Veda* (religious book) or participating in the veda religious ceremonies of the Brahmins/Aryas. Accordingly:

> If a sudra intentionally overhears the veda chants, he shall have his ears filled with molten tin and dark-red pigment. If a sudra dares to recite the chants himself, he will have his tongue cut out; and if he learns the chants by heart, his body shall be split in twain.

Thus, traditionally sudras/dalits were excluded from engaging themselves in reading and learning profession and participating in Aryan religious customs and ceremonies. There is more to it. Many other disabilities and restrictions were imposed on them. For instance, any dalit male who had sexual relations with a Brahmin woman would be punished by "having his penis severed and his wealth confiscated, and if the woman has a husband or patron of some kind, these above two punishments will be followed by death". Another scholar cites a rule from scriptures, which stated:

> If he assumes a position of equality with high caste men, either in sitting, or going along the road, he shall receive corporal punishment. A sudra committing adultery with women of the first three castes shall suffer capital punishment, or shall be burnt alive tied up with straw... if a sudra intentionally reviles a Brahmin or criminally assaults him; the limb with which he offends shall be cut off.

Manusmriti, the Hindu legal code, too contains similar kind of provisions. There are many provisions set down for the purpose of excluding dalits from places of worship. Regarding marriage between Brahmin men and dalit women, the *Manusmriti* pronounces, "from the moment of consummation they and all their progeny shall forever be of the sudra varna" or "be damned to hell." Heavy punishments, including sentences of death, were to be pronounced for sudras violating the rights of higher varnas, and the king was strictly directed "to ensure that sudras stay in a servile position (*dasya*) to the Brahmins." At another place, it is stated that "neither an untouchable, nor a pig, a cock, a dog, a menstruating woman, or an impotent man should be watching the priests dine." "The dwellings of untouchables and dog-Cookers should be outside the village; they must use discarded bowls, and dogs, and donkeys should be their wealth." The next verse stated, "Their clothing should be the clothes of the dead, and their food should be in broken dishes; their ornaments should be made of black iron, and they should wander constantly." "They should carry out the corpuses of people who have no relatives; this is a fixed rule". "They should take for themselves the clothing, beds, and ornaments of those condemned to death.". Rule 176 of Chapter 11 says "If a priest unknowingly has sex with untouchable women or very low caste women, eats (their food) or accepts (gifts from them), he falls if knowingly, he becomes their equal."

In principle, marriage was permitted within one's own caste. This rule was often broken, but any Brahmin male who took a sudra to be his wife would become the object of particular scorn. If a Brahmin male had only one wife and she was of sudra status, he would be considered to be in a state of ritual impurity and would be forbidden to attend family ceremonies like *sradha* (rites for the dead) ancestor worship. On the other hand, any sudra male who approached a Brahmin female, behaved like a Brahmin caste, or did any harm to a Brahmin person would be subject to serious punishment, sometimes even death.

Despite the above principles of discrimination concerning sudras, the Manusmriti, like the dharmasutras, has provisions for making compromises with reality. There are purification rites for those polluted by contact with sudras, conditions under which food cooked by sudras may be taken, cases in which marriage to sudra women can be permitted, and exceptions to the rules in times of distress, like "a Brahmin in distress may take alms from anyone", and "when life is endangered, it is permitted to take food from anyone".

For centuries, and even now, these untouchable castes have been subject to various restrictions in their movements or relationships with other people, especially the high caste persons. They still face many social disabilities, like denial or restriction of access to public facilities such as wells, schools, roads, post offices and courts; denial or restriction of access to temples where their presence might pollute the deity as well as the higher caste worshippers; and from rest-houses, tanks and shrines connected to temples. They have been denied access to services such as those provided by barbers, laundrymen, restaurants, shops and theatres, and are required to use separate utensils and facilities within such places. They face a lot of restrictions on style of life, especially in the goods indicating comfort or luxury. Riding on horseback, use of bicycles, umbrellas, footwear, the wearing of gold and silver ornaments (in fact, their abject poverty could never afford them to do so), the use of palanquins to carry bridegrooms were all forbidden for these people. Traditionally, they were required to have their homes/huts constructed outside the village and quite away from the high caste families; this practice is followed even now in almost all villages. This segregation is believed to have a divine sanction. While the touch of an animal was not considered polluting, the very sight of an untouchable was enough to pollute and called for the performance of special cleansing ceremonies. Domestic and agricultural animals could live and eat in the same house with high caste Hindus but the untouchables could not even live in the same town. For many orthodox

Hindus the cow dung is ritually so "clean", that a Brahmin priest will use it to wash away his impurities. Even now untouchability continues to be widely prevalent and is practiced in one form or another in most of the villages in India. This fact has been empirically established by a recent study of Action Aid India.

Constitutional Provisions for Equality

Article 14 of the Indian Constitution declares that the "State shall not deny to any person equality before the law or the equal protection of laws." Under Article 15, discrimination by the state on the grounds only of religion, race, caste, sex, and place of birth is proscribed keeping in view the problem of untouchability, Clause 2 of Article 15 further states that no person on grounds only of religion, race, caste, sex, or place of birth shall be subject to any disability, liability, restriction or condition with regard to:

— access to shops, public restaurants, hotels, places of public entertainment; or

— the use of wells, tanks, bathing *ghats*, roads and places of public resort maintained wholly or partly out of state funds or dedicated to the use of the general public.

Article 17 states that untouchability is abolished and its practice in any form is forbidden. The enforcement of any disability arising out of "untouchability" shall be an offence punishable in accordance with law. To give effect to this provision, the Parliament enacted the Abolition of untouchability (offences) Act, 1955, which was amended and renamed as the Protection of Civil Rights Act, 1976 and the scheduled Castes and scheduled Tribes (Prevention of Atrocities) Act, 1989. Article 23 prohibits traffic in human beings and forced / bonded labour practices. Article 24 provides that no child below the age of 14 shall be employed in any factory or mine or engaged in any other hazardous employment. Both these Articles are significant for dalits and tribals as majority of bonded /child labour belongs to these groups. To address these problems the Bonded labour (Abolition) Act, 1976, and Child labour (Prohibition and Regulation) Act, 1986 were enacted by Parliament. Article 25 (2b) provides that Hindu religious institutions of a public character shall be thrown open to all classes and sections of Hindus. This provision is relevant as some sects of Hindus, especially of higher castes, used to claim that dalits had no right to enter the temples. By the Constitution eighty–sixth Amendment Act, 2002, right to education as a fundamental right was added in the Constitution, which states, under Article 21A, that the state shall provide free and compulsory education to all children of the age of six to fourteen years in such manner as the state may by law, determine. Prior to 2002, the right to free and compulsory education of all children up to the age of 14 was a non-justiciable right (Article 45).

Notwithstanding the existence of national and international human rights laws, the dalits of India are facing many sociopolitical disabilities. Their human rights are violated. They are subject to many discriminations, subjugation, deprivations and violence. They are not integrated into the mainstream Hindu society. The affirmative action program for them has only marginally changed their status. They are still socially and educationally disadvantaged. They still experience the practice of untouchability by high caste Hindus.

Dalits and the Right to Education

The Universal Declaration of Human Rights (UDHR) declares under Article 26 (2) that:

> Education shall be directed to the full development of the human personality and to the strengthening of respect for human rights and fundamental freedoms. *It shall promote understanding, tolerance and friendship among all nations, racial or religious groups...* (Italics mine).

Besides the udHR, the International Convention on the elimination of All Forms of Racial discrimination is significant in the context of dalit rights. The Committee on Elimination of Racial Discrimination (CERD), the monitoring body of this treaty, in its interpretation of Article 1 of the Convention in general Recommendation XXIX stated that "discrimination based on 'descent' includes discrimination against members of communities based on forms of social stratification such as caste and analogous systems of inherited status." Furthermore, in its Concluding Observations on the reports submitted by India in 1996, the CERD affirmed, "that the situation of the scheduled Castes and scheduled Tribes falls within the scope of the Convention." Thus, in view of these positions taken by CERD, Article 7 of the Convention is relevant to the dalit issue and human rights education.

A progressive realization of human rights is dependent, and also possible to a large extent, on the popular awareness of and support for universally accepted human rights norms/standards. Although the importance of the teaching of human rights at all levels of education cannot be underestimated, teaching them at primary and secondary levels is most significant as the children develop their ideas, beliefs, attitudes, biases, and prejudices about other peoples, cultures and religions during these stages of education. Therefore, the objective of human rights education at these levels of schooling should not be to burden the students unnecessarily with specific texts of human rights but to focus on inculcating an attitude of self-esteem, respect for ideas and beliefs of other people and plurality of culture and of fostering an attitude of tolerance and removal of prejudices.

Education is one of the important means of reducing ignorance and inequality in society. It helps the individual to raise one's social status in various ways. Knowledge, skills, values, and attitudes acquired through education help one to lead a desired quality of life. Knowledge and education must be made available to all. As Dr. Ambedkar, the great dalit leader and chief architect of the Indian Constitution had said:

> In the complex world man lives at his peril and he must find his way in it without losing his freedom. There can, under these circumstances, be no freedom that is worthwhile unless the mind is trained to use its freedom. Deprive a man of knowledge and you will make him inevitably the slave of those more fortunate than himself... deprivation of knowledge is denial of the power to use liberty for great ends. An ignorant man may be free ... but he cannot employ his freedom so as to give him assurance of happiness.

The roots of educational deprivation of dalit communities must be traced back to their position as untouchables in the caste structure of traditional Hindu society. These were the most polluted of castes that were hereditarily assigned the most defiling of occupations. As per 2001 census, India's dalits numbered 167.2 million. There is a sizable population among the Muslims and Christians who are known as dalit Muslims (roughly estimated at forty two million) and dalit Christians (roughly estimated at sixteen million). Dalit Muslims and dalit Christians are not treated as scheduled Castes by the government, though they experience untouchability from their coreligionists, and are therefore not entitled to positive discrimination policies. On the other hand, dalits who are converted to sikhism and Buddhism do not face such deprivation.

The 1961 census revealed that only ten percent of dalits were literate. Sixty years after independence the situation has marginally improved. Low literacy rates for dalits are a clear indication of the ways in which the school system fails dalit children. The 2001 population census shows that literacy rate among dalits is 54.70 percent compared to 68.81 percent among others. There are many reasons for this sorry state of affairs.

Access to Schools

Poor accessibility of schools is one of the important factors for low literacy among dalits. By 1997, India had as many as 598,000 primary and 177,000 upper primary schools. However, easy access schooling has always been relatively poorer for the dalits as compared to the population in general, especially in rural areas. A study by National Council of Educational Research and Training (NCERT) reveals that schooling is available within a significantly smaller number of predominantly dalit habitations (37.03 per cent) as compared to general rural habitations (49.79 percent). With regard to upper primary schools, access within dalit habitations is lower (6.51 per cent) as compared to general rural habitations (13.87 percent).

Very few studies on social accessibility of schools are available. Aruna (1999, 1011-1014) in her study of Tamilnadu, a south Indian state, refers to "qualitative dangers" to schools and says that "in many habitations, the school is situated in localities inhabited by upper castes who are hostile to students belonging to the lower castes and minority groups". Ramaiah's observations of a village, Akramesi, in Tamil nadu where dalits form a small minority have disturbing implications for social accessibility of schools:

> None of the scheduled Castes were allowed to walk through the residential areas of dominant castes or through the village's main street running through the residential areas of the dominant castes. They had to walk a long way along the periphery of the village to reach their huts.

According to the sixth All India educational survey conducted by nCeRT, dalit communities mainly avail of government schooling. Of the dalit children in primary schools, 91.3 percent in rural areas and 64.6 percent in urban areas were in schools managed by state government and local bodies (municipalities or corporations). Many of these schools are plagued by various problems such as lack of basic infrastructure, classrooms, teachers, and teaching aids, dilapidated buildings, leaking roofs and mud floors appear quite common in schools and provide a depressing atmosphere for children. Teaching aids, apart from blackboards, are relatively absent. The conditions of the schools can be quite appalling as seen in this description of a school for dalit girls: "...the environment of this institution was reported to be very dirty as the ground was swampy and there were cow-dung heaps and firewood stocked all over." There is also the problem of absenteeism of students and teachers, etc. Thus dalit children do not have access to quality education. They also face discrimination and discouragement from higher caste community members who perceive education for dalits as both a waste and a threat. Their hostility towards dalits' education is linked to the perception that dalits are not meant to be educated, are incapable of being educated, or if educated, would pose a threat to village hierarchies and power relations.

Discrimination by teachers towards dalit children is commonly found in many schools. Teachers have been found to maintain discriminatory attitudes and practices that underlie caste relations in society. B.K. Anitha's study in karnataka revealed that dalit pupils were called 'kadu-jana' (forest people) who would not learn without being beaten. Anitha's research on classroom processes in Tumkur district of karnataka also found that the school day was significantly shorter in schools in the dalit concentrated villages as compared to the other schools studied. This was mainly because; "A majority of these teachers do not stay in the village and belong to the dominant castes, displaying a distinctive negative attitude towards the education of children of low castes." In their study in Rajasthan, Jabbi and

Rajlakshmi, found that fear of teachers and corporal punishment are factors that parents (especially of dalit Children) cite as constraining regular school attendance. Kancha Illaiah refers to his own teachers of higher castes in school who always used to say that "If he was a Brahmin he hated us and told us to our faces that it was because of the evil time because of kaliyuga, that he was being forced to teach 'sudras' like us."

Segregation in Schools

Dalit children's right to education free from discrimination is constantly undermined by the treatment they receive in school. Teachers maintain and impart discriminatory attitudes in their classrooms, forcing children to sit in the back of the room, segregating dalit children from non-dalits during lunchtime, forbidding non-dalit children from sitting next to dalit children or touching their plates, expressly limiting dalit student participation in class, subjecting them to verbal abuse and grading them unjustifiably low marks. Sometimes, their teachers often subject dalit children to corporal punishment. Instances of dalit students being made to sit/eat separately, their copies /slates not being touched by higher caste teachers, and children themselves not being touched are commonly reported like dalit students, even dalit teachers are segregated from non-dalit teachers in accessing food and water during lunchtime. Discrimination against dalit teachers at times turns violent. In December 2005, members of the dominant caste who could not accept the fact that their children were being taught by a dalit assaulted Satyanarayan Prasad, a dalit teacher, in a village in Bihar. When the teacher attempted to lodge a complaint with the police, the police termed the incident as "insignificant".

Biased attitudes of high caste teachers towards dalit students are well documented. As the UN Special Rapporteur on the right to education noted in his report before the 67th session of the then-Commission on Human Rights, "teachers have been known to declare that dalit pupils 'cannot learn unless they are beaten'. Noted journalist, Sainath, reported that in Rajasthan, one of the twenty eight states of India, children of the Balmiki (traditionally scavengers) caste, seen as most polluting of castes, "are made to sit on their own mats, often outside the room or at the door". Another study documented some of the discriminatory practices against dalit children in schools of Uttar Pradesh such as discrimination against dalit settlements in the location of schools; teachers refusing to touch dalit children; children from particular castes being special targets of verbal abuse and physical punishment by the teachers and low caste children frequently being beaten by higher caste classmates.

One of the important policy recommendations in this regard is that dalits are recruited as teachers in proportion to their representation in the population. Contrary to popular perception that the fifteen percent of dalits are recruited as teachers (as it is the government policy to provide fifteen percent job reservation to dalits), the nCeRT study (1998/99) reveals that dalits comprise only around eleven percent of teachers at primary stage, nine percent at upper primary stage, and five to six percent at secondary and higher secondary stages of education. This implies that non-dalit teachers, usually higher castes, by and large teach dalit children. If fifteen percent of the teachers at all stages of primary and secondary education are dalit teachers the situation of biased attitudes of teachers of high castes will be minimized. Moreover, their presence can act as deterrence to the incidents of discrimination and segregation.

Studies also suggest that the formation of peer groups is influenced by caste status of children and friendships are formed mainly within the boundaries of caste membership. In one of the government schools that Rekha Kaul studied, children:

> Complained that though prejudices and discrimination were not practised very openly in the classroom and the peer group appeared friendly in school, outside the school attitudes changed. Children of upper castes did not invite the kuruba or dalit children home for playing and there was no social intermixing outside the school.

Thus, it can be concluded that these practices of segregation in schools and discrimination serve to discourage and alienate dalit children, contributing to their high dropout rates. In fact, such practices serve to instil and reinforce dalit children's sense of inferiority, erode their sense of personal dignity and force them to internalize caste distinctions. Also, such segregations perpetuate "untouchability" practice by teaching the non-dalit children that "untouchability" is both an acceptable and necessary practice. It must be noted that such practices are in breach of international human rights norms. They violate Article 5 of the International Convention on the elimination of All Forms of Racial discrimination, as under this provision the states Parties agree to undertake to prohibit and to eliminate racial discrimination in all its forms and to guarantee the right of everyone, without distinction, notably in the enjoyment of various legal, political, civil, economic, social and cultural rights (among others, right to education and training) and the right of access to any place or service intended for use by the general public, such as transport, hotels, restaurants, cafes, theatres and parks. In 1997, the Human Rights Committee of the UN expressed its serious concern on caste discrimination and noted that scheduled castes "continue to endure severe social discrimination in India under the [ICCPR], *inter alia* inter-caste violence, bonded labour and discrimination of all kinds". It regrets that the *de facto* perpetuation of the caste system entrenches social differences and contributes to these violations. The Committee also recommended that further measures be adopted, including educational programs at national and state levels to combat all forms of discrimination against these vulnerable groups, in accordance with Article 2, paragraph 1 and 26 of the International Covenant on Civil and Political Rights. And as recently as 2004, the Committee on the Rights of the Child was "deeply concerned at persistent and significant social discrimination against children belonging to scheduled Castes and Tribes."

Dropout Rates of Dalit Students

As a result of discriminatory treatment, large number of dalit children drop out of school, especially in the early primary stages. According to the *2002 India Education Report*, school attendance in rural areas in 1993-1994 was 64.3 percent for dalit boys and 46.2 percent for dalit girls, compared to 74.9 percent among boys and 61 percent for girls from other social groups. According to a recent report of the national Commission for scheduled Castes and Tribes, "the drop out rate in scheduled Castes during 1990-91 was as high as 49.35 percent at primary stage and 67.77 percent at middle stage and 77.65 percent at secondary stage". It is interesting to note that due to increased interest in education and mobility the enrolment of dalit children has increased over the years. For instance, during 1999-2000 the enrolment of scheduled Caste and Tribes boys and girls reached an astonishing 92 percent. But it is regrettable to note that the drop out rate among them was alarming. According to a report of the Commission the national drop out rate among dalit children is 36.6 percent at primary, 59.4 percent at middle and 73.1 percent at secondary level of education.

Midday Meal Scheme and Caste Discrimination

As an incentive to increase the enrolment of children from marginalised communities various policies/schemes were initiated, such as free distribution of textbooks and uniforms and the Midday Meal scheme (MMs).

The incentive scheme of free distribution of textbooks and uniforms has no doubt improved school attendance and enrolment, as textbooks and uniforms are a major component of school costs. However, it must be noted that not all primary schools in the country were covered by the scheme. The nCeRT study (1998 / 1999) documents that in 1993 only 54.6 percent of primary schools were covered by the scheme of free textbooks and barely 10 percent of dalit students were beneficiaries while 29.3 percent of schools received free uniforms, a negligible 4.6 percent of dalit students were covered under this scheme. Midday meals were reported to cover 13.9 percent of schools, and barely 3.9 percent of the dalits benefited. Many studies have also pointed out that children do not receive incentives in time, and often do not receive them at all. Irregularities and delays in distributing textbooks and uniforms and other incentives as well as corruption have left little impact on these marginalised communities.

The MMs was initiated in 1995, as a means of addressing hunger and malnutrition among schoolchildren, following a supreme Court order. As a result of Public Interest litigation on the right to food, the supreme Court of India directed state governments and union Territories to implement a scheme providing every child in every government and government-aided primary school with a prepared midday meal. However, according to a study conducted by Indian Institute of dalit studies the states of uttar Pradesh and Bihar where a third of India's dalits live have refused to implement the MMs. This study points out that in many places MMs has been shelved because of upper caste community opposition; upper castes have also opposed the employment of dalit cooks for the program where the MMs is in place, dalit students' access to food has been restricted. In many places, the MMs has been organized in a higher caste locality, away from the dalit habitation. In two places in Tamil nadu, the meals are provided in a temple, "raising immediate questions of exclusion for dalit children, who are forbidden entry into temples, as well as non-Hindu children." In October 2006, an article in *Indian Express* quoted a primary school student, Shailesh Solanki, as follows:

> We are not allowed to sit with children of the other castes. We are always asked to sit separately. This is done every time we are served food at noon. Even the food served to us is less in quantity.

Objections to the segregation of dalit students in the MMs have been dealt with punitively. For instance, in december 2003, a school district in gujarat transferred seven teachers out of the district for objecting to this segregation.

Similar stories of segregation or discrimination can be found from other parts of India. Some instances are documented here. As per a report in *The Hindu* in a government primary school at Kontur in Medak district of Andhra Pradesh, thirty eight of the forty six students who were supposed to stay for midday meal reportedly leave the school without touching the food as it was cooked by two dalit women. Only fourteen dalit students eat at the school. On 10 September 2004, *The Pioneer* reported that the upper caste parents refused to allow their wards in Pooran-kheri village in Shivpuri District in Madhya Pradesh to eat the midday meal in school. The school authority had to maintain a separate kitchen for the school children belonging to the dalits and the tribals. The dalit women have been prevented from getting the job of cooks in schools under MMs because of their caste. In Kendrapara District of Orissa, the school authorities allegedly turned away dalit women who were applying for the job of cooks in schools under MMs for fear that upper caste students might not take the food cooked by dalits. This is contrary to the government directive for recruitment of women preferably from dalits and tribals in about 1,420 primary schools in the district. The national Human Rights Commission in december 2005 issued a notice to the district administration for not appointing dalit women as cooks in schools.

Treatment of Caste System in Curriculum

The treatment of the caste system in textbook and curriculums suggest that the official curriculum barely acknowledges the existence of dalit and tribal communities, despite the fact that they form nearly a quarter of India's population especially at the district and local levels in many states in the country. Recounting his own experiences of schooling, Illaiah also reveals that dalit and lower caste children are alienated from the language and course content as both the content of education and the medium through which it is transacted do not relate to their own cultural experiences.

The treatment of caste discrimination in textbooks and curriculums can strengthen caste division and prejudice. For instance, a report by the Mumbai-based non-governmental organization KHOJ found that even progressive curriculums either exclude any mention of caste discrimination or discuss the caste system in a way that suggests that caste inequities and discrimination no longer exist not only that the school text books may fail to mention caste discrimination, but also some of them may even attempt to justify the origins of caste discriminations. The Central Advisory Board on Education (CABE) subcommittee on "Regulatory Mechanisms for Textbooks and Parallel Textbooks Taught in schools Outside the government system", found that a social studies textbook approved for use by the gujarat state Board, is shocking as it describes the caste system as a "precious gift" given by the Aryans to the world and extols the virtues of the caste system for socially and economically organizing society on the basis of labour. The CABE subcommittee further added that school textbooks might attribute the unequal situation of dalits to their "ignorance, illiteracy and blind faith... because they still fail to realise [the] importance of education in life."

The transaction of the conventional curriculum in rural schools is a far cry from one that, according to a NCERT study, "encourages exploration, problem solving... participatory... interactive group learning...." A recent study by Bodh of schools in the villages of Madhya Pradesh and Rajasthan (a number of them predominantly inhabited by lower castes and tribes) reveals that curriculum transaction continues to be primarily textbook-based, directed by the teacher and dominated by rote learning. The boundaries between school and community knowledge are rigidly drawn with the textbook serving as the only source of "legitimate knowledge". Teachers rarely relate to the knowledge base of children.

There is another systemic problem in the Indian educational system. The authority of the teacher is unquestioned and children usually ask no questions, or are not encouraged to do so, even to clarify their doubts. Children listen to the teacher, copy lessons, memorize them and answer questions. In single- and two-teacher schools that predominate in the more backward regions, the situation is compounded as teachers are confronted with teaching children of many grades together, a situation that their training least prepared them for. They evolve their own coping strategies such as huddling children of two or more grades into one classroom, keeping students busy with writing work, and using punishment to maintain discipline. Learning becomes a casualty in the process.

Educational Problems of Tribal Children

Indigenous communities of India are commonly referred to as tribal or adivasi communities and are recognised as Scheduled Tribes under the Constitution of India. Although the Constitution does not define Scheduled Tribes as such, it designates these communities as those which are scheduled in accordance with Article 342 of the Constitution. According to Article 342 of the Constitution, the Scheduled Tribes are the tribes or tribal communities or part of or groups within these tribes and tribal communities which have been declared as such by the President through a public notification. The criteria followed for specification of a community, as scheduled tribe are indications of primitive traits, distinctive culture, geographical isolation, shyness of contact with the community at large, and backwardness. At present, 533 tribes in India have been notified under Article 342 of the Constitution with the largest number of 62 tribes belonging to the State of Orissa.

A large majority of tribals in India are landless and do not have a sustainable source of livelihood. The 1991 Census figures reveal that 42.02 percent of the Scheduled Tribe population were main workers (those who were employed for more than 183 days in the preceding year) of whom 54.50 percent were cultivators and 32.69 percent agricultural labourers. Thus, about 87 percent of the main workers from these communities were engaged in primary sector activities. While a majority of those employed do not receive even the statutory minimum wages, tribal women are found to be doubly exploited since they are paid even less than the tribal men. It is thus not surprising that poverty is widely prevalent among tribal population in India. Even when the overall levels of poverty for tribal population have reduced between 1993-94 to 1999-2000 from 51.94% to 45.86% among the rural tribal population and 41.14% to 34.75% among the urban tribal population, two important trends can be observed. Firstly, the rate of decline in poverty among the STs is much lower than that among the general population and secondly, the gap between poverty rates among tribal and general population is widening. A number of Scheduled Tribes living below poverty line have been provided economic assistance to enable them to rise above the poverty-line. However, this assistance has decreased from Rs. 9.98 lakh during 1999-2000 to 8.81 lakh during 2000-2001.

The sex ratio among the STs, although significantly higher than the general population, has been slowly declining. While there were 982 tribal females for every 1000 tribal males in 1971, the 1991 Census shows that there are only 972 females for every 1000 tribal males. This could be indicative of their poor access to health services.

Tribal children, like several marginalised groups of children in India, are trapped in an intergenerational vicious cycle of poverty, illiteracy and deprivation. This is evident in extremely poor adult literacy rates which are reproduced as low education levels among the children from ST communities. This section presents some key data points on educational status of ST communities as a whole as well as schooling status of tribal children.

The literacy rate of Scheduled Tribes is abysmally low at around 29.60 percent, as against the national average of 52.21 percent. A review of literacy rates among ST population in comparison with that of the general population indicates a growing gap between literacy rates of these two communities.

Female literacy is another significant indicator of educational development within any social group. Research studies have shown the importance of female literacy and education in uplifting the socioeconomic parameters of a given society. In the context of tribal women in India, illiteracy is so highly prevalent that their engagement with the mainstream society is seriously limited. While more than three-quarters of ST women are illiterate, 77 districts in India have tribal female literacy rates lower than ten percent and 14 districts have less than three percent tribal female literacy rate.

Inter-state differences in the literacy rates of tribal population is evident with tribes from North Eastern States of India showing high literacy rates. The highest literacy rate among tribals in Mizoram (82.73%) is attributed to a spread of Christian missionary educational institutions and a strong matrilineal family system among the Khasi and Garo tribes belonging to the State. Low literacy rates are seen among the tribals from Madhya Pradesh (21.54%) and Orissa (22.31%).

Lack of proactive governance in favour of the STs is not linked only to lack of resources. Governmental indifference and lack of political will are largely responsible for the callous state of affairs. The unutilised amount for tribal welfare for the years 1998-2001 for all the states combined was Rs. 40546.46 lakhs. States with high proportion of ST population also had high amounts of unutilised funds with Bihar (Rs. 8113.26 lakhs), Jharkhand (Rs. 4742.62 lakhs), Madhya Pradesh (Rs. 4721.61 lakhs) and Gujarat (Rs. 3721.72 lakhs) topping the order.

The School Experience

At school, the experiences of tribal children range from discrimination to a sense of complete alienation. Students from ST communities encounter a series of obstacles including commuting long distances to school in hostile environmental conditions, abuses and discrimination from teachers and fellow students from non-tribal backgrounds, difficulty in comprehending the language of instruction and negotiating space for themselves which was denied historically.

Children's denominational identities have always affected their school experiences. Ideally, the school teacher must play a vital role in supporting the struggles of first-generation learners. But it is found that although there is formal inclusion in the mainstream education system in the sense that children are officially enrolled, the teachers are often found to question the 'educability' of tribal children, revealing that nothing much has changed in the perceptions held about the 'other' by teachers who are generally drawn from mainstream social groups.

Research shows that tribal children are often subjected to overt discrimination by non-tribal upper caste school teachers who view them as 'slow learners' unable to learn despite several repetitions; as 'unclean' and are therefore given tasks of sweeping and swabbing the schools unlike non-tribal upper caste children who may be asked to fetch water or lock the school. Teachers also demean tribal children by calling their parents 'drunken', with no interest in schools and education. Untouchability is also found to prevail in schools, where upper caste teachers and students refuse to drink water from the same tap as the tribal children before washing it thoroughly. Even play activities and school transactions are sometimes segregated on the basis of these identities. The tribal children are repeatedly subjected to verbal abuse at the hands of upper caste teachers and this has a critical impact on the way these first generation students view themselves as learners.

Since the tribal languages are distinctly different from the medium of instruction in schools (which is usually the respective State language) tribal children often find it extremely difficult to cope with their studies and homework. This lack of language skills acts as a serious impediment when the teacher is a non-tribal and makes no effort to link the two linguistic experiences for the child. Aspirations among tribal children are also low considering that there are not many formally educated persons in such communities. The inability to secure jobs amongst tribals who have completed formal education have lead some to get disillusioned with the education system and question the futility of spending several years struggling to get educated. Some consider school educated children as unfit to carry out their hereditary occupations thereby rendering them 'useless' in their traditional lives. Yet, the motivation of a large number of tribal children to walk hours to reach school, tolerate the rebuke of teachers and fellow students, their efforts to identify with a language and curriculum that is alien to their own life worlds and their struggles to break free of their historical marginalisation is definitely striking.

In several societies, children's rights are intrinsically linked to respect for human rights and it would be almost impractical to separate rights of children from those of their families and communities.

Fulfilment of third generation of rights i.e. group or community rights is often imperative considering that it is not children's rights alone but those of an entire community which are under extreme risk. By bestowing children from such social groups rights that are not enjoyed by their families or communities, superficial lines get drawn between children and their families or communities while making a farce of realising children's rights. It also presumes that children's rights can be respected while the rights of their parents and communities are persistently violated. However, children's rights remain unfulfilled so long as the position of their social group is not improved. In the Indian context too, tribal children's rights are more likely to get realised if rights of tribal communities are holistically recognised and fulfilled. The following problems faced by tribal communities in India make it extremely difficult for tribal children to gain entry and sustain within the mainstream education system.

Displacement

Forced or voluntary eviction of tribals from their homes and habitats has been a serious problem since Independence. Large scale projects such as large dams, power plants, industrial units, large mining projects undertaken on tribal lands for the 'larger public good' very often provide little to the displaced communities. For years, questions have been raised about the unsatisfactory manner in which they have been rehabilitated. Research shows that between 1951 and 1990, a population of 21.3 million persons have been displaced in the states of Andhra Pradesh, Bihar, Gujarat, Maharashtra, Madhya Pradesh, Rajasthan and Orissa. Of this, 8.54 million are tribals (40 percent of the total) and of those only 2.12 million (24.8 percent) tribals have been resettled so far. In the absence of appropriate rehabilitation, displaced communities are uprooted and forced to migrate to newer areas. While they may settle down on forestlands in the new villages or in urban slums in case they migrate to cities, their settlement is considered illegal and they are therefore denied even the basic civic amenities. Children belonging to families of displaced tribal families are never able to continue schooling even if they were enrolled initially, and usually end up in wage employment in order to support the family's fresh set of challenges.

Land Alienation

Among tribal communities, land and its natural resources are sacrosanct and hold significant place in their socio-cultural and religious life. It is also the main source of livelihood and Minor Forest Produce (MFP) is known to help several communities to survive. Given the vulnerability of tribal communities in India, several of them have had to part with their treasured resource for reasons ranging from acquisition of land for public purposes, encroachments by non-tribals or 'outsiders', forcible evictions, etc. The Ministry of Rural Development data shows that as many as 4.65 lakh cases of alienation of tribal land covering an area of 9.17 lakh acres were registered in the states of Andhra Pradesh, Assam, Bihar, Gujarat, Himachal Pradesh, Karnataka, Madhya Pradesh, Maharashtra, Orissa, Rajasthan and Tripura in January 1999. Of these, only two lakh cases were disposed in favour of 1.56 lakh tribal families covering an area of 5.31 lakh acres. Among the states, land alienation is high in Andhra Pradesh (2.79 lakh acres), Madhya Pradesh (1.58 lakh acres), Karnataka (1.30 lakh acres), and Gujarat (1.16 lakh acres). An absence of political and administrative will to identify and hand over alienated land back to the tribals is considered to be a major obstacle in ensuring that the tribal communities get what is due to them. While on the one hand, tribals continue to loose their land to so-called large developmental projects, without being compensated or restored with lands adequately, questions are being asked about the so-called benefits of these projects percolating to the tribals themselves. In fact, due to lack of education and vocational training amongst tribals, projects set up in tribal areas rarely absorb the local tribals in employment. In many cases, tribals migrate at different times of the year to find employment. Children from such migrating families are either never enrolled in schools due to frequent transfers, or end up discontinuing education for the period that they are away which has an adverse impact on their educational attainments.

Overcoming the Barriers

The students from dalit communities have been facing discrimination of various kinds, despite the fact that such forms of discrimination are outlawed both in national law and the international law of human rights. They experience discrimination and restrictions in accessing schools, and getting midday meals, free textbooks and uniforms. They are segregated in classrooms and during midday meals. Their teachers curse themselves that in this life they are made to teach the most polluted people, the untouchables. The school curriculum does not include topics of caste discrimination and human rights education now the question is how to remove these caste biases and prejudices toward dalit students. What can be done to bring an end to the apartheid-kind of system that prevails in India?

One way of bringing an egalitarian system and an end to caste discrimination is to dismantle the caste system. The Constitution has provided a framework. On the one hand, it abolishes the practice of untouchability, and on the other hand, it introduces the positive discrimination measures to achieve integration of dalit communities into the mainstream society. If the laws prohibiting untouchability, such as untouchability Offences Act, 1955 (amended and renamed as Protection of Civil Rights Act, 1976 [1976 PCR Act]) and the Prevention of Atrocities Act, 1989 (1989 POA) are implemented in their letter and spirit and the perpetrators of atrocities against dalits are punished, the practices of discrimination in schools also will gradually come to an end.

But the perpetrators of atrocities against dalits and offences of untouchability are rarely punished. There is a big gap in the registration of cases of crimes against dalits in police stations and the rate of acquittals by the judiciary. Let us briefly look at the data. It is shocking to learn that during the decade 1990-2000 a total of 285,871 cases of various crimes against dalits were registered countrywide, of which 14,030 were registered under the 1976 PCR Act and 81,796 under the 1989 POA. This means that an average of 28,587 cases of practice of untouchability and atrocities against dalits were registered every year during the 1990s. These include, among others, 553 cases of murder, 2,990 cases of grievous hurt, 919 rapes, 184 kidnappings/abductions, 47 dacoities, 127 robberies, 456 cases of arson, 1,403 cases of caste discrimination and 8,179 cases of atrocities. In other words, every hour more than three cases of atrocities against dalits are registered, and every day three cases of rape and at least one murder are reported. Equally shocking is the data concerning high rate of acquittals. The Third and sixth reports of national Commission for SCs and STs reveal respectively, that in 1996, the conviction rate in these cases was fifteen percent, while the acquittal rate was eighty-five percent and that in 1999-2000 and 2000-2001, as much as eighty-nine percent of cases resulted in acquittals. This yawning gap between registration of crimes and acquittals of perpetrators needs to be drastically bridged, and the justice delivery system needs to be improved.

In relation to the schools, the following measures need to be undertaken: the curriculum must:

— acknowledge the existence of caste discrimination and the way the leaders from dalit communities (like Phule and Ambedkar) have fought for the abolition of untouchabilty, and

— address the issue of caste relations and human rights; teachers must be sensitized on caste discrimination during training programs; enabling pedagogies must evolve; and specific academic support to dalit children must be provided.

References

Ambedkar, B.R. 1987. *Writings and Speeches*, vol. 3. Mumbai: government of Maharashtra.

Centre for Human Rights and Global Justice (CHRGJ) and Human Rights Watch (HRW). 2007. *Caste Discrimination Against Dalits or So-Called Untouchables in India*, Report submitted to CERD, available at www.ohchr.org/english/bodies/cerd/docs/ngos/ chrgj_hrw.pdf

Derez, Jean and Haris Gazdar. 1996. "Uttar Pradesh: The burden of Inertia", in Derez Jean and Amartya Sen, editors, *India Development*. Delhi: Oxford university Press.

Illaiah, Kancha. 1996. *Why I am not a Hindu*. Calcutta: Samya Publications.

Jabbi, Mona and C. Rajyalakshmi. 2001. "Education of Marginalised Social Groups in Bihar", in Vaidyanathan, A. and P.R.Gopinath Nair, editors, *Elementary Education in Rural India: A Grassroots View*. New Delhi: Sage Publications.

5

Human Rights Issues of Dalit Women

India is a democracy and is a Party to most of the major human rights treaties. These treaties provide the same rights for men and for women. Because India is also a Party to the Convention on the Elimination of All Forms of Discrimination Against Women (CEDAW), the Government has an extra obligation to make sure that women can realise their rights. It is generally accepted in international law that governments have to do more than just pass legislation to protect human rights. The Government of India has an obligation to take all measures, including policy and budgetary measures, to make sure that women can fulfil their rights. It also has an obligation to punish those who engage in caste-based violence and discrimination. The government of India, as a modern country with a growing economy, has the means to fulfil its obligations.

The status of Dalit women in India needs special attention. They are one of the largest socially segregated groups anywhere in the world, and make up 2% of the world's total population. Dalit women are discriminated against three times over: they are poor, they are women, and they are Dalits. Dalit women constitute half of the ca. 200 million Dalit population, and 16.3 of the total Indian female population. The traditional taboos are the same for Dalit men and Dalit women. However, Dalit women have to deal with them more often. Dalit women are discriminated against not only by people of higher castes, but also within their own communities. Men are dominant in Dalit communities. Dalit women also have less power within the Dalit movement itself. Women are active in large numbers in the movement but most leadership positions in the organisations, local bodies and associations have until now been held by men.

Civil and Political Rights

India is a Party to the International Covenant on Civil and Political Rights. Based on this treaty, the Government of India has an obligation to make sure that Dalit women can enjoy a whole range of human rights, such as the right to life, freedom from torture or cruel, inhuman or degrading treatment or punishment, freedom from slavery, the right to be equal before the court, the right to recognition as a person before the law, the right to privacy, the right to marry only with free and full consent, and the right to take part in public affairs. The life and dignity of Dalit women depends on the realisation of these human rights. However, they are breached systematically.

An essential precondition for the realisation of civil and political rights of Dalit women is registration. Article 24 (2) of the Covenant provides that every child shall be registered immediately after birth. In India, 46 % of all children are not registered. There is also no system of registration of marriages. This is not only a barrier for the realisation of civil and political rights; it also prevents the protection of Dalit girls from sexual exploitation and trafficking, child labour and forced and early marriages.

Economic, Social, and Cultural Rights

India is also a Party to the International Covenant on Economic, Social and Cultural Rights (ICESCR). This treaty not only identifies a range of economic, social and cultural rights, but it also requires that all people have these rights, without discrimination. The treaty also discusses the ways in which states must work to realise the rights. The rights outlined in the ICESCR include the right to work and to just and favourable conditions of work, and to form trade unions, the right to social security, protection of the family, the right to an adequate standard of living, including food, housing and clothing, and the right to health. Dalit women hardly enjoy any of these human rights.

Millennium Development Goals and Dalit Women

In 2000, 189 countries accepted the Millennium Declaration and agreed to take the necessary action in order to attain eight specific goals: the Millennium Development Goals (MDGs). The realisation of human rights of Dalit women will have a major positive effect on the realisation of the MDGs. Dalit women are extremely poor, and make up 2% of the world's population. In India, 60 million children do not attend primary school; the majority of these children are Dalit girls. India's child mortality rate is one of the highest in the world and with its vast population and a rate of 540 maternal deaths per 100,000 live births, India accounts for more than 20 % of all global maternal deaths. A greater availability and accessibility of healthcare for women, including Dalit women, is needed.

Violation of Human Rights of Dalit Women

All human beings have the right to live as human beings. Human rights are not conferred or given. They already exist in society. The concept of human rights aims at protection of rights like right to life, liberty and property. These rights are attributed to human beings irrespective of class, caste, gender, colour and religion. The Universal Declaration of Human Rights was unanimously adopted by the UN General Assembly on December 10th, 1948. The preamble of Indian constitution adequately empowers the central and state government to eliminate human rights violation in the country.

Inspite of these international and national declarations and resolutions, human rights are violated in different countries all over the world. In Indian society, due to the social barriers such as castetism, untouchability, patriarchy, disparity, superstition, religious exploitation and class variations, specific groups are becoming weaker and marginalised. These groups are facing the problems of identity crisis, deprivation, discrimination and atrocities. These marginalised groups are also identified and recognised as dalits, SC (scheduled castes) ST (scheduled tribes), OBC (other backward castes) NT (nomadic tribes) DT (de-notified tribes) religious and linguistic minorities.

Violence on human beings in any form results in violation of human rights. Human rights of dalits and women in general are normally violated by high castes and powerful communities to practice and exhibit patriarchy and castetism. But human rights of dalit women are violated extremely and in peculiar form. Dalit women are in worst position than dalits in general, in terms of sex ratio, wages, employment, occupation, assets, education, health, social mobility and political participation. Hence, it is important to discuss the status of dalit women and various problems they face even after 60 years of independence.

Dalit women are one of the most marginalised segments in the society. The condition of dalit women is more vulnerable than non-dalit women. Dalit women are suffering from multi-disadvantages:

— Of being dalit i.e. socio-economically and culturally marginalised section,

— Being women and sharing the gender based inequalities and subordination.

Certain kinds of violence are traditionally reserved for Dalit women: extreme filthy verbal abuse and sexual epithets, naked parading, dismemberment, being forced to drink urine and eat faeces, branding, pulling out of teeth, tongue and nails, and violence including murder after proclaiming witchcraft, are only experienced by Dalit women. Dalit women are threatened by rape as part of collective violence by the higher castes. However, sexual assault and rape of Dalit women and girls also occur within their own communities. For Dalit men, the suppression and rape of women could be a way to compensate for their own lack of power in society. The Devadasi system of temple prostitution is the most extreme form of exploitation of Dalit women. Dalit girl children are forced to prostitution. The majority of cases of violence against Dalit women are not registered. The lack of law enforcement leaves many Dalit women unable to approach the legal system to seek redress. Women are often also unaware of the laws and their ignorance is exploited by their opponents, by the police, and by the judiciary system. Even when cases are registered, the lack of appropriate investigation, or the judge's own caste and gender biases, can lead to acquittal.

VULNERABLE STATUS OF DALIT WOMEN

It is easy for the historically dominating caste and gender to violate human rights of dalit women who are at the lowest rung of the hierarchical ladder. The type of violence inflicted on dalits is in the form of severest violation of human rights. Dalit and tribal women are raped as part of an effort by upper caste leaders, land lords and police to suppress movements to demand payment of minimum wages, to settle share cropping disputes or to reclaim lost lands.

The recent incident of Khairlanji Massacare is not something new. A dalit family had refused to let upper caste villagers built a road through their fields. Hence on September, 29th, 2006, Bhaiyalal Bhotmange's family, wife Surekha, daughter Prinyanka and two sons were killed by the villagers of Khairlangi in Bhandra district of Maharashtra. They were first attacked with huge iron chains and than abused by the other caste women of the village. Surekha and Priyanka were paraded naked and raped, and later, their bodies were mutilated and thrown into a pond.

This shows that dalit women are easy targets for any perpetrator Upper caste considers them to be sexually available. Hence they are largely unprotected by the state machinery. Further, there is prevalence of violence, making dalit women eat human excreta, parading them naked, gang- rape, murder, dacoity, robbery and burning of their huts or communities. These are the types of crime, which violate their human rights. According to SC/ST commission report between 1981 and 1986 about 4000 dalit women became victim of rape. In 1993–94 this figure rose to 798 and 992 respectively. This means annually about 700 dalit women fall prey to sexual assault by high caste people.

The main complaints of the poorer dalit women are that they have no good houses. In urban areas most of them stay in unhygienic slums and in rural areas their houses are away from main stream society. Under conditions of grinding poverty and severe exploitation at work place, dalit women also suffer caste specific ban on water access from upper castes and may be beaten up in their own houses as well. A poem by a dalit poetess Teressama, a teacher from Guntur puts the situation in the following words:

> *We go to work for we are poor But the same silken beds mock us, While we are ravished in broad daylight. Ill-starred our horoscopes are Even our tottering husbands Lying on the cots in the corner Hiss and shout for revenge If we cannot stand their touch*

At the outset, prevailing caste and secondary status of women in the society is largely responsible for violation of human rights of dalit women. To understand the root cause of the situation it is essential to examine basic factors responsible for their vulnerability.

Sociocultural and Religious Factors

First and foremost dalit women are victims of social, religious and cultural practices like Devdasis and Jogins. In the name of these practices, village girls are married to God by their helpless parents. These girls are then sexually exploited by the upper caste landlords and rich men and directed in to trafficking and prostitution. In his autobiography, Kale (1994) has described a ritual called 'chira'. The literal meaning of the word 'chira', is to cut or break. In this ritual when a girl from the lower caste community reaches the age of puberty, an elderly prestigious man from the higher caste breaks the hymen of the girl child by sexual act. This ritual is performed in a way to make the girl accept this fact as a routine practice.

The 28th report of SC/ST commission reported that in February 1986 there were about ten thousand Jogins belonging to SC in Nizamabad district of Andhra Pradesh. The survey submitted by the district collector to Schedule Caste Finance Corporation revealed prevalence of 15,850 cases. Eighty percent of these Jogins belonged to SC. This data is just an example of one district of the country. Practices such as Chira, Jogins, Devdasi which are prevalent even today are harmful and threaten the dignity of dalit women and violate their human rights.

Educational Status

Low level of education is a problem in itself and in turn gives rise to many other problems. In 1991, literacy among the dalit women was indeed quite low. In rural areas only 19.46 percentage women were literate. A report published by Ministry of Welfare, Government of

India in 1998 showed that there is much difference in the literacy rate of dalits and non-dalits in general, and gender specific. Literacy rate of non-dalits is 64.13 % and literacy rate of women is 39.29 %, where as dalit women's literacy rate is only 23.76 %. There is a large disparity in the literacy rate due to wide spread prejudice based on castetism and patriarchy against dalits and women in general and dalit women in particular.

Economic Deprivation and Unemployment

A careful look at the economic situation of dalit women reveals that their work force structure is such that they rarely own any land. A large majority of them are agricultural labourers. The rate of unemployment among them is also quite high. About 90% of women working in unorganized sector are mainly from lower castes. In 1991, about 71% of dalit women workers in rural area were agricultural labourers. Only 19% of them owned land.

A prominent researcher and sociologist while sharing her experience from a research on gender and land issue, informed that, when she enquired with dalit women about land owned by them in their names, they wondered about permissibility of owning land in their name. This indicates that neither do they own any land nor are they aware of their rights on land. When enquiries were made with Stri-mukti sanghatana and Prerana, Mumbai based organizations working on the issue of rag picking and prostitution respectively, to ascertain the proportion of dalit women in these occupations, it was learnt that NGOs usually do not keep record of caste. However, Human Rights Watch Report mentioned that a large number of dalit women are engaged in unclean, inferior occupation such as sweeping, scavenging and working in dumping grounds, rag picking and also in prostitution. These women have to face steep discrimination in the matters of social relation and employment due to their engagement in these occupations.

Health and Nutrition Status

Dalit women's daily diet is the leftover of family meals, inadequate in quantity and quality. Health services are either not available in case of illness or unaffordable even if available. In addition to that, due to early marriage and too many pregnancies their health is always at risk. If birth control is practiced at all, 91% cases of tubectomy are performed on the women who have to carry the burden of family planning. In an overall situation where dalits are prone to ailments in general, women suffer from more serious and more varied kind of sickness. More than 80% of women in reproductive age group (15 to 45) are anaemic. Poor health status of dalit women pushes her then into more vulnerable situation.

POLITICAL STATUS

Women constitute half of total population, but are unable to get equal share in active politics. Their socioeconomic status directly depends on their participation in politics. Political parties in India speak much about equality of women but have totally ignored the dalit women.

Traditionally, leadership in the village was confined to 'rural elites', who were aged and belonging to higher castes. In the year 1993, 73rd amendment in the constitution granted reservation to dalits, tribals and women in local government. This amendment made it compulsory that one third of the seats reserved for dalits be filled by dalit women. In some states, there has been little or no acceptance of reservation for the lower castes and dalit women by the upper castes. This has resulted in atrocities against panchayat members including women. Dalits who stood for election were beaten, and dalit women were raped and ill-treated. The members of the higher castes, who are not prepared to relinquish power to the lower castes, grabbed their land. An easier method to retain power is to put-up proxy candidates but keep the control in the hands of the dominant castes, always men.

The incapacity of women, particularly dalit women, to assert their rights is at the root of the problem. The reservation for dalits, particularly for women, is accepted in form but seldom in substance. Any change in the status quo is resisted. Dalit women's sitting on chairs is seen as threat to social hierarchy. So, the upper castes in the village vetoed chairs in the panchayat office.

Dalit women also faced many problems in performing their duties due to illiteracy, lack of information and dependency on the male members of their families. An important obstacle is the no-confidence motion against dalit women as pradhan by the dominant sections. Rural elites are unable to accept the power, which has been given into the hands of the poorer and disadvantaged women. Despite recognition and legal sanction for political rights, rigid caste system and patriarchy directly and indirectly has been suppressing dalit women and violating their political rights.

This proves that human rights of dalit women are violated right from her family to the society at large by one and all. All these factors are largely responsible for the precarious position of dalit women as far as their social, cultural, religious, economic, health and political status in the society is concerned. These factors force them to mutely allow violation of their civic and human rights. Thus they become victims of universal violence.

Efforts to Protect Human Rights of Dalit Women

With the realization that violence is one of the potent threats to the peaceful existence of human beings, whole hearted and all round efforts are made at international, national and local level. The preamble to the Universal Declaration of Human Rights (UDHR) serves as a foundation and philosophy of Human rights. There are a host of international conventions including those for prevention and punishment of genocide and elimination of all forms of racial and gender based discrimination.

The World Conference Against Racism (WCAR) related to racial discrimination, xenophobia and intolerance held in Durban, South Africa in 2001, brought the issue of caste and untouchability based discrimination on the agenda of UN Conference in Durban. Among the several organisations, the National Campaign on Dalit Human Rights (NCDHR) a collective of dalit NGOs, other NGOs, academicians', activists and large number of supporters spearheaded the national campaign in India for inclusion of the issue of caste and untouchability based discrimination in the Durban Conference.

The preamble of Indian constitution adequately empowers the central and state government to eliminate human right violation in the country. Article 17 of the constitution provides for removal of untouchability. Based on this article Protection of Civil Rights Act'

(PCR), was passed in 1955. However, there was no conviction/ under this Act hence, Thirty-four years after the introduction of PCR Act, the Scheduled Caste and Schedule Tribes (Prevention of Atrocities) Act 1989 was enacted to bring various forms of atrocities to an end. In this Act the complainant is given more weightage. There are stringent provisions against the police for negligence.

Formation of Dalit Women's organisations

Dalit women have been active throughout history, though often this has not been recorded. They were actively involved in the anti-caste and anti-untouchability movements in the 1920s. Today they are the strongholds of the Dalit movements in thousands of Indian villages. They continue to play a critical role in the movements for land rights. They are making their mark as independent thinkers and writers in the literary world and visionary leaders in the Panchayati Raj institutions. However, they are unable to put an end to the structural discrimination and exclusion. Violence and impunity are used to keep them in their place.

Since the late 1980s, therefore, Dalit women have increasingly felt and articulated the need for a separate platform created, developed and controlled by themselves through which they could forge their own identity, fight for their rights and find solutions to their particular problems as Dalits and as women. Conscious that the call for a separate platform could be interpreted as a divisive move by both Dalit men and non-Dalit women, the proponents of such a special forum emphasise that their initiative must not be mistaken for a separatist movement. Rather they assert that there is need for strong alliances between the Dalit movement, the women's movement and the Dalit women's movement if their common vision of social, economic and political equality and justice for all is to be realised.

The National Federation of Dalit Women (NFDW) was launched by Dalit women themselves and committed itself to undertake several tasks to bring about positive changes in the lives of Dalit women, such as legal action against caste based atrocities, political empowerment of Dalit women, economic empowerment against growing pauperisation, building self-confidence and leadership.

The focus on education of low caste women is one of the important factors responsible for the emerging identity of Dalit women. Reformist intervention by Savitribai and Mahatma Phule of opening school for untouchable girls way back in 1848 was a turning point for changing status of dalit women. Dr. Ambedkar's thought and action made important differences in the lives of dalit women. His movement and especially his organisations encouraged many dalit women to become educated to be active in public life and to gain leadership, self respect in the contemporary period encouraged women to participate in organisation for dalit women at regional, state and national level.

After independence in 1960's and 70's, the dalit movement and women's movement emerged to demand their rights against caste and gender respectively. However, specific problems of dalit women were not acknowledged by these movements. Hence in 1990's there were several special, independent and autonomous assertions of dalit women's identity; a case in point is the formation of National Federation for Dalit Women (NFDW) and All India Dalit Women's Forum (AIDWF) at the state level. The Maharashtra Dalit Mahila Sanghatana (MDMS) was formed in 1995. A year earlier, the women's wing of Bhartiya Republican Party (BRP) and the Bahujan Mahila Sangha (BMS) was set up the Bahujan Mahila Parishad. In December 1996, at Chandrapur, a Vikas Vanchit Dalit Mahila Parishad (VVDMP) was organised and a proposal to commemorate 25th December (the day on which Ambedkar had set Manu Smriti on fire) as Bhartiya Smriti Divas was advanced. The Christi Mahila Sanghatana, an organisation of Dalit Christian Women was established in 1997. These organisations have come together on several issues such as celebration of Bhartiya Stree Mukti Divas and on the issue of reservation for OBC women in parliament bodies. Indian Association of Women Studies (IAWS) network with dalit feminist across different regions had brought special issues on problems and identity of dalit women.

Several efforts have been made since independence to secure human rights of women in general and dalit women in particular. Despite this, human rights of dalit women are seen to be violated in different forms. Such infringement of human rights echoes the need of evolving suitable mechanism to empower dalit women to assert for equal rights and justice in order to live a dignified life.

Mechanism to Strengthen the Capacity of Dalit Women

To be human is to respond to human sufferings and pain with compassion and effective concern. It is not enough to feel with the dalit women in their pain, There is more need for effective action, otherwise it would be just sentimentalism. The needs and the problems of dalit women differ with city, village, area and caste. It is essential to keep in mind that dalit women are not mere individuals but belong to a sociological and dialectical system. Therefore to recognise the system and to prohibit violation, first and foremost proper perspectives about the issues has to be developed among all by considering following suggestions:

Awareness for Assertion

Extensive reading of available literature can be done by young generation to understand the profile and problems of dalit women. Factual incidents & success stories of dalit women namely, 'We made History Too' by Meenakshi Moon & Urmila Pawar can be included in the educational texts.

Access & Exposure Visits

Special exposure visits to dalit localities can be organised for school and college students to assess basic amenities accessible to dalit women namely, water, electricity, health and hygiene. Similarly dalit women's visit to urban structured colonies can be arranged to impress upon the importance of standard of living of non-dalits.

Academic Activities

Academic institutions need to be encouraged to undertake studies to assess the problems of violence and atrocities against dalit women as also the reasons therefore and to work out ways to overcome them. Thought provoking sessions on harmful social religions practices namely, Chira, Devdasi, Jogin need to be held for basic understanding and effective interventional strategies.

Campaigns and Sessions

Campaigns for equal and rational distribution of natural resources among weaker sections can be organised to secure their rightful means of livelihood. Proper rehabilitation and shelter can be provided to those communities, which are out of the social periphery (NT/DT) to protect them from the risk of sexual abuse.

Inclusion of Dalit Women in Various System

More dalit women in their population proportion (16.5% SC, 7.5% ST) should be given chance to enter in the system like police, judiciary, education, health and politics. Sessions can be organised for dalit activist and women activists to sensitize them about the magnitude of torture and oppression faced by the dalit women. Legal education dealing with protection of human rights of dalits and Prevention of Atrocities Act can be organised to prevent the problems of castism.

References

Ahuja, R. (1998). *Violence Against Women*, Rawat Publication, New Delhi.

Bandhu, P. (2003). *Dalit Women's cry for Liberation: My Rights Are Rising like the Sun, will you deny this sunrise"?* Edited in Rao (2003) *Caste and Gender*, Kali For Women, New Delhi.

Dietrich, G (2003). *Dalit Movement and Women's Movement*, Edited in Rao (2003) *Caste and Gender*, Kali for women, New Delhi.

Jogdand, P (1995) *Dalit Women, Issues and Perspectives*, Gyan Publication, New Delhi.

6

Tribal Land Issues

India's population of over a billion includes 70 million tribal people (8.6%). They are scattered throughout India, but most live in two contiguous areas. The first is the forested hills and mountains of the northeast, and the second is the broad belt of hilly, forested country across north–central India from Gujarat and Rajasthan in the west, through Madhya Pradesh and Chattisgarh, to Jharkhand and Orissa in the east.

The definition of the term "tribe" has long been a subject for discussion among anthropologists, but so far, there is no generally accepted definition. This leaves unresolved a basic question: Are there peoples who can be identified as tribal? For some scholars, identifying a tribal from a non-tribal is easy. Weiner claimed that "everyone in Chotanagpur can recognize a tribal. A distinctive racial type, known by physical anthropologists as belonging to the proto-Australoid stock, they are somewhat darker than other Indians and have features that are sometimes Mongoloid in appearance. They live in their own villages, many of which are wholly homogenous....Perhaps the most distinctive feature of tribal life is the very attitude toward life itself. In contrast with their Hindu neighbours, the tribals are a carefree people, hedonistic in their simple pleasures."

Several anthropologists hold the view that a tribe is no different from a caste. Tribe as a category, separate from the mainstream caste society, is an invention of the British administrators. As Singh put it, "[T]he notion of a tribe was introduced by colonial administrators. It was part of the universal trend to dichotomise the indigenous peoples and colonisers, the savage and the civilized, the tribals and non-tribals".

Beteille discusses four key criteria that have been used to distinguish a tribe from the rest of population: size, isolation, religion, and means of livelihoods. He points out that these criteria fail to support the contention that distinct tribal communities do exist in India. Beteille first considers the criterion of size and notes that anthropologists usually define tribal societies as small-scale social systems. For example, according to Lewis, "[I]deally tribal societies are small in scale, are restricted in the spatial and temporal range of their social, legal and political relations, and possess a morality, religion and world view of corresponding dimensions." Beteille agrees that this may be true of many tribes in Africa and elsewhere, but in India, he points out, tribes such as the Santhals, Gonds, and Bhils are large segments of the population, each numbering over a million and scattered over vast territories.

Beteille notes that the second criterion—that tribal societies are isolated and lack contact with non-tribals—is not true of Indian tribal communities, as most of them have long been living in close contact with Hindu castes and other communities. The third criterion—religion—also lacks validity, because India's major tribal groups do not practice an animism that is distinct from the country's mainstream Hinduism. In India, animism and Hinduism are often intertwined at the community level. Risley said that "no sharp line of demarcation can be drawn between Hinduism and Animism. The one shades away insensibly into the other." This is one reason why some Indian anthropologists identify tribal people as "Backward Hindus".

Regarding the fourth criterion, livelihood, Beteille notes that the archetypical tribal society lacks a clear division of labour; it does not split up tasks the way settled agriculture and family farming systems do. But Indian tribal populations do not fit that model. For example, the Birhors may follow a hunting and gathering way of life, but even they rely on some specialised households to supply baskets and utensils for daily use. In Jharkhand State, among the Mundas, the Hos, the Santhals, and the Oraons, settled agriculture is widely practiced, and, as Beteille pointed out, the family farm is key to these tribal social systems.

Constitutional Rights of Indian Tribals

The view that there are no tribal societies in India, as described in the anthropological literature, has now gained many adherents. This raises the question of why the Government of India came up with a list of "Scheduled Tribes" and wrote it into the Constitution. One argument is that historically, the invention and perpetuation of tribalism in India owe everything to the calculations of the governing elite. British administrators with their "classificatory urges" were the pioneers in preparing a list of "primitive tribes", with especially elabourate detail that was based on a 1931 census. In this regard, Beteille says that "it cannot be too strongly emphasized that the list of Primitive Tribes reflects the demands more of administrative and political circumstance than of academic or logical rigour".

The Indian Constitution refers to tribal people as the Scheduled Tribes, but it does not define tribe. Article 342 of the Indian Constitution declares that the scheduled tribes are "the tribes or the tribal communities or parts of or groups within tribes or tribal communities" that the President may specify by public notification. They were duly specified by the President through the Constitution (Scheduled Tribes) Order of 1950.

In addition to the "Scheduled Tribes", the Indian Constitution names other groups who are considered in need of special protection, such as "Scheduled Castes" and "Other Backward Castes". These communities, which occupy low ranks in India's caste hierarchy, have suffered through the ages socially, culturally, and economically. To uplift these castes, the Constitution provides certain protective measures such as reserving slots for them in education and employment. Some castes have sought recognition as "Other Backward Castes", feeling that they, too, deserve constitutional guarantees. A recent example of accession to that status is the politically powerful Jat community of Rajasthan.

The following were originally used as characteristics for awarding a community the status of a scheduled tribe: (i) the primitive way of living,

— habitation in remote and less accessible areas, and
— nomadic habits and love for drinks and dance.

In 1962, the Dhebar Commission took note of the fact that "the term tribe is nowhere defined in the Constitution and in fact there is no satisfactory definition anywhere". It proposed a definition of a "tribal area", recommending that an area be considered eligible if it met the following criteria:

— preponderance of tribal people in the population,
— compact and reasonable size,
— underdeveloped nature of the area, and
— marked disparity in economic standards of the people.

As with earlier criteria, these meet administrative and political decision-making purposes but are rather vague as distinct characteristics of a tribal community.

In independent India, successive governments have continued with the policy of "scheduling" areas, tribes, castes, and other backward classes despite the weaknesses and difficulties embedded in the process. This is primarily because political parties have found that it is easier to win the voters of "Scheduled India" than the voters of mainstreamed India. The scheduled tribes and castes usually have specific demands, and each political party presents solutions to their demands in its campaign in every general election. In several elections, the Congress Party greatly benefited from the support of scheduled castes and scheduled tribes in rural areas because of its elaborate schemes to assist such castes and tribes, listed in its election manifestos.

Identity Crisis

In recent decades, a view has emerged that there are many more communities that still need to be declared as scheduled tribes, and that the task of identifying such tribal groups should be done by the tribal people themselves. Such self-identification exercises, where carried out, have not only swelled the number of tribal people but also added groups that cannot be considered as tribes by the tribal characteristics discussed above. For example, the scheduled tribal population in the State of Karnataka has increased from 400,000 in 1980 to 2 million in 2000. This increase will continue as many more tribal communities still aspire to become scheduled tribes. The main reason is to gain political favours. In several other Indian states, many non-tribal communities have staked their claims to be listed as scheduled tribes and have even resorted to violence when denied. The current agitation of Gujjars in Rajasthan is a good example.

Scheduling has been criticized for its lack of a systematic and sound basis. While certain communities who do not possess tribal characteristics are included in the list of scheduled tribes as a political favour so that they can benefit from the special constitutional guarantees, others who are more deserving have been left out. This is the view of the Gujjar community in Rajasthan, which regard itself as better qualified to be a tribal community than the Meenas, who were among the first to get listed.

A World Bank consultation workshop held in Karnataka in 1998 recommended a list of characteristics that distinguish tribals from others:

— Isolation from the urban population
— Tracing of their origin to the oldest sections of the population
— Place of residence confined to scheduled areas
— Separate dialect that does not have a script
— Primitive and animist religious beliefs
— Distinct cultural features
— Particular name for identity
— A simple life
— Few or no links with the market
— A higher status accorded to women
— Production for consumption, not for sale

Communal Land Management

For aeons, tribal people have cultivated land and managed natural resources. Land and forest for them are essentially communal resources to be used according to their present and future needs. The judicious use of common property resources on which they depend heavily has become an integral part of their way of life. "Most indigenous peoples do not view land as a 'commodity' which can be bought or sold in impersonal markets, nor do they view the trees, plants, animals, and fish which cohabit the land as 'natural resources' which produce profits or rents. On the contrary, the indigenous view is that land is a substance endowed with sacred meanings, embedded in social relations and fundamental to the definition of a people's existence and identity. Similarly, the trees, plants, animals, and fish, which inhabit the land are highly personal beings (often a kinship idiom is used to describe these beings) which form part of their social and spiritual universes. This close attachment to the land and the environment is the defining characteristic of indigenous peoples". In a similar vein, a United Nations Development Programme (UNDP) report noted, "Indigenous people often have a special relationship with the land for many it is still their source of livelihood and sustenance and the basis of their existence as communities. The right to own, occupy and use land collectively is inherent in the self-conception of indigenous people, and this right is generally vested not in the individual but in the local community, the tribe or the indigenous nation".

The traditional communal land system, based on *jhum* (shifting cultivation) of common land, once flourished extensively in tribal areas but now survives only in some remote, inaccessible tracts, mainly in northeastern India among the Khasis, Garo, and Jaintia. It is generally believed that among these tribal communities in the northeast, all lands are necessarily communally owned. But this is a partial truth. There are lands that are owned by the entire village tribal community, but there are also some lands that are owned by the clan members within a village or by individual households. In several northeastern states, some jhum lands are not communal lands but are household property. Among tribes such as Adis, Noktes, and Mihomis, each household owns several plots of jhum land. For a few years, a household cultivates a plot and keeps the other plots fallow. Once the soil fertility of the plot diminishes, the household moves to the next plot. This movement lasts over several years. At the end of the shifting-cultivation cycle, a household returns to the first plot of jhum land that it had cultivated and starts the cycle again.

The jhum cultivation is also found in some parts of central and eastern India, especially among the Munda, Ho, and Khonds. The Khond society is based on group solidarity. They have a socialistic concept of property, and their creed of mutual help is based on the strong conviction that unity is their greatest strength. Their survival down the ages has been achieved by building up this rich community life. Even the layout of their villages reflects it. Houses are built in rows, with shared roofs and verandahs. They say, "We are in touch; we can call out to each other at night if a tiger comes down the street or anyone is ill".

The presence of communal land rights does not necessarily imply the absence of individual rights over land in a community. Communal land rights exist in various forms, and in each form, there is room for individual land rights. An individual, however, has access to land resources in a community only as a member of the community. In Nagaland, for example, when timber is extracted for sale from land belonging to an individual, a commission is collected from the buyer by the traditional village council for common village development programs. This indicates that communal land rights are primary and that individual rights over land emanate from them.

Traditional communal land tenure systems continue to exist even where formal land tenure systems emphasize individual property rights. Tribal people in Nagaland State have retained some of their communal land rights even after its integration into the Indian state. In fact, "even the state government has tried to make a synthesis of [common property resources] and the communal system. It has set up Village Development Boards through the authority of the traditional village councils. This ensures that the Board is rooted in the community and at the same time administrative rationality in operations is secured".

The tribal communities continue to follow communal land management systems as long as they serve a purpose. In fact, there are elements in communal land management that can be usefully integrated into tribal development programs, which rely on the active participation by the community. In support of this viewpoint, an Indian government committee chaired by Roy-Burman stated, "There is lot to be said for the view that forests should be managed primarily by the forest dwellers and backed by technical guidance of the Forest Department. This implies that wherever the community rights exist, they should be recognized and adopted to serve the urgent needs of soil and water management, and reforestation of the denuded tracts by suitable species".

The tribal people face numerous hurdles in trying to maintain their traditional communal land use and natural resource management practices. Some of these obstacles come from demographic changes, resulting from the growth of their own populations and the reduction of their traditional territories, which then make it difficult to continue shifting cultivation. But there are other factors, such as the unhelpful attitude that forest officials adopt, although their job is to assist the forest people. Often, the tribal people know nothing about their rights, and the forest officials exploit their ignorance. As Human and Pattanaik reported: "Various surveys have been conducted to find out what people know of their rights. They reveal confusion at best and at worst complete ignorance. It almost goes without saying that it suits both Forest officials and traders to keep it that way: the more ignorant or confused that people are, the less likely they are to assert their rights and less likely they are to fight exploitation that is perpetually visited upon them".

According to a widely held view, the communal land system is incompatible with the requirements of development. For example, the National Committee on Backward Areas in its report on northeast India advocated the individualization of communal resources for the sake of progress. In such an approach to development, tribal peoples face a formidable challenge regarding their efforts to maintain communal land use patterns and natural resource management practices. "Often the lands they use for productive purposes and to maintain historical and spiritual links are not secure and so are being taken over for logging, mining, tourism and infrastructure.…And not only their land is being coveted and taken so is their knowledge. Multinational corporations have discovered its commercial potential, and the race is on to patent, privatize and appropriate".

In recent years, national development processes and the emerging market system have influenced tribal life. One key factor is the conversion of land under shifting cultivation into land under permanent cultivation or under horticulture or in plantations. In tribal communities of the northeast, this conversion has encouraged the formation of private property. Private land development, leasing, and labour markets are slowly coming into existence. As a result of the privatization of forest ownership in the Khasi Hills, there is a large class of farmers who own forests.

Tribal people in India are also experiencing the impacts of globalization, which encourages private ownership. Globalization reaches local communities largely through the market. New goods may be seen on the television or noticed in other ways. But it is through the market that they become available to people. It is also through the market that producers come to know what they can sell. In turn, this growth of the market has led to a process of privatization of formerly communal land, of devolution of ownership from community or clan to the family. Tribal communities will find it increasingly difficult to resist the impact of such external forces and hold on to their traditional communal land management system. They themselves are gradually moving toward private ownership of items that they acquire from the market, making class divisions within a community more visible.

Displacement by Development Projects

Tribal lands are rich in hydrologic, mineral, oil, gas, forest, and other resources, and this easily makes them the most attractive sites to locate development projects of various kinds. Thus, many development projects in India are located in areas that are densely inhabited by tribal people. For multinational companies looking for investment opportunities, these areas are fast becoming the most favoured destinations. The fact is there is no such territory not coveted by some international corporation for its mineral wealth, its oil deposits, its pastures, its forests, its medicinal plants, its suitability for commercial plantation, its water resources, or its tourist potential.

One would normally expect a resource-rich region to be a boon for tribal people. In India, the rich natural endowment has, however, been of little avail to them. On the contrary, large-scale development projects undertaken in tribal areas have physically evicted significant numbers of tribal people. Tribal people constitute 8.6% of India's population, and about 40% of them have been displaced by development projects.

Until recently, dams were a major cause of displacement, but projects in other development sectors are now quickly catching up.

Urbanization and transport are among the development sectors that have seen a rapid rise in the number of persons displaced by development projects. In parks and protected areas, as many as 600,000 tribal people have been physically displaced. One important aspect of parks and protection-area development is that such programs often do not physically displace communities but restrict their access to forest produce on which they have traditionally subsisted. Such communities lack other skills to survive in different environments. Giesler argues that displacement from conservation efforts contributes to impoverishment in multiple ways. Conservation refugees are often poor at the outset of their ordeal. They are victims of displacement in part because of their combined poverty and powerlessness, which is then compounded by forced removal.

Development projects tend to displace tribal people more than others. A United Nations Environment Programme report cites the examples of the Karjan and Sukhi reservoirs in Gujarat State that displaced only tribal people. The Balimela Hydro Project in Orissa State displaced a large number of people, 98% of whom were tribal people. Equally disastrous were the consequences for tribal people affected by the Upper Kolar Dam. In this project, they constituted 96% of the total affected population. According to the World Commission on Dams, "Overall, 40 to 50% of those displaced are estimated to be tribal people, who account for barely 8% of India's total population of over a billion." A recent estimate is that at least 55% of those displaced by development projects in India are tribal people.

Much of the physical displacement could be avoided by careful planning. Large-scale displacement often occurs because of the callous attitude of the project authorities who acquire land. Often, they acquire large areas of land, which then turn out to be much more than needed and remain unused. In some cases, large areas are acquired for intended industries without proper planning. Such acquisition of land leaves the evicted people landless, without giving them in return any employment. Appa and Patel recount similar cases of unnecessary displacements from Gujarat that tore many lives asunder.

Displacement from Common Property Resources

Tribal people suffer from physical displacement mainly because of the laws that do not recognize communal customary rights of tribal people to their territories. The resettlement literature is full of case studies of how development projects ignore the customary rights of the tribal people and treat them as illegal occupants of government land. Such an approach invariably leads to the impoverishment of once settled communities, just the opposite of what development promises. For example, in the Upper Indravati Hydroelectric Project, the tribal people were forcibly removed from their lands despite having *patta* (legal title to land). In addition, they were given no compensation for losing their common resources—pastures, forest lands, water bodies, burial grounds, and quarries. Without those resources, their income and quality of life significantly deteriorated. Tribal people who are moved for development projects are impoverished by this loss of access to natural resources. "Such impoverishment is even more pronounced when people have to move from resource rich areas such as those targeted for conservation".

For many tribal and forest-dwelling communities, grazing lands, forests, ponds, fisheries, wildlife, riverbeds, and other such shared resources are a major source of sustenance. For example, 70% to 80% of the non-timber forest produce that forms a major component of many households' income comes from common resources. Development projects that involve involuntary resettlement abruptly terminate access to these resources. Sometimes it happens because the relocation site lacks similar resources. More often, it happens because the resettlement planners fail to consider the livelihood and social and cultural identities of the people they are moving. No thought is given to the important role of common resources in their lives. And because communal resources are considered government properties, the resettlers are given no compensation for losing access to them. For those without private land or other assets, the consequences generally prove catastrophic.

Displacement from common property resources has its harshest effects on women, because they are generally the ones who gather or are otherwise control the use of those resources. Firewood collection emerges as a major issue. In the Upper Krishna Irrigation Project, for example, nearly two thirds of the women reported the unavailability of fuel wood and fodder. In resettled areas of Kohadia villages in Korba in Madhya Pradesh State, women have no option but to buy firewood from markets instead of collecting it freely from nearby forests. This puts a serious drain on household budgets.

In tribal areas, it is women who generally control farm production and household economy, and hence their dependence on common property resources for earning or saving income is greater than that of men. The loss of access to those resources "results in the emergence of an unemployed and unemployable 'housewife' who is increasingly not only perceived to be but becomes almost solely dependent on her husband. Additionally, access to resources in the post-displacement scenario is almost always mediated via husbands, who now assume the role of 'sole' bread earners". There is a growing realization that projects that relocate people must compensate those who are dependent on common property resources. Not doing so will only lead to impoverishment among people who give up their livelihoods for the sake of development. That is not a happy development outcome.

Disastrous Displacement Effects

Involuntary resettlement worldwide seems to have been overwhelmingly disastrous for tribal people. Anyone would be harmed by displacement, but it is particularly disruptive of tribal livelihoods and cultures. They have to leave behind their land and the forests that are their sources of livelihood. They have no skills to start any other activity for a living. Thus, development projects in most cases have impoverished them economically.

The projects have also seriously wounded them socially and spiritually. People who are forced to relocate have to begin life anew in places that may be totally unfamiliar, if not altogether hostile. They have often lost their community, because the group they have been part of for generations is split up. With long-established social networks gone, economic recovery becomes doubly difficult, and people are left to face an uncertain future in straitened circumstances. The trauma of resettlement is exacerbated for tribal people because of their close spiritual ties to their homeland and their apprehension that once they move, their way of life will be lost forever.

As the World Commission on Dams pointed out, "Due to neglect and lack of capacity to secure justice because of structural inequities, cultural dissonance, discrimination and economic and political marginalisation, indigenous and tribal peoples have suffered disproportionately from the negative impacts of large dams, while often being excluded from sharing in the benefits." They face relatively more risks of impoverishment because they rarely go to courts to vindicate their rights or get the wrongs redressed. The legal system is cumbersome, dilatory, expensive, and often weighted against them because of their poverty, illiteracy, and low social status. Officials tend to deny them even what they are due by law. It is common for the officials to keep the project cost low by calculating cash compensation for land that is below the real value of the property.

Displacement is rarely achieved without the use or threat of force. In projects where tribal people are involved, displacement is sometimes carried out in a ruthless manner. Any sign of resistance invites police intervention. In Kacheipadar and Sunger, two villages of Orissa, a study team found overwhelming evidence of excessive use of coercive methods by district authorities against the tribal population who refused to move. Hundreds of people, including young boys and girls, were arrested. Tear-gas shells were fired in Kacheipadar to disperse crowds. In the Sunger area, Utkal Alumina International Ltd. let loose security guards to harass the villagers.

An elderly woman in Sunger village informed the observers that she had never in her life seen police until this incident and that now, policemen were frequently knocking on her door. Compensation, a critical issue in resettlement planning, is seldom addressed satisfactorily. Impoverishment that tribal people encounter soon after displacement mainly arises from delayed payment of compensation and the exclusion from compensation calculations of the common property resources on which they largely subsist. In addition, tribal people have little or no experience in handling large amount of cash. As a result, compensation paid in cash rarely helps them regain their previous standard of living. It quickly slips through their fingers for weddings and other festivities or ill-planned business enterprises. Yet, there continues to be heavy emphasis on issuing compensation in cash. Perera found even NGOs in the Singrauli region supporting cash compensation rather than other options that would generate livelihoods. Not only is cash compensation culturally inappropriate, but it leads to underpayment because of flawed valuation methods. For tribal people, the best settlement strategy would be to receive land to replace the land lost. This alternative, however, often is rejected because land is scarce.

Cultural Ignorance in Resettlement Planning

Many sites developed to resettle tribal people fail to attract them, as the communal character of their culture has not been taken fully into account. People are moved to an environment completely different from what they know. On arrival, they discover to their dismay that forests, pastures, and other common property resources that sustained them in their original environment do not exist. Additionally, resettlement disrupts their communal life when they are moved not as an integrated social unit but broken randomly into groups because there is no area large enough for the original community.

Tribal people leave the relocation site when they find that there is no forest land for collecting timber, firewood, and other forest products and no grazing land for their cattle. For example, the people of Karnaka Bas from the Sariska Project Tiger Reserve who first moved to Sirsawas and Bandipal found that the resettlement site lacked any communal resources. When they tried to return to their original village, the Forest Department would not let them in. They had to manage their own resettlement on the fringes of Kiraska and Kundelka, the two adjoining villages.

What makes resettlement sites particularly unattractive, often resulting in their complete abandonment, is the neglect of sociocultural aspects of tribal life in the planning process. Mathur found this to be the case in colonies built for the Bhil tribals displaced by the Kadana Dam on the Mahi River: "The colonies that the government agencies especially built for rehabilitation did not attract the Bhil oustees. The prospect of living in new settlements, with civic amenities not in accord with their lifestyle, was not very attractive. Like tribals elsewhere, the Bhils are deeply attached to their soil and their hamlets on forested hilltops, which are dispersed and separated from one another by long distances. Living in clustered colony conflicts with their traditional dispersed pattern of living on top of their own forested hills.... No wonder, then, that the number of oustees actually relocated to colonies is small, except in the colony at Dungarsaran.... The popularity of Dungarsaran as a resettlement sites lies in the fact that it comes closest to the hilly forest setting of a tribal village".

Similarly, a lack of attention to the sociocultural concerns of the tribal people backfired in a resettlement colony set up in Andhra Pradesh. The Gond tribals from two regions found their customs and manners so incompatible that they could not live together at the same place. One group then left the colony. People brought together from antagonistic segments are bound to carry with them the traditions of their past antagonism, making living together an impossible arrangement. Roy-Burman reported that such ignorance of tribal histories is a frequent reason that resettlement sites fail.

Tribals and Forest Rights

Commonly perceived as rights of local forest dwellers over forest products and forest land, forest rights have been a major area of concern as well as debate in India. In colonial and independent India, although a large tract of land would be recorded as "unclassed" forest in Government records, ownership was unclear, and because most of these forests were home to a large number of tribals, the land was acquired by the Forest Department without settling their rights over them. After Independence, supported by improper survey and settlement, large tracts of land were declared as "reserve forests," meaning no rights either existed there or would exist later and all who either resided or claimed rights would be termed as encroachers.

Forestry in colonial India was all about commercial exploitation and revenue and thus recognized no rights and concessions for forest dwellers, who were mostly tribals. There was no legislative framework to make forests available for meeting local livelihood needs and the colonial powers made no effort to hide their intention, i.e. forestry for commerce, especially timber. Forestry science was introduced by western colonial forces as a codified, printed, and formal curriculum to continue political domination that implied nonrecognition as well as opposition to the largely oral indigenous forest management traditions. This marked the beginning of a forest governance system that was alien, induced, and most importantly that excluded forest-dependent communities in the name of scientific forestry, public interest, national development, conservation, and industrial growth.

The national governments in the postcolonial phase inherited the colonial world view that not only aimed at the use of developing country forests to boost western industrial development, but also belaboured the nonexisting incompatibility between conservation and livelihoods.

Forest Rights in British India

The British established a mode of forest governance that imposed restrictions on local forest-dwelling communities through a definition of forests as national property for colonial objectives, which tried to acquire control of forests for commerce and national development at the cost of local forest-based livelihoods. Although the Forest Administration in British India put stress on national development, the primary focus of forest governance was commerce with limitations on the rights and privileges of local communities. Such regulation of rights was reflected in the classification of forests during colonial times.

As national property, forests were classified as conservation forests, commercial forests, minor forests, and pasture lands. The first two categories as the names would suggest were out of bounds for local forest-dependent communities. Minor forests were managed by *Panchayats* with a view to reducing the contact between subordinate forest officials and villagers. Pasture land, mostly grassland, was for grazing purposes.

During medieval India, forests were owned by local chiefs with access rights being awarded to local communities. Towards the beginning of the nineteenth century, the British wanted to undertake unhindered exploitation of timber, which required the Government to assert its ownership over forests and do away with the traditional systems of community forest management that existed in most parts of the country. This had nothing to do with conservation; it was a ploy to keep direct control over trees, timber, and forest routes. Teak was identified as a substitute for oak, already becoming depleted in England, to build ships for the Royal Navy and railway lines. With this objective, the East India Company acquired royalty rights over teak in 1807.

Table 1. Timeline of Control Established

Year	Controls and Rights Acquired	Remarks/Fall Out
1807	East India Company acquired royalty rights over teak	No locals allowed timber for domestic use. This meant prohibition of unauthorized teak felling and the Conservator becoming the sanctioning authority for teak felling and selling, more of an assumed power than lawfully given.
1846	Sanctioning authority over teak extended to all forests and forest produce	Prohibition of local use rights was supplemented by unrestricted extraction of timber from all forests.
1860	Company' ssovereignty extended to the total area of forest land	As an aftermath of the Sepoy Mutiny in 1857, during which time forests and forest-dwelling communities provided the rebels with safe hiding places, Company administration prohibited and withdrew all access rights and privileges to fuel, fodder, and other local uses.
1864	Formation of the Imperial Forest Department	In order to legitimize authority with legal and administrative backing, the Imperial Forest Department was created in 1864 to consolidate Government control over forests and forestry was made a scientific operation, making it inaccessible to forest dwellers.
1865 1878 1927	Series of Forest Acts promulgated	In order to legitimize Government control through scientific operations, a series of legal instruments were passed in the form of Forest Acts.

The Acts referred to in Table 1 empowered the Government to declare its intention to notify any area as a reserved or protected forest, following which a "Forest Settlement Officer" supposedly would enquire into claims of rights (to land, forest produce, pasture, etc.). The colonial forest administration camouflaged timber extraction as conservation (thus curtailing livelihood rights) through classification of forests and prohibition of customary use rights. There was no settlement of rights and no space for meeting local needs. On the contrary, valuable trees were reserved and elaborate provisions were made for punitive action in the event of violation. The 1927 Act remains India's central forest legislation and with minor modifications is still operational in independent India. Thus started deliberate Government intervention in forests and measures relating to scientific conservancy were promoted for legitimacy.

Forest Rights in Independent India

With Independence, local forest-dependent people expected to get their rights back. But far from improving, the rights situation actually worsened. Although the policy-makers changed, the policies remained more or less the same. In 1948, during the process of accession of the Princely States after Independence, the consolidation of Government forests continued. The Government proclaimed the lands of ex-Princely States and *zamindars* as Reserve Forests but no effective steps for settlement of rights were taken. This inevitably sowed the seeds of the future forest land conflicts between the tribals, nontribals, and the Government.

Forest governance in postcolonial India can be separated into three phases (Table 2).

Table 2. Phases of Forest Governance in Independent India

Phase	Time Frame	Developments/Remarks
Phase 1	1947–1970	This was the phase of commercial exploitation of forests for industrial development as well as for creating farmland for the large peasantry class.
Phase 2	1970–1988	This lasted till the commencement of the 1988 National Forest Policy; it was a phase of conservation with increased Government control. During this phase, forest conservation was made a directive principle, a fundamental duty in the Constitution, and brought to the Concurrent List for greater control of the Government. It was also the time when powerful legislative instruments like the Wildlife Protection Act and the Forest Conservation Act were put in place. This phase, like the previous one, had no space for forest dwellers and tribals in the protection and management of local forests.
Phase 3	1988 onwards	The third phase began with the introduction of the National Forest Policy in 1988, which not only made forest a local resource but also made the participation of local forest-protecting communities mandatory in the regeneration of degraded forests.

Conservation Continuity

The development of legal instruments in the second phase was a response to forest and wildlife depletion in the first phase. These instruments were extremely conservationist in nature, did not differentiate between local and external use, stressed excessive Government control in the form of Eminent Domain, and restricted or did not recognize existing local use rights. The assumption was that forest had been destroyed by the forest dwellers/tribals and needed to be protected/conserved from them, although in reality mindless exploitation of the forest and its wildlife were the handiwork of the rich and the influential. Although the Forest Conservation Act restricted forest diversion for nonforest use, by prescribing prior permission and a high conversion rate, it in effect made such diversion possible. However for the rich, forest land diversion was easier whereas the poor forest-dwelling tribals were termed as "encroachers" and a direction for their eviction was issued by the Ministry of Environment and Forests (MoEF) through the May 2002 circular. This incapacitation of forest-dwelling tribals was aggravated by the establishment of the Protected Area Network, which meant further inviolable areas with no or negligible rights over forests and forest land by the tribals; it enabled the State to evict local forest dwellers without settling their bona fide rights to residence. It is unfortunate that even the recent amendment to the Wildlife Protection Act of 2002 (WLPA) has made no reference to the Panchayat Extension to Scheduled Area (PESA) Act (PESA) and has withdrawn continuance of rights even after the final notification of a protected area. A constant and consistent process was initiated to make the conservation legislations like WLPA and the Forest Conservation Act (FCA) more powerful than right-providing legislations like PESA, although the latter was an amendment to the Constitution.

One of the residual features of the colonial Government that survived even in the post-Independence period was its obsession with technocratic expertise and utter mistrust and complete rejection of people's power and knowledge as important inputs for achieving national development goals. Development policy making in India, unfortunately, positioned itself on the astounding premise that people did not know anything. The prevailing social and political culture, the legal rational bureaucracy, and most dangerously the nation as a whole were made to believe in and sustain such an exclusionary development design, skilfully promoted by Government institutions. Curiously, almost all enabling- and right-conferring provisions were in the form of policies that had no legal sanction while the restrictive ones were in the form of Acts, which had legal backing. Besides, regulatory authorities and right-guaranteeing institutions mostly focused on commercial exploitation and conservation whereas the rights of local forest-dependent communities still remained an area of utter indifference.

Implications Pro-Tribal Forest Legislations in India

Since the primary intention of colonial laws was to take over lands and deny the rights of communities, the "settlement" process initiated during the late nineteenth and early twentieth centuries was hardly effective. Surveys were often incomplete or not done (82.9% of Madhya Pradesh's forest blocks have not been surveyed to date, while in Orissa more than 40% of State forests are "deemed" reserved forests where no settlement of rights took place). Where the claims process did occur, the rights of socially weaker communities particularly tribals were rarely recorded. The problem became worse particularly after Independence, when the lands declared "forests" by the Princely States, the *zamindars*, and the private owners were transferred to the Forest Department through blanket notifications. In short, what the Government records called "forests" often included large areas of land that were not and never were forest at all. Moreover, those areas that were in fact forest included the traditional homelands of communities. As such consolidation of Government forests did not settle existing claims on land; all people, mostly tribals, who lived in these forests, were subsequently declared "encroachers," as they did not have recognized rights and claims to their ancestral homelands.

The close relationship of tribal people with the forest was described by Elwin in a poetic yet accurate manner:

> To a vast number of the tribal people the forest is their well-loved home, their livelihood, their very existence. It gives them food—fruits of all kinds, edible leaves, honey, nourishing roots, wild game and fish. It provides them with material to build their homes and to

> practice their arts. By exploiting its products they can supplement their meagre income. It keeps them warm with its fuel and cool with its grateful shade. Their religion leads them to believe that there are many spirits living in the trees. There are special sacrifices to the forest gods; in many places offerings are made to a tree before it is cut, and there are usually ceremonies before and after hunting. Tribal folk-tales often speak about the relations of human beings and the sylvan spirits and it is striking to see how in many of the myths and legends the deep sense of identity with the forest is emphasized.... From time immemorial until comparatively recently the tribal people have enjoyed the freedom to use the forest and hunt its animals and this has given them a conviction, which remains even today in their hearts that the forest belongs to them.

This happy state of affairs for the tribal people was not to last forever, however. From about the middle of the 19th century, people from outside began to move into the forest, lured by its wealth of natural resources, and the colonial government, sensing the commercial potential of forests, gradually extended its authority over them in the name of scientific management.

The first move in this regard came in 1855 when the colonial government issued a memorandum titled "Charter of Indian Forests", which decisively changed the status of large areas of land including forests into government property. Then came the creation of the Forest Department and the passage of the Indian Forest Act of 1865, under which any land covered with trees or brushwood could be declared forest, and the government laid claim to it all. With a stroke, common property resources became a thing of the past. A succession of laws was then passed with the sole purpose of curtailing the traditional rights of tribal people in forests.

In 1952, after independence, a new national forest policy added further restrictions on tribal peoples. For example, under the old policy the forest land could be released for cultivation subject to certain safeguards, and free grazing was allowed. The new policy barred cultivation and required a paid permit for grazing, which was difficult to obtain. Elwin very aptly depicts the position of the tribal people in the changed circumstances:

> Thus the tribal who regarded himself as the lord of the forests, was through a deliberate process turned into a subject and placed under

> the Forest Department. Tribal villages were no longer an essential part of the forests but were there merely on sufferance. The traditional rights of the tribal were no longer recognised as rights. In 1894 they became "rights and privileges" and in 1952 they became "rights and concessions". Now they are regarded as "concessions".

At the same time, although the new policy expressed ecological concerns, vast forest lands in ecologically sensitive areas were destroyed to make way for big projects or clear-felled to raise revenue for the government.

The National Forest Policy of 1988 was a significant move in favour of both forest conservation and the livelihoods of forest communities. It endorsed the national goal of keeping one-third of the land area for forests, which had been recommended in 1952, and it incorporated specific provisions to safeguard the rights of tribal and other local people. "Indeed, meeting the needs of local populations dependent on the forest ecosystem was held to be the first charge on the forest. This meant that forests could not be exploited to meet the raw material demands of industry, nor earn revenue for the state at the cost of the local populations. The policy was, therefore, a significant departure from long-standing forest management practices whose emphasis had been on commercial exploitation and revenue raising". However, rules to implement the policy were not put in place until much later, and state governments in the meantime progressively reduced the traditional rights of the tribal people.

The question of forest rights is related to the modern concept of ownership, but notions of the forest people in this regard are quite different. The forest is the pivot around which the tribal life revolves, but for the state, the forest is simply a source of raw materials for industry and revenue for itself. In some states the Forest Department is a major source of revenue for the government. It is no wonder that successive plans, policies, and legislation have resulted in restricting the rights and usage of forests by millions of tribal people for whom forests are their only refuge and source of sustenance.

In 2006, as a result of a long campaign by forest rights activists, the Government of India enacted a new act entitled "The Scheduled Tribes and Other Traditional Forest Dwellers (Recognition of Forest Rights) Act 2006". Those in support of the act regard it as the long overdue recognition of the rights of scheduled tribes and forest dwellers to the lands they have occupied for centuries. It will save them from being treated as encroachers and evicted for development purposes without compensation, as has often happened in the past. It is also contended by the tribal rights activists that secure tenurial rights will lead to sustainable management of land. Those who are opposed to the act fear that it will undermine the fast-dwindling forests and sound the death knell for the endangered tiger population.

The implementation of this law is not going to be smooth. Tribal and for-est-dwelling people will not get the rights to forestland automatically. Only those families who have been primarily residing in forest areas for three generations (nearly 75 years) will be entitled. The verification procedures to determine eligibility are not simple and could be quite time consuming, as disputes may arise among the forest-dwelling communities themselves.The act also prevents the use of forestland for development purposes such as mining, reservoir construction, and industrial plants without the consent of the tribal people who live in forests or in the vicinity through *gram sabhas* (village assemblies). But there is a risk that politically connected commercial interests could manipulate gram sabhas to obtain such lands for commercial purposes. The tribal rights activists also warn against the machinations of some bureaucrats, especially those in the Forest Department who think that the department is the master of all forests in India. This could obstruct the implementation of the act and deny its benefits for tribal people.

Communal Rights

Land and territorial rights of the tribal people often receive no explicit legal recognition. When laws do recognize such rights, they are seldom defended in practice, especially if they conflict with wider national development goals. The Panchayats (Extension to Scheduled Areas) Act of 1996, or PESA as it is commonly known, is a major move to recognize the rights of the tribal people over the natural resources that they manage, and on which they depend for their livelihoods. However, the act has not been implemented, and the communal management of forests remains a mere promise. In fact, despite the opposition from tribal people, the forest areas in Orissa and other mineral-rich states are being allocated to corporations to invest in mining and other projects.

Tribal people feel that development projects, especially those of large-scale corporations, will take over more and more of the lands that are in their possession. The most worrisome aspect is the leading role of the state, which is handing over tribal lands to industries and corporations in violation of the Constitution and national laws. The tribal people in Schedule V Areas as defined in the Constitution enjoy certain rights over land, forests, water bodies, and other resources. In September 1997, the Supreme Court of India delivered a landmark judgment upholding these rights of tribal peoples to life, livelihood, land, and forests in a case that dealt with issues of mining in tribal land. Samatha, a nongovernment organization (NGO) in Andhra Pradesh, fled the case on behalf of the affected tribal people. The Supreme Court held that forests and lands in scheduled areas, irrespective of whether owned by the government or by a tribal community, cannot be leased out to non-tribal people or to private companies for mining or industrial uses. It restricted mining activity in these areas to be carried out only by the State Mineral Development Corporation or a cooperative of the tribal people. All leases granted by the state governments were declared to contravene Schedule V of the Constitution and were declared null and void. The judgment, known as Samatha Judgment, is a significant check to restrain the state from encouraging indiscriminate exploitation of land, forests, water bodies, and other resources for commercial purposes, especially in tribal areas.

The central government and state governments, however, chose to file an application to the Supreme Court in early 2000 asking for a review of the Samatha Judgment. The court dismissed the request, but efforts to circumvent the Samatha decision—which reinforced constitutional protections for tribal people are continuing. Under pressure from multinational corporations, the Government of India as well as state governments are still looking for an escape route. In July 2003, the Government of Orissa went as far as constituting a state subcommittee chaired by the chief minister to discuss the implications of the Samatha Judgment. The committee concluded that the judgment is not binding on the state. The reasoning was that there are enough laws in the state to ensure protection of tribal interests and that therefore; Orissa could stay outside the purview of the Supreme Court's ruling. On the basis of this interpretation, the government decided to allow the transfer of land in areas covered by Schedule V of the Constitution for mining and industrial purposes. This is a patently wrong inference because the ruling was applicable to all states.

After the Samatha judgment, the Government of India issued executive instructions in 1998 to set up systems for consulting with the gram sabhas and detail the procedure for land acquisition in Schedule V areas. But in Orissa, the state government circumvented the gram sabhas and gave their power to the *zila parishad* (divisional councils). This was a manipulation of the PESA that undermined its intent and effectively denied tribal people their rights to be consulted on land acquisition for projects.

Panchayats Extension to Schedule Areas Act, 1996

During the 1990s, the Eminent Domain of the Government was challenged by activists and human rights movements. Rights of the tribals over local resources were considered sacrosanct and non-negotiable and a move was initiated to secure Constitutional recognition for these rights. The sustained campaign led first to the 73rd Amendment of the Constitution to give recognition to decentralized governance in rural areas and then the constitution of the Bhuria Committee to look at tribal rights over resources through extension of the provisions of this Amendment to the Schedule V areas. Based on the recommendations of the committee, Parliament passed a separate legislation in 1996 as an annexure to the 73rd Amendment specifying special provisions for *Panchayats* in Schedule V areas. Known as the Panchayats Extension to Schedule Areas (PESA), 1996, it decentralized existing approaches to forest governance by bringing the *Gram Sabha* centre stage and recognized the traditional rights of tribals over "community resources"—meaning land, water, and forests.

PESA was important not just because it provided for a wide range of rights and privileges, but also because it provided a principle as well as a basis for future law making concerning the tribals. According to the Central Government law, the states promulgated their own laws supposedly giving rights to tribals over local resources.

It is almost a decade since PESA came into effect, but the obstacles in enforcing its provisions have remained largely unaddressed. Its avowed objective of power to the people has yet to take shape. The states are struggling to devise definitive procedures to define rights over forests and minor forest produce. Meanwhile, some states like Maharastra, Gujurat, and Orissa, in an effort to perpetuate State control over forest resources, tried to dilute the provisions of PESA although they had no legal jurisdiction to do so. The Government of Orissa, for example, has circumscribed the provisions of PESA by adding a clause, ".... consistent with the relevant laws in force," while incorporating the constitutional provision concerning the competence of the *Gram Sabha* to manage community resources and resolve disputes according to the customs and traditions of the people. This clearly implied that tribals could have rights over forests and minor forest produce, only if existing laws allowed it. Instead of changing State laws inconsistent with PESA, the Government of Orissa changed the provisions of the Act, thus negating the rights conferred on the community by the Constitution. The original objective of the Central Act was that state governments should change their laws according to central legislation. But the Government of Orissa, on the contrary, tampered with the central legislation to suit its own ends.

The Central Act talked about providing ownership rights over minor forest produce to the *Gram Sabha.* The MoEF constituted an expert committee to define ownership, which recommended that "ownership means revenue from sale of usufructory rights, i.e. the right to net revenue after retaining the administrative expenses of the department, and not right to control." The case of Andhra Pradesh is even more interesting. It gave ownership rights to the *Van Suraksha Samitis* (VSS, forest protection committees) with respect to all non-wood forest products (NWFPs) for which Girijan Cooperative Corporation (GCC) did not hold the monopoly rights. Similarly, there is no clarity on the issue of "community resource." The states have their own interpretations and legislations. While Orissa and Andhra Pradesh are silent about what constitutes community resource, Madhya Pradesh has defined it as land, water, and forest. This implies that the powers given by PESA to exercise rights over community resources are almost nonexistent in many states.

Although the Central Act leaves no room for doubt that reserve forests should be considered community resources under the purview of PESA, the official assumption is that reserve forests are out of the PESA domain. For instance, the NTFP Policy of 2000 in Orissa restricts the *Panchayat's* control over minor forest produce in reserve forests. It says that the *Gram Panchayats* shall not have any control over minor forest produce collected from the reserve forests whereas the PESA, in its spirit, sought to extend ownership of forests to any forest located in the vicinity of the village that the people had been traditionally accessing. The policy-makers knew very well that it would be foolish to create such a distinction because it was almost impossible to differentiate between produce collected from reserve forests and that from others. Nevertheless, they went ahead with putting in place the proviso that reserve forests cannot come under the purview of PESA because the relevant laws laid down that no rights can exist in the reserve forest area.

The Scheduled Tribes and Other Traditional Forest Dwellers (Recognition of Forest Rights) Act, 2006

The Supreme Court of India in an important case held that the tribals have a definite right over the forests and any sort of forest diversion or eviction should have their informed consent. Following suit, in an affidavit to the Apex Court, in June 2004, the Government of India made a significant admission by holding that "historical injustice" had been done to the tribal forest dwellers of the country, which needed to be immediately addressed by recognizing their traditional rights over forests and forest land. What made this admission particularly crucial was its acceptance that colonial perspective on forest management had failed and alienated a large chunk of the forest dwellers, especially tribals from forests and forest-based livelihood options. Besides, it could not have come at a better time just months after the eviction of about 168,000 families from over 150,000 hectares effected by the May 2002 Government order of eviction of forest encroachers. This led the Government of India to introduce the Scheduled Tribes (Recognition of Forest Rights) Bill, 2005 in Parliament on 13 December 2005. This legislation is now widely accepted and revered as a major step towards achieving social justice and a milestone in the tribal empowerment process.

Pressure mounted on the Government by tribal bodies and supportive progressive forces to introduce structural changes in favour of the forest-dependent people resulting in constitution of the Joint Parliamentary Committee (JPC) to take a fresh look at the Bill and recommend measures to meet their demands. Considering the fact that tribals were served with eviction notices in May 2002 for being "encroachers" as they could not produce residential evidence in forests before 25 October 1980 according to the FCA 1980, the JPC recommended that the cutoff date for the settlement of rights be extended to 13 December 2005, the date on which the Bill was first tabled in Parliament. It further recommended inclusion of non-scheduled tribe "traditional forest dwellers" living in the forest for three generations within its ambit. The recommendations also included the identification of the "critical wildlife habitat" by an independent and participatory scientific process, and relocation of the residents, if necessary, through mutually acceptable terms.

The JPC also recognized multiple land use for shifting cultivators and removed the land ceiling of 2.5 hectares for land rights. Besides, considering the heavy dependence of tribals and other forest dwellers on NWFPs, and the associated exploitation of these hapless people by intermediaries, it urged for ensuring a minimum support price for minor forest produce. Furthermore, the JPC made the *Gram Sabha* the final authority in the process of rights settlement. In matters relating to forest land diversion for nonforest use, consent of the *Gram Sabha* was made mandatory. Representation of the *panchyatiraj* institutions at all levels was also strongly recommended, the *Gram Sabha* being a core unit, in all matters relating to selection and identification in the rights settlement process. In recommending changes to the Bill, the JPC made PESA a reference point by bringing the *Gram Sabha* centre stage.

Like most other progressive legislations, the JPC recommendations were hailed by everyone in the field as one of the most revolutionary contributions to the tribal lawmaking process in India, with the exception of the forest bureaucracy and the conservationists who regarded it as the "death knell" for forests in the country. But the Government probably had different motives and ideas. After these recommendations were introduced in the legislature and came out as law, the offspring had very little resemblance to its parentage. It raised serious doubts about its ability to undo the injustices it was supposed to address in the first place. The Bill which was hurriedly passed in December 2006 completely obliterated the preeminent position that was given to the *Gram Sabha.* PESA, which formed the very basis of the JPC recommendations, was ignored and quietly forgotten. The result was predominance of the limiting provisions over the enabling ones. The unhindered power and strength of the forest bureaucracy, conservationists, and the mining and industrial lobby were to a large extent reinstated and reinforced.

Unfortunately the pre-eminence given to the *Gram Sabha* in matters of forest governance by the JPC has been substantially reduced. It is now neither the final authority in settlement of rights nor is its consent mandatory in diversion of forest land for nonforest purposes. The authority has been transferred to the subdivisional committee. Representation of forest-dwelling tribes in the subdivisional-level committee has been excluded from the Bill providing opportunity to the departmental officers to exercise their authority on the decisions. The *Gram Sabha* has no role when it comes to either demarcation of a protected area or in deciding the critical wildlife habitat. The Government reserves the right to decide the area, whether there would be eviction or not, and the *Gram Sabha* would only give its informed consent on the resettlement package. The *Gram Sabha* does not have the right to disagree. Besides, the role of the *Gram Sabha* for determining the rights has been limited only to initiating this process.

Even after several months of the Act coming into force, there is a misconception amongst many that the Government will give/distribute 4 hectares of forest land afresh to tribals for homestead and cultivation. This, they think, will destroy the forests as anybody can acquire 4 hectares of forest land and obtain the desired recognition. The truth, however, is that an individual claiming forest rights has to produce sufficient proof not only in terms of documents to support his/her claim but also needs an endorsement from the *Gram/Palli Sabha* about such claims. Thereafter the Forest Rights Committee will initiate the process of determination of such rights. This claim will then be verified first by the subdivisional-level committee and then the district-level committee and can either be settled or refused. The proviso about 4 hectares of forest land does not necessarily mean that all claimants will be provided with that amount of land. On the contrary, it should be interpreted to mean that no claimant will get more than 4 hectares.

With the promulgation of the Act, the age-old debate "tigers or tribals" has been revived once again. There is a fear that the Act will wipe out the remaining big cats in the country. Therefore, one of the most contentious issues influencing the realization of forest rights within a protected area has been the declaration and demarcation of the "critical wildlife habitat" (CWLH), a crucial aspect of the Forest Rights Act.

Controlling through Definition and Classification

In the last couple of decades, debates around forest rights have focused basically on two areas: definition and classification of forests and the nature and extent of departmental control over different types of forests. Although classification is indicative of designated control, there are still some areas where community control is more than visible strictly from a conservation and sustainable dependence point of view. During British India, a good number of people resided on parcels of land where ownership was unclear. As discussed earlier, the situation was even worse after Independence due to inadequate and improper survey and settlement. The Government continued declaring reserve forests without settling the rights of the people who dwelt there. There are thousands of cases of local inhabitants claiming that they were in occupation of notified forest lands prior to initiation of forest settlements under the Indian Forest Act. There are various cases of *pattas*/leases/grants said to be issued under proper authority but which have now become contentious issues between different departments, particularly the Forest and the Revenue Departments. The problem is compounded by the fact that in many cases there is no clear demarcation of forest lands. In fact most of the disputes and claims relating to use and access to forests have lingered on and evaded resolution in the past because of the failure to demarcate precisely the extent of the forest.

Frequent changes in the definition and classification of forests have not helped in determining and settling forest rights. Different laws, policies, and orders defined and classified forests differently. Read between the lines all the definitions and classifications have specific control regimes attached to them. For example, forest was first defined in the Indian Forest Act, 1865 as "land covered with trees, brushwood and jungle," because its purpose was timber extraction. In 1996 the Supreme Court, as part of the interim judgement on the Godavarman case, defined forests as an extensive area covered by trees and bushes with no agriculture.

As recently as 2007, the MoEF has proposed a definition that says forest is "an area under Government control notified or recorded as forest under any Act, for conservation and management of ecological and biological resources." If the proposed definition becomes operative, then it is expected to put private forest lands out of the purview of forest laws and may come in conflict with the 1996 verdict of the Supreme Court.

Through this definition, an effort is being made to address the limitations on afforestation on forest land and also restrictions on cutting and transport of trees mandated by the Indian Forest Act, 1927 and the Forest Conservation Act, 1980. This definition is bound to have enormous implications for the corporate actors, especially those active in the plantation sector. With private forest lands taken out of the purview of forest laws, large tracts of revenue land would now have forest species on them, timber from which can be safely harvested without attracting any forest law. It is now becoming increasingly clear why the MoEF, in the recent past, has exhibited such missionary zeal in considering proposals to place large areas of forest land in the hands of industries for afforestation.

With this definition, diversion of a parcel of land legally defined as forest can be possible. What an irony! The MoEF, which so faithfully carried out the Supreme Court order as regards not giving land to the tribals and even termed them as "encroachers" in their own homes, instead is now ready even eager to take on the same mighty institution in favour of the corporate sector. The same MoEF never bothered when the Supreme Court banned collection of minor forest produce from within protected areas. It even went a step further and amended the Wildlife Protection Act according to the Supreme Court order. One more example of what money and influence can do in this country and what the voiceless and powerless are destined to endure!

Modern Trends

In tribal areas, the communal management of land and other resources is facing a major challenge from markets and globalization. Communal systems are being rapidly transformed, with far-reaching consequences that Nathan and Kelkar have aptly described as "civilizational change."

Globalization, although seen as a threat to the survival of tribal people, could work to their advantage. It has indeed made it possible for them to organize, raise funds, and network with other groups around the world, with greater political reach and impact than before. Without networking globally, the Narmada Bachao Andolan (Save the Narmada Campaign) against dams on the Narmada River could not have become a rallying point for attack against projects that displace people not only in India but all over the world.

Addressing the concerns of indigenous peoples will require global, national, and corporate policies that advance human development goals. International institutions are already looking for ways to mitigate some of the problems, including acknowledging the right of indigenous peoples to land in their territories and respecting their traditions and cultures. For example, the World Bank in 2001 commissioned a review of extractive industries to determine how such projects can assist in poverty reduction and sustainable development. Based on extensive discussions, the review recommended public and corporate governance that works on behalf of the poor, effective social and environmental policies, and respect for human rights as key pillars of poverty reduction and development in areas where such industries are concentrated.

In today's globalizing world, the concerns of indigenous peoples can no longer be ignored or suppressed. They have become better organized and capable of demanding equality in sharing benefits from development protects in both national and international forums, and they are searching for ways to overcome obstacles to the eradication of their poverty and underdevelopment. "Indigenous peoples have dynamic living cultures and seek their place in the modern world. They are not against development, but for too long they have been victims of development and now demand to be participants in—and to benefit from a development that is sustainable".

A quick look into the current management approaches reveals some startling trends with regard to community rights over forest resources. On the one hand, the limitations of the so-called progressive legal framework are getting slowly exposed. On the other, there are equally disturbing developments like changing definition of forests, forest diversion becoming easier with the preeminent role of the mining lobby, large-scale plantation projects taken up to create carbon sinks in natural forests with no or negligible local access rights, gradual withdrawal of the State machinery from the forest-based livelihood sector, especially NWFPs, and the missionary zeal exhibited to renew the industrial–commercial approach to forest management further marginalising local users and putting a major question mark on their continued dependence on forests.

The colonial legislations had no pretensions whatsoever to protect and promote local access rights. Therefore, forest management was expected to adopt a welfare approach in independent India. But somehow, this did not occur. On the contrary, when it came to transferring rights to the local forest-dependent communities, laws, Acts, and Supreme Court orders were introduced to obstruct such transfer. Even when no such legal and judicial hurdles were there, bureaucratic apathy, inactivity, and reluctance combined to obstruct their effective implementation. Needless to say that in both the situations, the forest dwellers, mostly tribals, continued to remain at the receiving end. But the process of the marginalisation of forest dwellers does not end with Acts and policies alone; Government-sponsored programs and projects faithfully reflect the dominant world view of creating more space for the private players, implying penury for the perennially marginalised "public," i.e. the forest-dwelling tribals. In order to substantiate the current argument, it may be relevant to focus on some of these programs and approaches.

The strict conservation orientation of the plantation projects implemented to create carbon sinks in the protected forests, to a large extent, has limited local access rights. The only right that is recognized is the right over NWFPs. The approach of such projects is to remove potential threats of deforestation, and manage forest areas so as to minimize human impact. Interestingly, carbon payments would be supposedly used to develop local income sources, outside protected forests. In other words, it is an endeavour to shift the livelihood focus from forests to other non-farm sources, and conserve forests exclusively for carbon sinks so as to create carbon credits for payments that states could use in infrastructure development.

Closely observed, these developments would reveal a very interesting, although disturbing, trend. Now, with the aforementioned developments taking place, the major land mass of the country is expected to come under the purview of plantation projects. On the one hand, the State Forest Departments will use bilateral donor funding for plantation in forest lands; on the other, the private sector, armed with a new definition of forest, will go in for large-scale plantation activities with deceptive use of jargon like "public–private partnership." In the process, they will occupy and usurp a major portion of the revenue land, especially from the cultivable wasteland category. As discussed, the locals will have no access rights in the plantation forests not to mention any such rights in the private plantation areas. The states, as well as the corporate sector, are expected to earn a fortune in the process through selling of carbon credits as well as through timber trade.

If a major chunk of the revenue land of the said category is leased out to the corporate sector for taking up plantation projects, this is definitely going to have a serious repercussion on the process of land distribution to the landless under different Government schemes. Because of the huge revenue gain for the Government, revenue lands, which could have otherwise been settled in favour of the landless, will now go to the private sector. Besides, with large-scale industrialization, the Government also has to find land, especially of the nonforest category, for industries to take up Compensatory Afforestation, where locals will have no access rights. Besides, in matters of forest land being given to industries for compensatory afforestation, no rights assessment is done before such forest land is transferred. It is assumed that all rights are settled in a forest land area. There are instances in Keonjhar District in Orissa, India, where shifting cultivation areas have been given for compensatory afforestation. The forest-dependent communities are losers both ways. On the one hand, their livelihood options are closed within the protected forests; on the other, they have no entitlement over cultivable wasteland either. Such processes are expected to create a situation where the landless will remain so indefinitely.

As if all this was not enough, the hapless tribal now has to contend with the gradual closing of the NWFP option his last remaining source for some cash income. Under the misleading pretext of falling international prices and procurement of certain commonly traded NWFPs, state governments are now increasingly trying to wriggle out of their responsibility to manage, monitor, and promote collection and trade of NWFPs. Rather than acknowledge the fact that the drop in procurement and prices of NWFPs is a result of their own policies and inaction and find ways to reverse the trend, they have chosen to place primary gatherers completely at the mercy of ruthless market forces. Their decision to curtail their involvement in the NWFP sector is based purely on calculations of profit and loss and is a complete abrogation of their welfare obligations.

References

Antony, P., H. Dayal, and A.K. Karan, eds. (2003). *Poverty and Deprivation Among Scheduled Tribes in India.* Delhi: Institute for Human Development.

Bailey, F.G. (1960). *Tribe, Caste, and Nation: A Study in Political Activity and Political Change in Highland Orissa.* Manchester University Press.

Cernea, M.M. (1998). Impoverishment or Social Justice? A Model for Planning Resettlement. In Mathur, H.M., and D. Marsden, eds. *Development Projects and Impoverishment Risks: Resettling Project-Affected People in India.* Delhi: Oxford University Press.

Davis, S.H. (1993). Introduction. In Davis, S.H., ed. *Indigenous View of Land and the Environment.* Washington, DC: World Bank.

Elwin, V. (1963). *A New Deal for Tribal India.* Delhi: Government of India/ Ministry of Home Affairs.

Fabricius, C., and C. de Wet. (2002). In Chatty, D., and M. Colchester, ed. *Conservation and Mobile Indigenous Peoples: Displacement, Forced Settlement, and Sustainable Development.* New York and Oxford: Berghahn Books.

Government of India. (1976). *Report of the National Commission on Agriculture* (vol. 9: *Forests*). Delhi: Ministry of Agriculture and Irrigation.

7

Reservation Policy

In the ancient period of India, the backward castes had been denied all kinds of social and economic endowments. Hence, they had been lagging behind in the process of development. The social and economic deprivation among Scheduled Castes had been most common during pre- and post-Independence. Therefore, there was a need of number of special safeguard policies. One of that is, 'Reservation Policy' in the Government Recruitment. The objective of the reservation policy is to eradicate the social and economic disparities which existed in the society.

Article 15 (4) and 16 (4) of the Indian constitution has made provision of reservation for backward classes in educational institutions and public employment. The reservation policy has to be followed by both, Central and State government. "When the first Backward Classes Commission was constituted on 29th January, 1953 under the chairmanship of *Kakasaheb Kalelkar*, he wanted economic backwardness to be the criterion and not caste in deciding backwardness. But he had to field to the majority of the members who wanted caste to be the criterion, to decide the backwardness".

Finally, the government accepted the reservation policy. The social and economic upliftment of SCs/STs could be made through the reservation policy. Social inequality is a product of Hindu-Caste System. Hence, protective discrimination policy like 'reservation policy' must be adopted. The Government of India has been following this policy in the recruitment. The reservation policy is being followed in recruitment and also in education.

BACKGROUND FOR CAST RESERVATION

The 'Sudras' were classified as inferior and the last varna to other three varnas, in ancient social system in India. Along with this several social, economic and political restrictions were imposed on them. This classified 'Sudras' includes various caste groups, which have suffered social and economic inequity since ages. They had to stay outside the village. The concept of pollution was attached to them and they were treated as untouchable castes. These untouchables or castes were officially defined as depressed castes in 1932 and they were systematically listed in the 1931-Census of India. Gandhi named the untouchables as *'Harijans'*. *'Hari'* means 'God' and 'Jan' means 'People', i.e. 'People of God'. The meaning of this word in *Hindi, Marathi* and other languages is, ' a child, whose father's identity is unknown'. Therefore the name *'Harijan'* was opposed and hated by the untouchables.

The Simon Commission in 1935 first coined the term 'Scheduled Castes'. All the untouchable castes, which were listed in 1931-Census of India, came to be known as the 'Scheduled Castes' (SCs) through the Government of India Act of 1935. In the mean time, the Government published a list of Scheduled Castes under the Government of India (Scheduled Castes) Order, 1936. The Government of India in post-independence period carried the same idea. According to the Constitution of India, under article 341(1), the President of India, after consultation with the Governor, may specify, "the castes, races, tribes or parts of groups within castes or races, which shall be deemed to be Scheduled Castes". Accordingly the President has notified the Scheduled Castes in the order called 'Constitution (Scheduled Castes) Order-1950' and the 'Scheduled Castes and Scheduled Tribes List (Modification) Order-1956'.

However, under article 341(2), the Parliament of India by law can include or exclude the above-mentioned groups from the list of the Scheduled Castes. In a simple way, in contemporary period, the Scheduled Castes are defined under article 366 (244) of the Constitution of India as, " the Scheduled Castes means such Castes, Races, Tribes or parts of or groups within such Castes, races or tribes, deemed under article 341 to be Scheduled Castes for the purpose of this

Constitution." Thus the Scheduled Castes are those castes which are listed as Scheduled Castes in the Constitution of India.

The Scheduled Castes constitute a significant demographic strength in India. In the year 1935, the Scheduled Castes were estimated as about 5 Crores., in the year 1981, estimated as 10.475 crores and in the year 1991, population was estimated as 13.822 croes, which constitutes 16.48 per cent of the total population. The decadal growth of Scheduled Castes in India over 1991 was 30 per cent, which is more than decadal growth of general population 81 per cent of Scheduled Castes are living in rural area. Nearly 84 per cent of the SCs. population live in ten states. In the states of 'Himachal Pradesh', 'West-Bengal' and 'Uttar Pradesh', 25.34 per cent of its total, 23.62 per cent of its total and 21.04 per cent of its total population, respectively, belongs to Scheduled Castes. In 'Maharashtra', 11.10 per cent of its population is SCs, interestingly, 28 per cent of the total population of 'Punjab' belong to 'Scheduled Castes'. Other states like 'Bihar' (14.56 per cent of its total), 'Haryana' (19.75 per cent of its total), 'Karnataka' (16.38 per cent of its total), 'Madhya Pradesh' (14.54 per cent of its total), 'Orissa' (16.20 per cent of its total) 'Andhra Pradesh' (15.93 per cent of its total) and 'Tamil Nadu' (19.18 per cent of its total) have significant strength of Scheduled Castes population.

According to the 2001 Census, the Scheduled Caste population in India is 166,635,700 persons, constituting 16.2 per cent of the country's total population. Being rural people, four fifth (79.8 per cent) of them live in rural areas and rest one-fifth (20.2 per cent) live in urban areas. The sex ratio of 936 females per thousand males is slightly higher than national average of 933 sex ratio. The highest percentage of Scheduled Caste population to the total Scheduled Caste population of the country live in Uttar Pradesh (21.1 per cent) followed by West Bengal (11.1 per cent) and Bihar (7.8 per cent), Andhra Pradesh (7.4 percent) and Tamil Nadu (7.1.percent). In fact, more than 57 per cent of total Scheduled Castes population inhibit in these five States. Proportionately, the largest proportion of population of the Scheduled Castes to total population of the State is in Punjab (28.9 per cent), followed by Himachal Pradesh (24.7 per cent) and West Bengal (23 percent). In Andhra Pradesh, Karnataka and Pondicherry proportion of SC population is exactly equal to the National average of 16.2 per cent. The smallest concentration of the Scheduled Caste population is in the

North-Eastern tribal States such as Mizoram (with negligible or only 272 persons) followed by Meghalaya (0.5 per cent) and Arunachal Pradesh (0.6 per cent).

Implementation of Reservation Policy

The Central Government recruitment has been an important and largest area, where the reservation policy can be implemented effectively. But over the years, the status of reservation in this area has been weak. Immediately, after the independence, since, the educational status of Scheduled Castes (SCs) was poor, this factor must be considered. The class of the post can be classified into four, namely, 'Class I', 'Class II', 'Class III' and 'Class IV'. The Class I posts are very important, which are involved in the decision making process. Whereas, Class II posts are also equally important. But Class III and Class IV posts are classified as inferior posts. It includes, *'peons', 'sweeper'* etc. Over the years, the representation of SCs in class I posts, has been increasing at a steady rate. It was just 0.35 per cent to the total number of posts in 1953, which reached to 10.13 per cent in 1995. The prescribed quota of reservation for SCs is 15 per cent of the total posts. Yet there remains a backlog of about 4.87 per cent of the total. At national level, this figure may include hundreds of posts. It means, the SCs have been kept away from the decision making process. This could be stated as, one important reason, for huge backlog of SCs in the recruitment. Similar trend could be found in Class II posts, where the representation of SCs was 1.29 per cent in 1953, which reached 13.13 per cent in 1995. Here also backlog could be estimated at about 1.87 per cent of its total posts. Altogether, Class I and Class II backlog in the reservation has been in significant size. The growth of reservation in the recruitment has been slow.

The reservation status of SCs in class III posts in 1953 was 4.52, which increased to 15.46 per cent in 1995. The representation in the present era is satisfactory. More interestingly, In Class IV, the representation of SCs has been higher from the beginning, i.e. in the year 1953, it was 20.52 per cent and in the year 1995, it was 20.46 per cent. The reservation status in Class IV has more than the requirement. This is because, except SCs/STs and other backward castes, no one from upper castes, applies for the post like 'sweeper'. It means, in the government recruitment also, there could be found a *'Varna'* System. The caste system has been percolated in the government services. The main part of the reservation policy is that, the Class I and II backlog must be filled as soon as possible. But the problem is that, in the contemporary period, the government is adopting 'Zero Recruitment Policy'. In this situation, the SCs., may be losing its posts or the rights of reservation. This could be stated as an injustice to the SCs.

Table 1. Reservation Status of Scheduled Castes in Central Government Recruitment

Year	Class I	Class II	Class III	Class IV
1953	00.35	01.29	04.52	20.52
1965	01.64	02.82	08.88	17.73
1970	02.36	03.84	09.27	18.09
1975	03.43	04.98	10.27	18.64
1979	04.83	08.07	11.54	19.16
1992	09.70	11.60	15.80	20.70
1995	10.13	13.13	15.46	20.46

Disparities in Reservation

The reservation policy for Scheduled Castes is most important, since it is linked with their social and economic identity. Reservation is the right of the Scheduled Castes, however, there have been high rate of disparity in the implementation of reservation policy in India. The rate of disparity can be calculated after 1979-80, since before, the educational level of Scheduled Castes was not satisfactory. But in the present context, the Scheduled Castes have achieved a satisfactory level of education all over India. As per the Government of India, the reservation quota for Scheduled Castes is 15 per cent. The rate of disparity over the years has been declining. In Class I posts, the disparity was higher (67.8 per cent) in 1979, which declined to 35.3 per cent in 1992 and further declined to 31.3 per cent in 1995. However, there still exists a significant level of disparity in the implementation reservation policy. In case of Class II posts, the disparity was 46.2 per cent in 1979, which declined to 22.66 per cent in 1992 and then to 12.6 per cent in 1995. In these two categories of the posts, there exists significant level of disparity in the implementation of reservation.

These posts are important, which are part of decision-making process. Chart No. 1 explains the trend in the rate of disparity over the years in comparison to other categories of posts. In case of Class III & IV posts, the implemented reservation is more than the prescribed. This indicates negative disparity. These posts are inferior level posts, hence, except the SCs, hardly any one is ready to work. This is a result of 'Hindu Caste System'. And once, in the government sector, the caste structure has been strictly established through the occupations.

Table 2. Disparity in the Implementation of Reservation Policy in India for SCs. (All Figures in Per cent)

Year	Class I		Class II		Class III		Class IV	
	AIR	Disp.	AIR.	Disp.	AIR.	Disp.	AIR.	Disp
1979	04.83	67.8	08.07	46.2	11.54	23.06	19.76	-31.7
1992	09.70	35.3	11.60	22.66	15.80	-5.3	20.70	-38.0
1995	10.3	31.3	13.13	12.6	15.46	-3.0	20.46	-36.4

Note: (1). Rate of disparity in the reservation has been Calculated on the basis of above data. (2). A.R.=Actual Implemented Reservation, Disp. = The Rate of Disparity

Economic Consequences

The disparity in the implementation of reservation policy for SCs has resulted into serious economic consequences, which are closely connected to their life. When one person from SCs family gets a job, the whole family remains dependent on him. The dependency ratio in SCs family is higher. Therefore, the disparity has resulted into huge economic losses to the SCs, as a whole. Although the government is trying to reduce the disparity, in the phase of globalisation, large number of posts have been wiped by the government itself. Therefore, The disparity has affected adversely, the social, economic and cultural life of the Scheduled Castes. According to the report of the Working Group on the Empowering of Scheduled Castes, over 1,13,450 job opportunities were lost by the scheduled castes in the Central Government during the period 1992-97. Eradication of reservation posts on large scale could be seen in all state Government. The reasons for such step are given as 'Excess Recruitment', 'Globalisation', 'Efficiency' etc. During the last few years, several lakhs of reservation posts have been wiped out. Majority of these posts were high-class posts, which can play important role in the determination of the economic position of the society. This is social injustice; above all, this is an violation of Indian constitution. In the light of economics, the Scheduled Castes lost huge number of sources of livelihood. This policy may create once again, the economic slavery, in the economic system.

Castes, Reservation and Globlisation

The international capitalist economy is undergoing a process of fundamental transformation in the organizations of production accompanied by institutional arrangements necessary for such transformation. Neo-liberalism, the structural adjustment policy of the World Bank and the International Monetary Fund and the WTO followed by the new GATT agreement constitute the institutional framework for transnational capitalism. This transformation since last two decades is known as a process of Globalisation.Two more processes, namely, Privatisation and liberalization accompany it. In fact the phenomenon of globalization is not new to the world. Because the historical processes of wealth and poverty creation are interconnected. From ancient days trade and transport have brought the world together. Earlier there were attempts like Napoleonic wars, industrial revolution, Russian revolution etc. However their impact remained limited. The present process of globalization is qualitatively and radically different from the earlier ones. Since 1970's it has brought a radical restructuring of the world economy. Now there is a new political economy in the making and it is information driven. Capitalism and IT are the driving forces. It is holistic, multi-dimensional and therefore truly global in nature.

Globalisation is making a considerable impact on all the aspects of human life in all the countries in the world. It is imperative to understand this process and study the nature of the impact on various communities. It is making its impact even on developed countries. The impact is social, economic, political, cultural and even moral in nature. Since the globalization is truly universal in nature, it naturally involves competition and quality. No individual would escape from these. And there is no point in avoiding these. Quality and competition are the watchwords in the age of globalization. Fortunately Indian society has all the potentialities of these two. Moreover unlike the United Nations, the WTO expects the members to accept at present any one service to be thrown open to all the members in the world. Therefore, there is no alternative to competition. And without quality, competition would have no meaning. Here the other processes of liberalization and Privatisation are going to play an important role. Therefore, what is necessary?

India is a plural society having many sections based on religion, caste, class etc. These sections have different types of impact at different levels. It will be academically unfair to think about the impact of globalization unilaterally. Different sections or groups in a heterogeneous society have different problems. Even after sixty years of independence various social groups are not empowered to face the challenge of competing equality. Even now they need the positive support of the welfare State. In view of this what is necessary is to have a rational balance between empowerment of weaker sections and the achievement of quality to face the competition.

Few societies have condemned one of their sections to physical segregation as the Hindu society has done in the case of the former untouchables. The mere physical touch of an untouchable was a sin, an abomination. The segregation of a section of the Hindus as untouchables, precluded from such elementary rights as entry to public temples or the use of public wells and tanks, and whose physical touch contaminated a member of higher castes, constituted a most inhuman form of social oppression. The untouchables were the outcastes of Hindu society. Hallowed with tradition and sanctified by religion, the unsociability continued to exist in all its barbarous vigour for centuries.

After independence, in 1950, the Constitution of India abolished untouchability (Article 17) and in 1955, the Parliament passed the Untouchability Offences Act. The national movement had created an atmosphere sympathetic towards the untouchables. It made it possible for the Government to provide protective discrimination in an attempt to pull out the untouchables from traditional segregation. Among the multitude of difficult tasks facing the new nation of India in 1947, none was more challenging than the integration of the most deprived 15 percent of its population-the untouchables-into unequal partnership in the emerging modern republic. Since the Govt.of India Act 1935, the untouchables became known as the Scheduled Castes. But even though untouchability and discrimination on the basis of caste are constitutionally outlawed, despite the constitutional legal support and also efforts by various voluntary agencies, it is commonly observed that they continue to be deprived of their rightful place in society. And upper castes have generally denied equal treatment to the Schedules Castes.

The backwardness of the Scheduled castes will be evident from their unemployment, dependence on agriculture, illiteracy and social segregation. In terms of residence, housing and health conditions, the condition of the Scheduled Castes is precarious. Even now in many villages they have to suffer residential segregation and direct and indirect social boycott. There are many among them who are too poor to build their houses. On account of their poverty and unhygienic living conditions, they, in large numbers, suffer from malnutrition, physical disabilities and diseases such as tuberculosis, leprosy, malaria, and general diseases.

This is not to say that post-independence period has not brought any socioeconomic and political change in the life of the Scheduled Castes. Constitutional provisions, political process since independence and the impact of leadership of Dr. B.R. Ambedkar have created a wave of rising expectations in the life of Scheduled Castes in general and in the life of the neo-Buddhists in particular. Gradually, since then, the Scheduled Castes are slowly becoming aware of their rightful place in society and are asserting for the reordering of society for their betterment and advancement. This has created a number of pressures and pulls resulting in sociopolitical tensions in Indian society. Renaming Marathwada University agitation after Dr. Ambedkar was one such occasion.

Present Scenario

There are a good number of studies on the neo-Buddhists, the dominant Scheduled Caste in Maharashtra. However there are very few studies on other Scheduled Castes like *Mang, Chamar, Dhor, Mochi Bhangi* etc. Moreover most of the studies are based on single or two variables like caste or/and class. It is to be remembered that in a complex society like India. Single factor analysis gives one-sided picture, which is far away from reality. It is therefore necessary to study the nature and impact of Scheduled Castes movement, impact of government policies, also the impact of the efforts of the voluntary agencies and most importantly the impact of the political process during last sixty years. Owing to the democratic process since independence, increasing means of communication and the spread of education, there is increasing awareness among all the sections of society and the Scheduled Castes are not exceptions to it.

The Constitution has released the forces of liberalism. Because of these forces, an era of politicisation has started in all walks of life and traditional gap between politics and society has come to an end. Now politics has become a new instrument for achieving socioeconomic development. Socioeconomic development of the Scheduled Castes would be the precondition for their integration in the mainstream of society, which the constitution has visualized. Much has been done by way of constitutional provisions, administrative efforts and proper response from a larger section of the upper castes. However, whatever is done is not enough to match the rising expectations of the weaker sections including then Scheduled Castes. Still they are unorganized and constitute the larger chunk of the population. On the other hand, the organized sections even in Scheduled Castes have grabbed the benefits of socioeconomic development.

Need of Political Education

We have accepted a democratic form of government in an undemocratic society. It is, therefore, necessary to give political education to the people about the need and genesis of welfare policies for the weaker sections. Political education means education about nature, working and the functions of a political system in which you live. This was the duty of the elites and the leaders in the political process. Unfortunately both have miserably failed in their tasks. As a result of it, there is a lack of understanding about the problems of weaker sections which results in social tensions...

Lack of Political Will

There is a lack of political will regarding the development of

Scheduled Castes. There is increasing populism to fetch the votes of Schedules Castes and very few sincere efforts for their development. Many a times the political process has divided the Scheduled Castes. It is observed that the welfare schemes remain on paper but because of the policies there is a backlash among the upper castes.

Challenge of Globalisation

Infact it is a high time that the leaders in the political process and academicians give a serious thought to the consequences of Liberalisation, Privatisation and particularly Globalisation.

On the lines of the Scheduled Castes. In globalization the old concepts like nationalism, sovereignty are gradually waning and the there is an erosion of a nation-state. Samuel Huntington argues that now the culture would be an important variable in international politics and not the concepts like nationalism or sovereignty. There is increasing international interdependence on the one hand giving rise to internationalism. On the other hand, the narrow and parochial loyalties are playing significant role.

Globalization needs quality and the quality assumes acquiring various skills necessary for individual and social development. Because of changing nature of economy and social conditions now there are new needs, which have arisen in society, now new sections have come up in society and they have non-traditional needs. They include the needs of senior citizens, the employed married couples in metropolitan cities, and the demand for creche is on increase. Multiplexes, food malls, shopping malls, etc. have changes the life style of the middle class. In this way new needs can be found out and an attempt can be made to give response to these demands by way of providing service to them. The 21st century is a century of multi- skills and a person having more than one skill will have definitely a bright future.

Dr. Ambedkar gave a message—"educates, agitates and organizes." But what kind of education? Present education is fast becoming irrelevant to the changing needs. It is to be understood that the present education system is the product of the colonial rule and the post-independence period governments have done very little to change the same. In addition to increasing educational opportunities, our demand should be to make the education system more meaningful and more relevant to the changing needs in society. It may be remembered in a way, that present unemployment is mostly false one. It is unemployment of the unskilled people. Therefore an attempt is to be made to improve the quality of the people. It can be achieved by way of acquiring knowledge, skills and attitudes in the changing context.

Neo-Buddhists can be a good model for other Scheduled Castes for their development. During last sixty years the neo-Buddhists have done a remarkable progress. In all walks of life. It was found in 1971 census that their literacy has become equal to that of the Brahmins and all other castes and Scheduled Castes lag behind them. The neo-Buddhists have modernized themselves, removed superstitions among themselves and entered into various professions and occupations. They speak on behalf of all weaker sections. They assert for removal of injustice, equal opportunity, organize them and have a clear perception of development. Now there are many more doctors, engineers, pleaders, professors, technicians, artists in films and on the stage, administrative officers. They have surpassed the dominant Maratha caste in many respects. They have ably utilized the policy of reservation in particular and policy of protective discrimination in general. They have made use of the Constitution and the political process in an efficient manner. There would be surprise if any other community has made such a remarkable development in such short period in the history of the world. Progress made by the neo-Buddhists is more because of the strong will for development created by their leader Dr. Ambedkar. The spirit among the neo-Buddhists consists of removal of inferiority complex, willingness for hard work, sense of responsibility etc. This spirit is lacking in other Scheduled Castes. They may not follow the neo-Buddhists in totality. But the inspiration from them would be very useful for their development. The other Scheduled Castes should follow this model.

The policy of reservation should be viewed as a part of the total policy for the development. Efforts should be made to observe that it is being implemented sincerely and honestly. However it would be well to remind us that the reservation would not be enough for the development. Manysided development, as described above, would be required.

An effort should be made to seek the help from the liberal Hindus. Contrary to general belief, there is a strong element of liberalism among the Hindus. Dr. Ambedkar made its use wisely in the fight against untouchability. There should be fight against the conservative elements and not all the Hindus. It should not be treated as a cold war between Scheduled Castes and the Hindus.

In post-independence period, every caste is now roughly divided in to three classes. The elites, middle class and the masses. They have different attitudes. What are necessary are the efforts for the development of the masses in Scheduled Castes. They badly need it. Globalisation has posed a challenge to all and more to the Scheduled Castes. Unless such efforts are done the values in the constitution would not be materialized.

References

Desai, A.R. (1996), *Social Background of Indian Nationalism*, Popular Prakashan, Bombay.

Gail Omvedt. (2006), *Dalit Visions: The Anti-caste Movement and the Construction of an Indian Identity*, Orient Longman.

Johnson, Glen, and Sipra Bose, *Social Mobility Among Untouchables*, in Gupta.

Sachchidanand, (1977), *The Harijan Elite, Thompson Press, Faridabad,* p. 162.

Kakade, S.R. (1990), *Scheduled Castes and National Integration*, Radiant publishers, New Delhi.

8

Welfare Schemes for Dalits and Tribals

The Ministry of Social Justice and Empowerment is committed towards educational development, economic empowerment and social empowerment of persons belonging to Scheduled Castes, Other Backward Classes, rehabilitation of persons with disabilities, victims of drug abuse, aged etc.

WELFARE PROGRAMMES FOR SCHEDULED CASTES

National Commission for Scheduled Castes

The National Commission for Scheduled Castes, a Constitutional body monitors the safeguards provided for Scheduled Castes and also reviews issues concerning their welfare. The Commission has wide powers to protect, safeguard and promote the interests of the SCs. The Commission has been conferred powers of a civil court trying a suit, to summon and enforce the attendance of any persons from any part of India and examining on oath, receiving evidence on affidavits. The Commissioner submitted its first report on 17-7-2006.

National Commission for Safai Karmacharis

The National Commission for Safai Karmacharis, a statutory body has, inter-alia, been empowered to investigate into specific grievances as well as matters relating to implementation of programmes and schemes for welfare of Safai Karmacharis.

Protection of Civil Rights Act, 1955 and Scheduled Castes and Scheduled Tribes (Prevention of Atrocities) ACT, 1989

Protection of Civil Rights Act, 1955 provides for preventing any person on grounds of untouchability, from enjoying the rights accruing on account of abolition of untouchability. Provisions for legal aid to Scheduled Castes in cases relating to untouchability have been made by 22 States/Union Territories. Special Cells have been set up in 21 States for initiating and exercising supervision over prosecution for contravention of provisions of the PCR Act. 22 special Mobile Courts have been set up in Andhra Pradesh for expeditious disposal of such cases. Necessary guidelines and instructions are issued to States from time to time for effective implementation of the provisions of the PCR Act.

The Scheduled Castes and Scheduled Tribes (Prevention of Atrocities) Act, 1989, specifies offences, which are considered as atrocities, and provides for deterrent punishments for commission of the same. Comprehensive Rules were also framed under the SCs and STs (POA) Act in 1995, which among other things provided for relief and rehabilitation of the affected people. It also envisages preventive measures, and State have to evolve schemes, among and Union Territories except Arunachal Pradesh and Nagaland have specified special courts for trial of offences under this Act. 137 Exclusive Special courts have also been set up in Andhra Pradesh, Bihar, Chhattisgarh, Gujarat, Karnataka, Madhya Pradesh, Rajasthan, Tamilnadu and Uttar Pradesh, 11 States (Andhra Pradesh, Bihar, Gujarat, Jharkhand, Karnataka, Kerala, Madhya Pradesh, Maharashtra, Orissa, Tamilnadu and Uttar Pradesh) have been identified atrocity prone areas.

Under the Centrally sponsored scheme for implementation of both the Act, State Governments are funded on 50:50 basis and Union Territories are given cent percent central assistance. During the year 2006-07 Rs. 36.44 crore were released to States/UTs.

A Committee under the Chairpersonship of the Hon'ble Minister of Social Justice & Empowerment has been constituted for effective coordination to devise ways and means to curb offences of untouchability and atrocities against SCs and STs and their effective administration/implementation. The first meeting of the Committee was held on 18.09.2006 at New Delhi and the second meeting was also held on 15.01.2007 at Jaipur. The Inter-State Council Meeting was held on 9th December 2006 exclusively on the subject 'Offences of untouchability against Scheduled Castes and Scheduled Tribes'. This meeting was chaired by the Hon'ble Prime Minister and attended by the Chief Ministers and other senior officials. As a follow up the Hon'ble Minister (SJ&E) had addressed a d.o. letter dated 24.4.2007 to all chief Ministers of States to ensure that the year 2007-08 turns out to be an untouchability and atrocity free year.

The Ministry of Social Justice & Empowerment has launched National Awards to be given to Non-Governmental Organizations (NGOs) or individual Human Rights Activists who have done outstanding fieldwork in the area of eradicating untouchability and in combating offences of atrocities under the Protection of Civil Rights Act, 1955 and the Scheduled Castes and the Scheduled Tribes (Prevention of Atrocities) Act, 1989. There will be four awards every year. Award to individual activist shall carry an amount of Rs. 2.00 lakhs and Rs. 5.00 lakhs to an Institution. The Award will be given to outstanding NGOs or Human Rights Activists in each of the four regions of the country namely North, South, East and West for rendering yeomen services in the said fields. The award may be shared by more than one recipient or organization. The Award was instituted in 2006 and is given annually. The date of receipt of the nominations for the award is 31st October of the respective year.

Educational Development

Pre-Matric Scholarships for Children of those engaged in Unclean Occupation: Under the Scheme, the Children of families engaged in unclean occupations such as scavenging, flaying and tanning are assisted to pursue education upto matriculation level. The scholarship is provided through State Governments and Union Territory Administrations. Central assistance is provided to the State Governments on 50:50 basis and to the Union Territory Administration on 100 per cent basis over and above their committed liability. Students amongst target groups with disabilities are also assisted. There is no income ceiling prescribed under the scheme.

The scheme provides scholarship of Rs. 40 per month in classes I to V, Rs. 60 per month in classes VI to VIII and Rs. 75 per month in classes IX to X in respect of day scholar; for hostellers Rs. 300 per month in classes III to VIII and Rs. 375 per month in classes IX to X.

The duration of scholarship in an academic year is ten months. The Day Scholars and hostellers are eligible for ad-hoc grant of Rs. 550 and Rs. 600 per students gap annum respectively. During 2006-07 Rs. 20.25 crores has been released to States/UTs for covering about 6.54 lakh students.

Post-Metric Scholarships for SC Students: Under the scheme, financial assistance is provided to Scheduled Caste students for pursuing studies beyond matriculation in recognised institutions. The assistance include maintenance allowance for various categories of courses, reimbursement of compulsory non-refundable fee charged by the institutions and other allowance such as study tour charges, thesis typing/printing charges and book grant, revisions of income ceiling to Rs. one lakh per annum for eligibility Scholarship is disbursed through respective State Governments and UT Administrations.

The scheme provides for 100 per Central assistance to the State. Governments and UT Administrations over and above the perspective committed liability of the States/UTs. The committed liability of the North Eastern States has, however, been dispensed with. During the year 2006-07 an amount of Rs. 526 crores has been released to the States/UTs for covering over estimated 29.58 lakh students.

Rajiv Gandhi National Fellowship Scheme: A new Scheme named Rajiv Gandhi National Fellowship (RGNF) for Scheduled Caste Students has been introduced during the current financial year 2005-06. Fellowships, in the form of financial assistance, are to be provided to students belonging to Scheduled Castes to pursue higher studies leading to award of M.Phil and Ph.D. degree. A student, belonging to Scheduled Caste registered in a regular and full time M.Phil/Ph. D course in a University/Academic institution will be eligible for the fellowship. The fellowships will be on the same scale as that of the University Grants Commission (UGC) Junior Research Fellowships. In total, 1333 fellowships each year are to be awarded initially during 2005-06 and 2006-07. The scheme is being implemented through the University Grants Commission. An amount of Rs. 34.18 crores was released to UGC during 2006-07 under the scheme.

National Overseas Scholarship and Passage Grants for Higher Education: Under this scheme assistance is provided to meritorious students for pursuing higher studies of Masters level courses, Ph.D and Post Doctoral research Programmes abroad in specified fields like Engineering, Technology and Science only. Rate of maintenance allowance was enhanced to US$ 8,200 or Pounds Sterling 5,200 per annum per candidate. The contingency allowance for books, essential apparatus, study tour charges, typing and binding of thesis, etc. was also revised to US $ 550 or Pound Sterling 400 per annum for candidates in U.K. the scheme provides for air passage, visa fee, equipment allowance, incidental expenses charged by the institution as per actual and insurance premia, etc. The awardees were permitted to undertake research/teaching assistantship. Financial assistance under the scheme is provided for a maximum period of four years for Ph.D. research, for 3 years for Master's Programme. Students whose family income exceeds Rs. 18,000 per month are not eligible for assistance and only one child of the same parents/ guardians is eligible to get benefit under the scheme. The prospective awardees should not be more than 35 years of age. During 2006-07, Rs. 1.05 crores was disbursed to 20 students that include 17 SCs, two students from de-notified nomadic and semi-nomadic tribe and one student from landless agricultural labourers and traditional artisans.

Upgradation of Merit for SC Students: The main objective of the scheme is to upgrade the merit of Scheduled Caste students by providing them with facilities for all-round development through education in residential schools. The scheme provides for 100 per cent Central assistance to States/UTs for arrangement of remedial and special coaching for SC students studying in class IX to XII. Financial assistance is provided to students as package grant of Rs. 15,000 per year per student, out of which Rs. 5,000 is for boarding and lodging, Rs. 1,000 for pocket expenses, Rs. 2,000 for books and stationery and Rs. 7,000 as an honorarium to Principals/experts involved in providing the remedial/special coaching. SC students with disability enjoy additional benefits. During the year 2006-07 Rs. 3.00 crores were released to the States/UTs.

Coaching and Allied Scheme for Weaker Sections including SCs, OBCs and Minorities: The scheme aimed to equip aspiring students for preparing them for various competitive exams. Aspiring students take their guidance and coaching from the centres run by State Governments/UTs, Universities and NGOs. These centres are extended Central assistance to provide coaching to students. During 2006-07, Rs. 3.91 crores was released to the implementing agencies in pre-revised schemes.

Hostels for Scheduled Caste Boys and Girls: The objective of the Scheme is to provide hostel facilities to SC Boys and Girls studying in middle schools, higher secondary schools, colleges and Universities. The financial assistance is provided for construction of hostels. The maintenance of hostel, boarding and lodging of students, however, rest with the respective States/UTs. The Scheme provides for release of Central Assistance to State Govts. on 50:50 matching share basis and 100% to UTs and also 90% to Central Universities. Other Universities can also get Central Assistance upto 45% and the remaining amount has to be provided by their respective States (45%) and themselves 10%. The NGOs also get assistance on the basis of 45:45:10 through their States/UTs for extension of their existing hostels. During the year 2006-07 Rs. 25.23 crores was released for construction of 109 boys hostel and Rs. 28.811 crore for construction of 204 girls hostels.

Dr. Ambedkar Foundation

The main objective of the Foundation is to propagate the ideology and message of Baba Saheb Dr. B.R. Ambedkar among the masses in India as well as abroad. The following were achievements under different schemes during the year. A sum of Rs. 6.25 lakhs was released for benefiting 25 persons under Dr. Ambedkar Medical Scheme. A sum of Rs. 58.39 lakhs were released for maintenance of Dr. Ambedkar Chairs in Universities/Institutions for research for the year 2006-07. The Foundation also published collected works in Tamil and Urdu under Samajik Samta Kendra Yojana.

Economic Development

Special Central Assistance to Scheduled Castes Sub Plan (SCSP):

Under Special Central Assistance (SCA) to Scheduled Castes Sub Plan (SCSP) (earlier known as SCP), cent percent assistance is provided to State and Union territories as an additive to their Special Component Plans. The assistance would be used to give an added thrust to the development programmes for SC persons living below poverty line. During the year 2006-07 Rs. 459.15 crores was released to States/UTs.

National Scheduled Castes Finance and Development Corporation: The National Scheduled Castes Finance and Development Corporation (NSFDC) provides concessional finance for employment generation to the persons belonging to the Scheduled Castes living below double the poverty line (i.e. Rs. 40,000 p.a. in rural areas and Rs. 55,000 p.a. in urban areas), skill development through training, entrepreneurial development and innovative projects. The Corporation is also implementing 'Mahila Samridhi Yojana' The Corporation has assisted 53,315 beneficiaries during the year 2005-06.

National Safai Karamcharis Finance and Development Corporation: National Safai Karamcharis Finance and Development Corporation (NSKFDC) extends concessional finance assistance to the Safai Karamcharies beneficiaries for establishments 'Mahila Samridhi Yojana'. The Corporation has assisted 77,970 beneficiaries during 2006-07.

State Scheduled Castes Development Corporation: State Scheduled Castes Development Corporation (SCDCs) are functioning in 26 States/Union Territories. The Central Government contributes 49 per cent to the authorised share capital of the SCDC's against the 51 per cent contributed by the State Government. During the year 2005-06 Rs. 16,902 lakhs was released as Government of India's contribution to benefit anticipated 77,970 beneficiaries.

Scheme for Rehabilitation of Manual Scavengers: A new Self Employment Scheme for Rehabilitation, of Manual Scavengers (SRMS) was launched from January 2007 for rehabilitation of scavengers and their dependents by March, 2009 with total expenditure of Rs. 735.60 crores. The Central Govt. has released Rs. 56.00 crores during 2006-07 to NSKFDC as Grant in aid for implementation of the scheme.

Voluntary Organisations Working for Scheduled Castes: The objective of the scheme is to utilise the services of capable and reliable voluntary organisations in the process of social-economic development of scheduled casts. Under this scheme, grant-in-aid is given to the voluntary organisations to the extent of 90 per cent of each project cost for activities such as general/technical/vocational education including preschool education, medical centres, dispensaries and income generating activities.

Welfare Programmes for Scheduled Tribes

The tribal people of India, who come under the category of *'Scheduled Tribes' (STs)* in terms of the provisions of the Constitution of India, number 8.43 crore—constituting 8.2 per cent of the population of the country.

Scheduled Areas and Tribal Areas

Scheduled Tribes live in contiguous areas unlike other communities. It is, therefore, much simpler to have an area-approach for development activities and also regulatory provisions to protect their interests. In order to protect the interests of Scheduled Tribes with regard to land alienation and other social factors, provisions of "Fifth Schedule" and "Sixth Schedule" have been enshrined in the Constitution.

The Fifth Schedule under Article 244(1) of Constitution defines *"Scheduled Areas"* as such areas as the President may by Order declare to be Scheduled Areas after consultation with the Governor of the State.

The Sixth Schedule under Article 244 (2) of the Constitution relates to those areas in the States of Assam, Mehalaya, Tripura and Mizoram which are declared as *"Tribal Areas"* and provides for District Councils and/or Regional Councils for such Areas. These Councils have been conferred with wide ranging legislative, judicial and executive powers.

The Fifth Schedule Areas

The criteria for declaring any area as a *"Scheduled Area"* under the Fifth Schedule are :

— Preponderance of tribal population,
— Compactness and reasonable size of the area,
— A viable administrative entity such as a district, block or taluk, and
— Economic backwardness of the area as compared to neighbouring areas.

The specification of "Scheduled Areas" in relation to a State is by a notified Order of the President, after consultation with the State Governments concerned. The same applies for altering, increasing, decreasing, incorporating new areas, or rescinding any Orders relating to "Scheduled Areas".

The advantages of *Scheduled Areas* are that:

— The Governor of a state, which has Scheduled Areas, is empowered to make regulations in respect of the following:
  — Prohibit or restrict transfer of land from tribal people;
  — Regulate the business of money lending to the members of Scheduled Tribes. In making any such regulation, the Governor may repeal or amend any Act of Parliament or of the Legislature of the State, which is applicable to the area in question.
— The Governor may be public notification direct that any particular Act of Parliament or of the Legislature of the State, shall not apply to a Scheduled Area or any part thereof in the State or shall apply to such area subject to such exceptions and modifications as he may specify.
— The Governor of a State having Scheduled Areas therein, shall annually, or whenever so required by the President of India, make a report to the President regarding the administration of the Scheduled Areas in that State and the executive power of the Union shall extend to the giving of directions to the State as to the administration of the said area.
— Tribes Advisory Council (TAC) shall be established in States having Scheduled Areas. The role of TAC is to advise the State Government on matters pertaining to the welfare and advancement of the Scheduled Tribes in the State as may be referred to it by the Governor. The TAC will consist of not more

than twenty members of whom about 3/4 are from ST-MLAs. (The TAC may also be established in any State having Scheduled Tribes but not Scheduled Areas on the direction of the President of India.

— The *Provisions of the Panchayats (Extension to Scheduled Areas) Act, 1996 (PESA),* vide which the provisions of Panchayats, contained in Part IX of the Constitution, were extended to Scheduled Areas, also contain special provisions for the benefit of Scheduled Tribes.

The Sixth Schedule-Tribal Areas

The Sixth Schedule under Article 244 of the Constitution identifies Autonomous districts in the Tribal Areas in the states of Assam, Meghalaya, Tripura and Mizoram. It also makes provisions for recognition of Autonomous Regions within these Autonomous Districts. These have been specified in Parts I, II, IIA & III of the table appended to paragraph 20 of the Sixth Schedule. In other words, areas where provisions of Sixth Schedule are applicable are known as Tribal Areas. The State-wise details of Tribal Areas are as under:

Part-I	Assam	1. The North Cachar Hills District
		2. The Karbi-Anglong District
		3. The Bodo Land Territorial Area Districts
Part II	Meghalaya	1. Khasi Hills District
		2. Jaintia Hills District
		3. The Garo Hills District
Part IIA	Tripura	Tripura Tribal Areas District
Part III	Mizoram	1. The Chakma District
		2. The Mara District
		3. The Lai District

The administration of Autonomous Districts and Autonomous Regions is done through District Councils/Regional Councils. These Councils are elected bodies and have powers of legislation, administration of justice apart from executive, developmental and financial responsibilities. The District or Regional Councils are empowered to make rules with the approval of the Governor with regard to matters like establishment, construction or management of primary schools, dispensaries, markets, cattle ponds, ferries, fisheries, roads, road transport and waterways in the district.

The Autonomous Councils of the North Cachar Hills and Karbi Anglong have been granted additional powers to make laws with respect to other matters like secondary education, agriculture, social security and social insurance, public health and sanitation, minor irrigation, etc.

The Councils have also been conferred powers under the Civil Procedure Code and Criminal Procedure Code for trial of certain suits and offences, as also the powers of a revenue authority for their area for collection of revenue and taxes and other powers for the regulation and management of natural resources.

Procedure for Declaration as ST

The term *''Scheduled Tribes''* is defined in the Constitution of India under Article 366(25) as *''such tribes or tribal communities or parts of groups within such tribes or tribal communities as are deemed under Article 342 to be Scheduled Tribes for the purposes of this Constitution''*. Article 342 prescribes the procedure to be followed in the matter of specification of Scheduled Tribes.

In terms of Article 342(1), the President may, with respect to any State or Union Territory, and where it is State, after consultation with the Governor thereof, notify tribes or tribal communities or parts thereof as Scheduled Tribes. This confers on the tribe or part of it a Constitutional status invoking the safeguards provided for in the Constitution, to these communities in their respective States/UTs.

Thus, in terms of Article 342(1), only those communities who have been declared as such by the President through an initial public notification will be considered as Scheduled Tribes. Any further amendment in the list is to be done through an Act of Parliament (Article 342(2)). Parliament may, by law, include in or exclude from the list of Scheduled Tribes, any tribe or tribal community or parts of thereof.

The list of Scheduled Tribes is State-specific. In other words, a community declared as Scheduled Tribe in one State need not be so in another State.

Scheduling and De-Scheduling of Tribes

Thus, the first specification of Scheduled Tribes in relation to a particular State/ Union Territory is by a notified order of the President, after consultation with the State Governments concerned.

The criteria generally adopted for specification of a community as a Scheduled Tribe are:

— indications of primitive traits;

— distinctive culture;

— shyness of contact with the community at large;

— geographical isolation i.e. backwardness.

These are not spelt out in the Constitution but have become well established. They take into account the definitions in the 1931 Census, the reports of the first Backward Classes Commission 1955, the Advisory Committee on Revision of SC/ ST lists (Lokur Committee) 1965 and the Joint Committee of Parliament on the Scheduled Castes and Scheduled Tribes Orders (Amendment) Bill, 1967 (Chanda Committee) 1969.

There are over 700 tribes (with many of them overlapping in more than one State) as notified under Article 342 of the Constitution of India, spread over different States and Union Territories of the country. It is worth noting that no community has been specified as a Scheduled tribe in relation to the States of Haryana and Punjab and the Union Territories of Chandigarh, Delhi and Puducherry.

Ascertaining ST Status of Individuals

General

Where a person claims to belong to a Scheduled tribe by birth, it should be verified:

— that the person and his parents actually belong to the community claimed;

— that the community is included in the Presidential Order specifying the Scheduled Tribes in relation to the concerned State;

— that the person belongs to that State and the area within that State in respect of which the community has been scheduled;

— he may profess any religion;

— that he or his parents/grandparents, etc., should be permanent resident of the State/UT on the date of notification of the Presidential Order applicable in his case;

— a person who is temporarily away from his permanent place of residence at the time of the notification of the Presidential Order applicable in his case, say for example to earn a living or seek education, etc. can also be regarded as a Scheduled Tribe, if his tribe has been specified in that order in relation to his home State/ Union Territory;

— but he cannot be treated as such in relation to the place of his temporary residence notwithstanding the fact that the name of his tribe has been scheduled in respect of that State where he is temporarily settled, in any Presidential Order;

— in the case of persons born after the date of notification of the relevant Presidential Order, the place of residence for the purpose of acquiring Scheduled Tribe status, is the place of permanent abode of their parents at the time of the notification of the Presidential Order under which they claim to belong to such a tribe.

This does not apply to the STs of the Lakhadweep Islands for whom there is a requirement of being born in the U.T. in order to be eligible for ST status.

Scheduled Tribe Claims on Migration

— Where a person migrates from the portion of the State in which his/her community is scheduled, to another part of the same State in respect of which his/her community is not scheduled, the person will continue to be deemed to be a member of the Scheduled Tribe, in relation to that State

— Where a person migrates from one State to another, he can claim to belong to a Scheduled Tribe only in relation to the State to which he originally belonged and not in respect of the State to which he has migrated.

Scheduled Tribe Claims through Marriages

The guiding principle is that no person who is not a Scheduled Tribe by birth will be deemed to be a member of Scheduled Tribe merely because he or she has married a person belonging to a Scheduled Tribe. Similarly a person who is a member of a Scheduled Tribe will continue to be a member of that Scheduled Tribe, even after his or her marriage with a person who does not belong to a Scheduled Tribe.

Issue of Scheduled Tribe Certificates

The candidates belonging to Scheduled Tribes may get Scheduled Tribe certificates, in the prescribed form, from any one of the following authorities:

- District Magistrate/Additional District Magistrate/Collector/ Deputy Commissioner/ Additional Deputy Commissioner/ Deputy Collector/1st Class Stipendiary Magistrate/City Magistrate/Sub Divisional Magistrate/Taluka Magistrate/ Executive Magistrate/Extra Assistant Commissioner *[not below the rank of 1st Class Stipendiary Magistrate]*.
- Chief Presidency Magistrate/Additional Chief Presidency Magistrate/ Presidency Magistrate.
- Revenue Officers not below the rank of Tehsildar.
- Sub-Divisional Officer of the Area where the candidate and/or his family normally resides.
- Administrator/Secretary to the Administrator/Development Officer [Lakshadweep Islands].

Punishments for officials issuing Scheduled Tribe Certificates without proper Verification

Action is to be taken under the relevant provisions of the Indian Penal Code if any official is found to have issued a Scheduled tribe certificate carelessly and without proper verification. This will be in addition to other action to which they are liable under the appropriate disciplinary rules applicable to them.

Liberalization of procedure for issue of Scheduled Tribe certificates to Migrants from other States/Union Territories.

Persons belonging to a Scheduled Tribe who have migrated from one State to another for the purpose of employment, education etc. experience great difficulty in obtaining ST certificates from the State from which they have migrated. In order to remove this difficulty, it has been decided that the prescribed authority of a State Government/ Union Territory Administration may issue a Scheduled Tribe certificate to a person who migrated from another state, on the production of the genuine certificate issued to his father/mother by the prescribed authority of the State of the father/mother's origin except where the prescribed authority feels that a detailed enquiry is necessary through the state of origin before issue of the certificate.

Procedure for Inclusion in or Exclusion from the list of STs

In June 1999, the Government approved modalities for deciding claims for inclusion in, or exclusion from, the lists of Scheduled Tribes. According to these approved guidelines, only those claims that have been agreed to by the concerned State Government, the Registrar General of India and the National Commission for Scheduled Castes and Scheduled Tribes will be taken up for consideration.

Whenever representations are received in the Ministry for inclusion of any community in the list of Scheduled Tribes of a State/ UT, the Ministry forwards that representation to the concerned State Government/UT Administration for recommendation as required under Article 342 of the Constitution. If the concerned State Government recommends the proposal, then the same is sent to the Registrar General of India (RGI).

If RGI is satisfied with recommendation of the State Government and recommends the proposal to the Central Government, the Government refers the proposal to the National Commission for Scheduled Tribes for their recommendation. If the National Commission for Scheduled Tribes also recommends the case, the matter is processed for the decision of the cabinet after consulting the concerned administrative Ministries. Thereafter the matter is put up before the Parliament in the form of a Bill to amend the Presidential Order.

Demographic Features of Scheduled Tribes

According to the 2001 Census, the population of Scheduled tribes in the country was 8.43 crore—i.e., constituting 8.2 per cent of the total population of the country.

Table 1. Demography of Scheduled Tribes

S. No.	India/State	Total population	ST Population	% of STs to total population in the State
1.	Mizoram	888,573	839,310	94.5
2.	Lakshadweep	60,650	57,321	94.5
3.	Nagaland	1,990,036	1,774,026	89.1
4.	Meghalaya	2,318,822	1,992,862	85.9
5.	Arunachal Pradesh	1,097,968	705,158	64.2
6.	Dadra and Nagar Haveli	220,490	137,225	62.2
7.	Manipur	2,166,788	741,141	34.2
8.	Chhattisgarh	20,833,803	6,616,596	31.8
9.	Tripura	3,199,203	993,426	31.1
10.	Jharkhand	26,945,829	7,087,068	26.3
11.	Orissa	36,804,660	8,145,081	22.1
12.	Sikkim	540,851	111,405	20.6
13.	Madhya Pradesh	60,348,023	12,233,474	20.3
14.	Gujarat	50,671,017	7,481,160	14.8
15.	Rajasthan	56,507,188	7,097,706	12.6
16.	Assam	26,655,528	3,308,570	12.4
17.	J&K	10,143,700	1,105,979	10.9
18.	Maharashtra	96,878,627	8,577,276	8.9
19.	Daman and Diu	158,204	13,997	8.8
20.	Andaman and Nicobar	356,152	29,469	8.3
21.	Andhra Pradesh	76,210,007	5,024,104	6.6
22.	Karnataka	52,850,562	3,463,986	6.6
23.	West Bengal	80,176,197	4,406,794	5.5
24.	Himachal Pradesh	6,077,900	244,587	4.0
25.	Uttarakhand	8,489,349	256,129	3.0
26.	Kerala	31,841,374	364,189	1.1
27.	Tamilnadu	62,405,679	651,321	1.0
28.	Bihar	82,998,509	758,351	0.9

29.	Uttar Pradesh	166,197,921	107,963	0.1
30.	Goa	1,347,668	566	0
31.	Haryana	21,144,564	0	0
32.	Punjab	24,358,999	0	0
33.	Chandigarh	900,635	0	0
34.	Delhi	13,850,507	0	0
35.	Puducherry	974,345	0	0
	India	1,028,610,328	84,326,240	8.2

The tribal population are normally seen to be living in the following three categories of locations:

1.	North-Eastern Region (NER)	Arunachal Pradesh, Assam, Manipur, Meghalaya, Mizoram, Nagaland, Tripura and Sikkim
2.	Central Tribal Belt (CTB)	Rajasthan, Gujarat, Maharashtra, Madhya Pradesh, Chhattisgarh, Andhra Pradesh, Orissa, Bihar, Jharkhand West Bengal, Dadra and Nagar Haveli, and Daman and Diu
3.	Other States/ UTs	Himachal Pradesh, Uttar Pradesh, Uttarakhand, Karnataka, J and K, Tamilnadu, Kerala, Andaman and Nicobar Islands, and Lakshadweep.

The Tribal communities live in about 15 per cent of the country's area, in varying ecological and geo-climatic conditions, plains, forests, hills and inaccessible areas. Tribal groups are at different stages of social, economic and educational development. They have their presence in the States and Union Territories except Haryana, Punjab, Chandigarh, Delhi and Puducherry. The predominant tribal-populated States of the country (i.e., those with tribal population of more than 50 per cent of the total population of the State are: Arunachal Pradesh, Meghalaya, Mizoram, Nagaland, Union territories of Dadra & Nagar Haveli and Lakshadweep. If a comparison is made amongst ST population alone, more than half the ST population of the country is concentrated in the States of Madhya Pradesh, Chhattisgarh, Maharashtra, Orissa, Jharkhand and Gujarat. The largest number of tribes (i.e. 62) are in the State of Orissa. The next major concentration is in the North-Eastern States.

Primitive Tribal Groups (PTGs)

While some tribal communities have adopted a mainstream way of life at one of the spectrum, there are 75 Primitive Tribal Groups (PTGs) in 17 States and Union Territories of Andaman and Nicobar Islands, who are characterized by:

— a pre-agriculture level of technology,
— a stagnant or declining population,
— extremely low literacy, and
— a subsistence level of economy.

Their total population as per the 1991 census was about 24.12 lakh. Most of these groups are small in number, have attained various levels of social and economic progress and generally live in remote habitat, with poor administrative and infrastructure back up.

Population Profile

Many indicators in respect of Scheduled Tribes like their demography, sex-ratio, education, livelihood profile, health profile have been compiled periodically through the Census operations or by the National Sample Survey Organisation (NSSO) or the Central Statistical Organisation (CSO).

The population of Scheduled Tribes has been on the increase since 1961. The census reveals that the tribal population had grown at the rate of 24.45 per cent during the period 1991-2001. The decadal population growth between the Census Year 1981 to 1991 in respect of the tribal population had been higher (31.64 per cent) than that for the overall population (23.51 per cent). However during census years 1991 to 2001 it had been 24.45 per cent against the growth rate of 22.66 per cent for the entire population.

As compared to the sex ratio for the overall population (933 females per 1000 male), the sex ratio among Scheduled Tribes is more favourable, at 978 females per 1,000 males (2001 census).

Literacy

The literacy rate for overall population has increased from 52.2 per cent to 65.38 per cent between 1991 to 2001. In case of Scheduled

Tribes the increase in literacy has been from 29.62 per cent to 47.10 per cent. The literacy rate among tribals (47.10 per cent) is however far below the overall literacy in the country (64.8 per cent).

The female literacy rate among tribals during the period 1991 to 2001 increased from 18.2 per cent to 34.8 per cent, which is lower by approximately 20 per cent as compared to literacy rate of the females of the general population. However, the significant point is the increase in the total as well as the female literacy among tribals. These disparities are compounded by higher dropout rates in formal education, resulting in a disproportionately low representation in higher education.

Job profile

According to the 1991 Census figures, 42.02 per cent of the ST population were main workers, of whom 54.50 per cent were cultivators and 36.09 per cent agricultural labourers. Thus, about 82 per cent of the main workers from these communities were engaged in primary sector activities.

Indicators of Backwardness

Not surprisingly, the cumulative effect has been that the proportion of Scheduled Tribes below the poverty line is substantially higher than the national average. A majority of Scheduled Tribes continue to live below the poverty line, have poor literacy rates, suffer from malnutrition and diseases and are vulnerable to displacement.

The Central Government and the State Governments have been implementing schemes/programmes for the upliftment of STs like reservation in Services, Tribal Sub-Plans, Central Schemes, Centrally Sponsored Schemes, etc. However, a lot more is required to be done to achieve the desired development goals for STs.

Development of STs

We have seen that the HDI (Human Development Indices) of tribal population is quite low as compared to the rest of the population. This is mainly because they live in clusters generally in far-flung areas, which are remote or in the vicinity of forests. The development programmes meant for the general public often elude the tribal population for the reasons of inaccessibility and difficult terrain. Nevertheless the Government of India and the State Governments have taken a number of measures over the years to improve the conditions of STs and for their development. But a lot more needs to be done. This emphasis on development of STs is quite visible in the Agenda Items of the National Common Minimum Programme (NCMP) adopted by the Central Government in May 2004.

Tribal Sub-Plan (TSP)

Upgradation of administration through the innovative strategy of the Tribal Sub-Plan (TSP) for STs was launched at the beginning of the 5th Five Year Plan in 1974-75, covering 21 States and 2 U.T.S., where Scheduled Tribes constitute a sizeable population. This special strategy was expected to ensure that all the general development sectors, both at the Central and State levels, earmark funds for STs in proportion to their population so that adequate benefits from all the concerned sectors flow to this disadvantaged group. Thus the TSP strategy seeks to ensure adequate flow of funds for tribal development not only under every State Plan funds, but also from all the Central Ministries/Departments. TSP is a part of the overall plan of a State/UT or a Central Ministry/Department, and is therefore called a Sub-Plan.

The TSP to promote development activities through legal and administrative support. The TSP strategy is being implemented through 195 Integrated Tribal Development Projects (ITDPs)/ Integrated Tribal Development Agencies (ITDAs), 259 Modified Area Development Approach (MADA) and 82 Clusters. The benefits of the Tribal Sub-Plan are also extended to the scattered tribal population. The TSP is financed by four sources namely, flow from Centrally Sponsored Schemes. Special Central Assistance, State Plan, and Institutional finance. The Central Ministries have also been requested to utilize at lease 8% of their budget for the welfare and development of Scheduled Tribes.

Special Central Assistance for Tribal Sub-Plan

In support of TSP, the Government of India launched the SCA scheme in 1974 to the States and the UTs, as an additive to fill up the gaps, especially in the family based income-generating programmes. As a result, there has been a substantial increase in the flow of funds during the Ninth Five Year Plan for the development of STs besides enlargement of the share of benefits for STs under all the development programmes. The SCA to TSP is provided by the Ministry of Tribal Affairs to 21 Tribal Sub-Plan States including North Eastern States of Assam, Manipur and Tripura. Since 2003-04 the Ministry of Home Affairs is releasing the funds under SCA to TSP meant for the UTS.

The SCA is to be utilised in conjunction with the TSP flow with a view to meeting the gaps, which are not otherwise taken care of by the State Plan. The objective and scope of SCA to TSP was originally meant for filling up of the critical gaps in the family-based income-generation activities of the TSP. From the Tenth Five Year Plan, the objective and scope of SCA to TSP has been expanded to cover the infrastructure incidental to income-generation.

The funds released under SCA to TSP to State Governments/UT Administrations are as follows:

(Rs. in crore)

Five Year Plan	Fund released
V	119.31
VI	486.11
VII	846.95
VIII	1484.12
IX	2009.61
X	2960.83
XI (2007-08)	631.80

Grants under the First Proviso to Article 275(1) of the Constitution: The Constitution of India under the First Proviso Article 275(1) of the Constitution provides for assured special financial assistance for promoting the welfare of STs and for raising the level of administration of the Scheduled Areas to that of the rest of the State.

Programme for Development of Forest Villages

Development of forest villages is one of the thrust areas of tribal development during the 10th Five Year Plan. The Planning

Commission allocated Rs. 450 crore to the Ministry of Tribal Affairs for the development of forest villages at an average allocation of Rs. 15 lakh per village. There are about 2,474 such forest villages at an average allocation of Rs. 15 lakh per village. There are about 2,474 such forest villages in 12 States, which are still managed by State Forest Departments. It is estimated that there are about 2.5 lakh tribal families in these villages. A process of conversion of these forest villages into revenue earning villages is underway.

The funds released under the scheme are as follows:

(Rs. in lakh)

Year	Fund Released
2005-06	19180.86
2006-07	22097.09
2007-08	4646.82
2008-09 (till 30.6.08)	13931.55

Releases made in various Plans under Article 275(I)

Plan	Rs. in crore
V	60.00
VI	80.00
VII	100.00
VIII	340.00
IX	741.00
X	1662.70
XI	390.28

Scheme for Primitive Tribal Groups (PTGs): A Central Sector Scheme was introduced in 1998-99 for the all-round development of these groups under which financial assistance is made available to Integrated Tribal Development Projects, Tribal Research Institutes and Non-Governmental Organisations for undertaking projects/activities not covered by any of the existing schemes.

Scheme of Construction of Hostels for ST Boys and Girls: Under the scheme, Central assistance is given to States/UTs for construction of new hostel buildings and/or extension of existing hostels. In this scheme till 2007-08 the cost of the construction of the hostel building was equally shared between the Centre and the State in ratio of 50:50. In case of UTs, the Central Government bore the entire cost of the building. The cost of construction is based on the State PWD schedule of rates or local CPWD schedule of rates, which is lower. Maintenance of the hostel is the responsibility of the concerned States/UTs. The number of seats in a hostel was 100. The scheme of Construction of Hostel for ST Boys and Girls is being continued in the 11th Five Year Plan period with the following modifications:

— Central Assistance for Construction of ST Girls Hostels in all States/UTs/ Universities will be 100% of the cost of construction.
— Central Assistance for Construction of Boys' Hostel for ST Boys will be 100% in identified naxal-affected areas and will remain at 50% in all other areas.

  Universities in naxal-affected area as would be entitled to receive 100% Central assistance.
— Central assistance would also be given on the same pattern in respect of vocational training centres if sought by States/UTs.
— The construction period for the hostels has been reduced from 5 years to 2 years.

(Rs. in crore)

Plan Period	Outlay	Actually Released	No. of Hostels Constructed	No. of Beneficiaries
During the 10th Plan both schemes were merged)	104.00	88.41	389	24379
2007-08	37.00	37.00	314	28146

Establishment of Ashram School in Tribal Sub-Plan Area: The scheme of Ashram School has as its objective the establishment of residential schools for STs in an environment conducive to learning to increase the literacy rates among the tribal students and to bring them at par with the other population of the country. The funding for the scheme with the State is done on matching (50-50) basis, while cent percent assistance is given to UTs.

(Rs. in crore)

Plan period	Outlay	Actually Released	No. of Ashram Schools constructed	No. of seats
X	78.30	42.97	232	17650
2007-08	147.60	20.00	97	16839

Upgradation of Merit of ST Students: The objective of this scheme is to upgrade the merit of ST students by providing them remedial and special coaching in classes IX to XII, to prepare the students for competitive examinations for seeking entry into professional courses like Engineering and Medical disciplines. The scheme provides for 100 per cent Central assistance to the States/UT's.

(Rs. in crore)

Plan period	Outlay	Actually Released	Physical Achievements
IX	4.20	3.60	329 students*
X	5.56	4.58	3352 students
2007-08	1.75	1.38	1031 students

* the number of beneficiaries from 1997-98 to 1999-2000 are for SCs & STs.

Post-Metric Scholarships for Scheduled Tribes Students

The objective of the scheme is to provide financial assistance to students belonging to STs pursuing Post-Matriculation recognized courses in recognized institutions. The scheme covers professional, technical, nonprofessional and nontechnical courses at various levels. It also includes correspondence courses including distance and continuing education and is implemented by the State Government and UT Administrations, covering 100% Central Assistance over and above the committed liability which is required to be borne by them from their own budgetary provisions. Budget Allocations, actually released and beneficiaries are given below:

(Rs. in crore)

Plan period	Outlay	Actually Released	Physical Achievements
IX	221.55	260.65	2639088
X	389.09	683.98	3744000
2007-08	201.24	200.03	1028903

Vocational Training in Tribal Areas: The main aim of this scheme is to develop the skill of the tribal youth in order to gain employment/self employment opportunities. This scheme was introduced in 1992-93 as Central Sector Scheme and implemented through the State Governments/UT Administrations, Institutions or Organisations set up by Government as autonomous body, educational and other institutions like local bodies and cooperative societies and Non-Governmental Organizations. The capacity of each vocational training centre is 100 with hostel facility for 50. Each centre caters to five vocational courses in traditional skills depending upon the employment potential of the area. Each tribal boy/girl is trained in two trades of his/ her choice, the course in each trade being of three months duration. Each trainee is attached at the end of six months to a Master Craftsman in a semi-urban area for a period of six months to learn his/ her skill by practical experience, the practical experience if each trade being of three months duration. There is a provision for monthly stipend and for raw material for the trainees.

Budget Allocations, actually released and beneficiaries are given below:

(Rs. in crore)

Name of the Five year Plan	Outlay	Actual Released	No. of VTC
IX	30.25	17.44	203
X	33.56	24.35	290
2007-08 (other than NGO	6.75	6.75	48
XI (2007-08) (NGO)	2.25	2.25	14

Education of Girls in Low Literacy Pockets: Launched in 1992-93 the scheme envisages setting up of residential educational complexes for ST girls from I to V standard with facility for upgradation in order to raise the literacy level of tribal females. This scheme is implemented through the voluntary organizations and autonomous bodies of the State Government. During 10th Pan period an amount of Rs. 33.34 crores was released benefiting more than 8000 (appro..) ST Girls each year.An amount of Rs. 19.75 crore was released to 76 complexes during 2007-08 benefiting 10379 ST girls.

With the beginning of financial year 2009 the scheme has been revised and renamed as 'Strengthening Education among Scheduled Tribes Girls in Low Literacy Districts'. The revised scheme covers 54 identified districts where the ST population is 25% or more, and ST female literacy rate below 35% as per 2001 census. The scheme also covers blocks in districts other than 54 identified districts which have ST population 25% or more, and ST female rate below 35% and PTG areas. Naxal affected areas are given priority and the Ministry provides financial assistance under the scheme for Girls Hostel where schools under "Sarva Shiksha Abhiyan". Kasturba Gandhi Vidhyalayas or other schemes of Education Departments are available. Where such schools are not available, complete complex including hostel & school are considered. Besides free schooling, boarding/lodging, uniforms, books, food cast stipend and incentive to girls students are also provided. In addition, the organization running the educational complex is also required to impart Vocational/ Skill development Training among ST girls.

Grants-in-Aid to Voluntary Organisations: The prime objective of the scheme is to enhance the reach of welfare schemes of Government and fills the gaps in service deficient tribal areas in the sectors such as education, health, drinking water, agro-horticultural productivity, social security net etc. through the efforts of voluntary organizations and to provide an environment for socioeconomic upliftment and overall development of the Scheduled Tribes (STs). The Ministry gives Grant-in-aid to voluntary organizations working for the welfare of STs for projects like residential schools and nonresidential, hostels, hospitals, mobile medical units, computer training centres, libraries and audiovisual units, agriculture training etc. The grant is generally restricted to 90 per cent of the approved total cost of the project and the balance 10 per cent is borne by the guarantee organizations. During the 10th Five Year Plan period 146.16 crores were released under the scheme. An amount of Rs. 34.00 crore was released during 2007-08. During the 11th Five Year Plan, from 2008-09, the scheme and its financial norms has been revised.

Rajiv Gandhi National Fellowship (RGNF): The objective of the scheme is to provide fellowship in the form of financial assistance to students belonging to Scheduled Tribes to pursue higher studies. The fellowship under RGNF will be on the pattern of UGC Fellowships awarded to research students pursuing regular and full time M.Phill and Ph.D. Courses.Under the scheme, 776 students have been awarded fellowships during the 10th Plan and 667 new students are expected to benefit in the year 2007-08.

National Overseas Scholarship Scheme for Scheduled Tribes (Non-Plan): The Scheme provides for financial assistance to meritorious students for pursuing higher studies abroad in specified fields of Master level courses, Ph.D. and Post-Doctoral research programmes, in the field of Engineering, Technology and Science for Scheduled Tribes, De-notified, Nomadic and Semi-nomadic tribes. The selected candidates are provided the cost of tuition and other educational fees charged by the foreign university, etc., maintenance and other grants along with travel expenses. In addition passage grants are also available to candidates belonging to ST who are in receipt of merit scholarship for postgraduate studies, research or training abroad (excluding attending seminars, workshops, conferences) from a foreign government/organisations or under any other scheme where cost of passage is not provided. The Scheme of NOS has been revised in 2004-05.

The scheme provides financial assistance to meritorious ST students for pursuing higher studies abroad in specified fields of Master level courses, Ph.D. and Post-Doctoral research programmes, in the field of Engineering, Technology and Science.

Budget Allocations, funds actually by released and beneficiaries are given below:

Plan period	Outlay	Funds Actually Released	Physical Achievements
IX	114	50	5 students
X	418	50	5 students
2007-08	100	0.14	8 students

Scheme of Top Class Education for ST Students

The Ministry of Tribal Affairs has introduced a new scheme of Top Class Education of ST students from 2007-08 with the objective of encouraging meritorious ST students for pursuing studies at degree and post degree and post degree level in any of the selected list of institutes of excellence, in which the scholarship scheme would be operative. There are 127 top-rated institutes approved under the scheme in both the Government and private sectors covering the field of management, medicine, engineering, law and commercial courses. Each institute has been allocated five awards, with a ceiling of a total of 635 scholarships per year. The family income of the ST students from all the sources shall not exceed Rs. 2.00 lakh per annum.

The ST students will be awarded scholarship covering full tuition fee and other non-refundable dues in respect of Government/ Government-funded institutions. However, there will be a ceiling of Rs. 2.00 lakh per annum per student for private sector institutions and Rs. 3.72 lakh per annum per student for the private sector flying clubs for Commercial Pilot Training. In addition to the above, the scholarship also provides for:

— living expenses @ Rs. 220/- per month per student subject to actual,

— books and stationery @ Rs. 3,000/- per annum per student and

— cost of a latest computer system along with its accessories limited to Rs. 45,000/- as one time assistance during the course.

Grants-in-Aid for Minor Forest Produce (MFP) Operations: This is a Central Sector Scheme, with 100 per cent grant, available to the State Tribal Development Cooperative Corporations, Forest Development Corporations, and Minor Forest Produce (Trading and Development) Federations for taking up the minor forest produce operations. The funds under the scheme is available to the State TDCCS/FDC's for:

— increasing the quantum of MFP handled by setting off operational losses, if need be:

— strengthening the share capital base of the Corporation for undertaking MFP operations thereby increasing the quantum of MFP presently handled;

— setting up of scientific warehousing facilities, wherever necessary;

— establishing processing industries for value addition with the objective of ensuring maximum returns on the MFPs for the tribals;

— giving consumption loans to tribals; and

— supplementing Research & Development (R&D) efforts.

Exchange of visits by STs: The Scheme "Exchange of Visits by Tribals" providing wider exposure and experience sharing to the tribals by visits to the more developed areas of the country.

National Scheduled Tribes Finance and Development Corporation

With a view to pay a focused attention and accelerate the pace of economic development of Scheduled Tribes, the erstwhile National Scheduled Castes and Scheduled Tribes Financial Development Corporation was bifurcated and National Scheduled Tribes Finance and Development Corporation (NSTFDC) was set up in April, 2001 under the Ministry of Tribal Affairs. The NSTFDC has been granted license under Sec. 25 of the Companies Act (A Company not for profit). The Authorized Share Capital of the NSTFDC is Rs. 500.00 crore and paid up capital is Rs. 230.50 crore as on date.

In order to achieve the mandate set for the NSTFDC, financial assistance is extended by NSTFDC to the Scheduled Tribes, who are having annual family income upto double the poverty line. NSTFDC also provides financial assistance as grant for skill and entrepreneurial development of the target group. The financial assistance is channelised through Government owned agencies nominated by the respective Ministries/State Governments and UT Administrations. This is aimed to raise the level of income and improve socioeconomic status of the eligible Scheduled Tribes. NSTFDC also provides financial assistance for procurement and marketing/minor forest produce so as to avoid the distress sale of produce/products by the Scheduled Tribes.

Eligibility criteria for the beneficiary: The beneficiary (ies) should belong to ST community and annual family income of the beneficiary (ies) should not exceed double the poverty line (DPL) income limit (presently DPL is Rs. 39,500/- per annum for the rural areas and Rs. 54,500/- per annum for the urban areas).

In the case of Self Help Groups (SHGs), all the members of the SHG should belong to the ST community having annual family income upto Double the Poverty line (DPL). Similarly for Cooperative Society, loan is extended to the eligible STs through cooperative Society having minimum 80% or more STs as member of the said cooperative society.

NSTFDC is implementing following programmes for the economic development of STs.

Term Loan for Income generating activities:

— NSTFDC provides term loan for viable scheme(s)/project(s) costing upto Rs. 10 lakh per individual unit/profit centre.

— Financial assistance upto 90% of the cost of the scheme(s)/ project(s) is provided by the NSTFDC. Promoter's contribution is not insisted upon for the scheme/project costing upto Rs. 1 lakh. However, only 2-5% of the total cost of the scheme(s)/project(s) costing above Rs. 1 lakh per unit/profit centre is required as promoter's contribution depending upon the cost of unit.

— NSTFDC charges concessional rate of interest, which is 3% per annum for the scheme/project having NSTFDC's share upto Rs. 5 lakh per unit/profit centre and 5% for the schemes having NSTFDC's share more than Rs. 5 lakh/unit/profit centre. The SCAs are allowed to charge interest at the rate of 3% per annum over and above the interest rate charged by NSTFDC from the beneficiaries.

— The loan is to be repaid in quarterly/half yearly instalments, as the case may be, within a maximum period of 10 years including suitable moratorium period.

Bridge Loan: Bridge loan is provided by the NSTFDC against subsidy/ capital incentives etc. available for the scheme(s)/project(s) through the SCAs to meet the gap in funding requirement of scheme(s)/ project(s) costing upto 10 lakh per unit/ profit centre.

Schemes for Self Help Groups (SHGs):

— NSTFDC has introduced specific scheme for extending financial assistance for Self Help Groups (SHGs) and financial assistance is extended for the scheme(s)/project(s) having unit cost upto Rs. 25 lakh per SHG.

— Financial assistance is extended upto 90% of the cost of the scheme/ project subject to investment per member not exceeding Rs. 50,000/- per unit.

— Minimum promoter's contribution under the scheme is 10% of the cost of the unit.

Marketing Support Assistance:

— It is provided for financial support for meeting the working capital requirement of the Central/State Government owned agencies and national level federations for undertaking procurement and/or marketing of minor forest produce/agricultural produce collected/grown by the STs and/or related product/services.

— Marketing Support Assistance extended to the beneficiaries through the SCAs, the interest is at par with rates of interest for long term loan.

— For Marketing Support Assistance extended to the Central/State/UT owned organizations, national level federations directly involved in procurement, the interest rate is 7% per annum.

Assistance by way of grant: Grant to meet up to 100% recurring cost in respect of regular training programmes conducted for imparting skill and entrepreneurial development training to the eligible STs through the Government/semi Government/ autonomous Government bodies is extended by the NSTFDC to its SCAs.

Special Schemes

Adivasi Mahila Sashaktikaran Yojana (AMSY) is an exclusive scheme for the economic development of ST women, at a highly concessional rate of interest. Under the scheme, NSTFDC provides Term Loan for scheme(s)/project(s) costing upto Rs. 50,000/- per individual unit/profit centre. Financial assistance up to 90% of the cost of the scheme(s)/project(s) is provided by the NSTFDC. The SCAs may charge a maximum interest @ 4% per annum from the ultimate women beneficiaries.

Micro-credit scheme-launch of a new scheme: Micro Credit Scheme is meant to provide financial assistance for undertaking small self-employment ventures/ activities by the eligible STs through existing profit making SHGs. SCAs shall provide eligible amount of subsidy or margin money as per their scheme(s) for the target group and remaining amount may be provided as term loan by NSTFDC. In case of no subsidy and or no share of SCAs/banks as SCAs. NSTFDC may provide 100% of the funds required as term loan subject to maximum of Rs. 15,000/- per member.

Performance of NSTFDC during 2006-07: Till 31.03.2008, NSTFDC has cumulatively sanctioned 937 schemes/projects under its income generating programme having its share of Rs. 466.59 crores (net) for providing self employment to the 1.73 lakhs Scheduled Tribes. The above includes sanctions of Rs. 64.17 crores for assisting about 45,000 scheduled tribe women. Besides NSTFDC has also sanctioned loans of Rs. 65.00 crore for produce and marketing of the Agriculture/Forest produce and other produce etc. for 19.11 lakh number of Scheduled Tribes.

Tribal Cooperative Marketing Development Federation of India Ltd. (TRIFED)

The Tribal Cooperative Marketing Development Federation of India Limited (TRIFED), was set up in 1987 as a national level apex body under the Multi State Cooperative Societies Act, 1984.

After the enactment of the Multi-State Cooperative Societies Act, 2002 (MSCS Act, 2002) TRIFED is deemed to be registered under the latter Act and is also listed in the Second Schedule to the Act as a National Cooperative Society.

The Bye-laws of TRIFED were revised in April 2003 in tune with the new Multi State Cooperative Societies Act, 2002 read with the Multi State Cooperative Societies Rules, 2002. Under its revised mandate TRIFED has stopped bulk procurement in Minor Forest Produce (MFP) and Surplus Agricultural Produce (SAP) from tribals. (This procurement is now done by the State-level Tribal Cooperatives Societies/ Federations). TRIFED now functions as a 'market developer' for tribal products and as 'service provider' to its member federations. This way TRIFED is now striving to provide economic benefits to a large number of this unorganized section of the society.

TRIFED is now engaged in the marketing development of tribal products (natural and organic products, handicrafts, ratification etc.) through its own shops ('TRIBES India') and shops selling its products on consignment basis.

Recognition of Forest Rights of STs: The Scheduled Tribes and Other Traditional Forest Dwellers (Recognition of Forest Rights) Act, 2006 seeks to recognize and vest the forest rights and occupation in forest land in forest dwelling Scheduled Tribes and other traditional forest dwellers Sho have been residing in such forests for generations but shoes rights on ancestral lands and their habitat were not adequately recognized in the consolidation of State forests during the colonial period as well as in independent India resulting in historical injustice to them. The Act has been notified for operation with effect from 31.12.2007.

The Scheduled Tribe and Other Traditional Forest Dwellers (Recognition of Forest Rights) Rules, for implementing the provisions of the Act, were notified on 1.1.2008 and they envisage the constitution of various Committees under the Act, viz, the Sub Divisional Level Committee, District Level Committee and the State Level Monitoring Committee, by the State Governments.

All the States have been requested to nominate the nodal officer for implementing the provisions of the Act. The State Government were also requested to take necessary steps to:

— Ensure that awareness is created about the objectives, provisions and procedures of the Act and the Rules through various measures including awareness programmes and printed material such as posters in the regional languages;

— Ensure the translation and publication of the Act and the rules in all the regional languages and arrange to distribute to all Gram Sabhas, Forest Right Committees and all departments of the Government including Panchayati Raj, Rural Development, Tribal and Social Welfare and Forest Departments;

— Undertake the orientation of officials, civilian representatives and non-Government organizations in the State, who can then be called upon to assist as resource persons in the awareness programmes;

— Sensitize the Sub-Divisional and District Level Committees on the objectives, provisions and procedures of the Act and the Rules:

As per the Act, the responsibility for recognition and vesting of forest rights and distribution of land rights resets with the State Government, as per the Rules notified for implementation of the Act. All the State Governments have been directed that the entire process of vesting of forest rights as per the Scheduled Tribes and Other Traditional forest Dwellers (Recognition of Forest Rights) Act, 2006 should be completed at the earliest.

Welfare Programmes for Other Backward Classes

The Other Backward Classes (OBC) constitutes estimated 52 per cent of population as per Second Report of Backward Classes popularly known as Mandal Report. After the Mandal Judgement in 1992 the OBCs started getting various benefits for their educational development, economic development and reservation in services.

Statutory Body

National Commission for Backward Classes: In pursuance of the Supreme Court Judgement popularly known as Mandal Judgement (1992), the National Commission for Backward Classes was set up in 1993 as a permanent body for entertaining, examining and advising the Government on requests for inclusion and complaints of over-inclusion and under inclusion in the lists of Other Backward Classes (OBCs) of citizens. As per the provision of the Act, the advice tendered by the Commission shall ordinarily be binding upon the Government.

Educational Development

Pre-metric Scholarships for OBCs: The Scholarships are awarded to the students belonging to OBCs whose parents'/guardians' income from all sources does not exceed Rs 44,500 per annum. The scholarships are given to the students in class I or any subsequent class of pre-metric stage in the case of day scholars and class III or any subsequent class of pre-metric stage in the case of hostellers. The scholarship will terminate at the end of class X. The duration of the scholarship in an academic year is 10 months. The scholarship is tenable in such institutions and for such pre-matriculation courses, which have been duly recognised by the concerned State Government and Union Territory Administration. Under the scheme, 50 per cent Central assistance is provided to the State Governments and 100 per cent in case of UTs over and above the committed liability. An amount of Rs. 25.27 crores was released under the scheme to 12 states during 2006-07 for covering 9,57,338 beneficiaries.

Post-Metric Scholarships for OBCs: The objective of the scheme is to provide financial assistance to the OBC students studying at post-matriculation or post secondary stage to enable them to complete their education. These scholarships are available for studies in India only and awarded through the State Governments/UT Administrations to which the applicant actually belongs. These scholarships are given for study in recognised institutions. Unemployed students whose parents/ guardians income from all sources does not exceed Rs. 44,500 per annum are entitled for scholarships under the scheme. Under the Scheme, 100 per cent Central assistance is provided to State Governments/UT Administrations over and above the committed liability. An amount of Rs. 55.73 crores was released under the scheme to 16 states/ UTs for covering 4,16,765 beneficiaries during the year 2006-07.

Hostels for OBC Boys and Girls: The scheme aims at providing better educational opportunities to students belonging to socially and educationally backward classes notified as such in the Central/State/ UT lists of OBCs, generally referred to as Other Backward Classes (OBCs). Under the scheme, 50 per cent Central assistance is provided to the States and 100 per cent to UTs for constructions of hostels. These hostels are constructed for middle, secondary, college and university level students. The expenditure on procurement of land, staffing and other maintenance shall be borne by the State Governments/UT concerned. During 2006-07 an amount of Rs 19.58 crore was released 11 States/UTs for construction of 82 hostels and for covering 4520 OBCs inmates.

Assistance to Voluntary Organisations for Welfare of OBCs: The objective of the scheme is to involve the voluntary sector for improving the educational and socioeconomic conditions of the OBCs through skill upgradation and enables them to start income generating activities on their own or get gainfully employed. Under the Scheme, 90 per cent of approved expenditure in form of grant-in-aid is given to NGOs for running vocational training courses such as carpentry, computer, craft, electrician, motor winding and fitting, photography, printing, composing and bookbinding, type and shorthand and welding and fitter training, etc. An amount of Rs 2.22 crore was released in 2006-07 to 85 NGOs so as to benefit 4316 OBC beneficiaries.

Economic Development

National Backward Classes Finance and Development Corporation: The National Backward Classes Finance and Development Corporation (NBCFDC) provides credit facilities to beneficiaries whose annual income is less than double the poverty line for various income generation activities including implementation of Mahila Samridhi Yojana. The corporation extended credit facilities to 1,32,108 beneficiaries.

Reservation in Services

Reservation is given to Scheduled Castes (SCs), Scheduled Tribes (STs) and Other Backward Classes (OBCs) in services under the control of Government. Reservation is also provided to persons with disabilities and the ex-servicemen in certain categories of posts. The quantum of reservation for SCs, STs, and OBCs in direct recruitment on all-India basis by open competition is 15 per cent, 7.5 per cent and 27 per cent respectively. In direct recruitment on all-India basis otherwise than by open competition, reservation is 16.66 per cent for SCs, 7.5 per cent for STs and 25.84 per cent for OBCs. In case of promotion SCs and STs get reservation at the rate of 15 per cent and 7.5 per cent respectively. There is no reservation for OBCs is case of promotion. Three per cent of vacancies are kept reserved for persons with disabilities. Ten per cent of the vacancies in the posts of the level of Assistant Commandant in all paramilitary forces, 10 per cent of the vacancies in Group-C posts and 20 per cent of the vacancies in Group-D posts are reserved for the ex-servicemen.

Article 341 and 342 of the Constitution define as to who would be the SCs and the STs with respect of any State or Union Territory. The Government has prepared a list of OBCs has been prepared by the Government. The interstate area restrictions have been imposed so that the people belonging to the specific community residing in a specific area which has been assessed to qualify for SC, ST and OBC status only benefit from the facilities provided for them. Definition of 'ex-servicemen' for the purpose of getting reservation in services is contained in Ex-servicemen (Re-employment in Civil Services and Posts) Rules, 1979 and conditions for reservation to persons with disabilities are given under the Persons with Disabilities (Equal Opportunities, Protection of Rights and Full Participation) Act, 1995.

To ensure that reserved vacancies are filled by candidates belonging to appropriate category, certain relaxations and concessions like relaxation in upper age-limit, etc., are provided. Liaison officers have been appointed for SCs/STs and OBCs in each Ministry/ Department to ensure proper implementation of reservation policy for them.

The Scheme of reservation is being followed by public sector undertakings including nationalised public sector banks. State governments have also provided for reservation of posts for SCs, STs and OBCs, etc., and have taken steps to increase their representation in State services. Reservation in State government services, however, is under the exclusive jurisdiction of respective State Governments.

REFERENCES

Bhowmik, K.L. (ed.) (1988). Development of Scheduled Communities. *Current Anthropological and Archaeological Perspectives*, Vol. 6. New Delhi: Inter-India Publications.

Corrie, B.D. (1995). A human development index for the Dalit child in India, *Social Indicators Research* 34: 395-409

Freeman, J.M. (1986).The consciousness of freedom amongst India's Untouchables. In D.K. Basu & R. Sisson (eds) *Social and Economic Development in India*. New Delhi: Sage.

Galanter, M. (1986). Pursuing equality. An assessment of India's policy of compensatory discrimination for disadvantaged groups. In D.K. Basu & R. Sisson (eds) *Social and Economic Development in India*. New Delhi: Sage.

Joshi, B. (1987). Recent developments in inter-regional mobilization of Dalit protest in India, *South Asia Bulletin* 7, 86-96.

Mahar, P. (1960). Changing religious practices of an Untouchable caste, *Economic Development and Cultural Change* 8.

Maurya, R.L. (1991). Changing status of the Scheduled Castes. In R.S. Tripathi & P.D. Tiwari (eds) *Dimensions of Scheduled Caste Development in India*. New Delhi: Uppal.

9

Dalit Rights Movement

The word "dalit" means broken or downtrodden in Sanskrit and was "used as far back as 1931 in journalistic writing". Popularized by Dr. B.R. Ambedkar in the 1920s and 30s, and later by the Dalit Panthers movement in the 1970s, the term became a new secular identity for millions of those formerly known as 'untouchables' in India. Today, modern dalit identity is in a discursive competition with various religious identities for control of between one-fourth and one-fifth of India's billion-person population, which is classified as scheduled caste (SC). The life and thought of Dr. B.R. Ambedkar, the father of dalit rights and assertion, as well as the modern Indian constitution, was foundational to this discursive competition, which can be clearly seen in the following quote from Gangadar Pantawane, the founding editor of *Asmitadarsh*, a journal devoted to dalit literature:

> To me Dalit is not a caste. He is a man exploited by the social and economic traditions of this country. He does not believe in God, Rebirth, Soul, Holy Books teaching separatism, Fate and Heaven because they have made him a slave. He does believe in humanism. Dalit is a symbol of change and revolution

Compared to the rhetorical calls by Trailokya Bauddha Mahasangha, Sahayak Gana (TBMSG) activists to work towards a time when "all India will be Buddhist," the above quote provides a stark secular-focused contrast to Indian social activists' penchant for citing religious ideals in order to galvanize the identity of followers. Pantawane's conception privileges dalit as symbolic of a post-modern identity in which caste distinctions have become irrelevant.

Yet, it was the life and legacy of Dr. B.R. Ambedkar that laid the foundation for this competition to win the hearts and minds of dalits. As both a social reformer from within the government, and then later a cultural reformer from the outside, Dr. Ambedkar's life itself represented a balancing between these two, not incompatible, identities. While many people outside the Indian subcontinent are familiar with Mahatma Gandhi, few who live outside of India know much about Dr. Ambedkar, or about the movement he helped spawn. Both his political significance as the foremost representative of the Mahar 'untouchable' community in Maharashtra, and the religious importance he played in changing the social identity and spiritual commitments of that particular community of dalits through a revival of Buddhism, are unrivalled throughout India's long historical development. Ambedkar's prolific legacy culminating in his chairmanship of the drafting of the Indian constitution, as well as his call to all former 'untouchables' to convert to Buddhism has made his continued influence among scheduled castes unrivalled. Though his life narrative is so compelling that Indians of all persuasions have appropriated his image, like other low-caste social reformers, both before and after him, Dr. Ambedkar struggled to create intra-caste bonds; bonds that were lacking even among the lowest of caste groupings who were divided and aggrieved.

Dr. Bhimrao Ramji Ambedkar, affectionately known by his followers as Babasaheb, overcame the cultural and economic impasses of being born an 'untouchable' Mahar, one of three lowest-caste segments of Maharashtra society, in late 19th Century Hindu-dominated India. Breaking through countless stereotypes, Ambedkar was taught early of the importance of education, and he used the social cleavages that the British administrative policy provided to transcend his socially prescribed role. Rising to the post of Law Minister in Nehru's first independent Indian cabinet, he was appointed chairman of the drafting committee for the new constitution. From this vantage point, Ambedkar was well-placed to destroy the legal foundations of the caste system, and in 1948 Ambedkar presented his draft of the Indian constitution, which was accepted a year later. In it can be seen Ambedkar's push to get social change codified legalistically. This part of Ambedkar's legacy culminates in Article 17 of the Indian Constitution, which states:

> 'Untouchability' is abolished and its practice in any form is forbidden. The enforcement of any disability arising out of 'untouchability' shall be an offense punishable in accordance with the law

But despite this important legal success, Dr. Ambedkar slowly began to realize that structural reform was only one means to his larger goal of social change in India. Increasingly frustrated that change was not coming to his people fast enough, he began to believe that social revolution was necessary, which could come only from actively critiquing the cultural structure of Hinduism, as opposed to attempting to change it from within. Similar to later conflict resolution scholars, the trailblazing Ambedkar seemed to ask: "Will we contribute to harmony through conflict resolution, but do so at the cost of accepting the continuation of some injustice? Or should we pursue justice for a particular group, knowing that this pursuit may increase conflict rather than resolve it?". Gradually coming to believe the answer to these questions was a resounding commitment to pursue justice, Dr. Ambedkar began to focus more on societal rather than structural change. By organizing political parties, educating low-caste people, and agitating for change, Dr. Ambedkar pursued broad based change by re-conceiving the meaning of justice in society, not only its structures, but also its social realities.

Ambedkar's identity evolved throughout his life to one of social activist, and the evolution of his growth and thought can be seen clearly in his prolific writings. During the latter part of his career, Ambedkar increasingly began to see religion as a valuable means to realize change through sociocultural critique. As an answer to his discontent with the structural violence imposed by the caste system, religion provided a vehicle to restructure social discourse and remake the foundational values of the social system two important aims of legions of young dalit activists. It was also with a lifelong desire to understand religion that Ambedkar conditioned his analysis of caste. Thus, by 1935, Ambedkar had decided that Hinduism was the root cause of the 'untouchable' problem and had resolved to change his religion as a result. This, he believed, was the best solution for the Mahar 'untouchables' that he now led. Encouraging other 'untouchables' to join this cause.

But Ambedkar saw religion as a social vehicle as much as others saw it for its soteriological commitments to explain life. For Ambedkar choice of religions was a means to social change in the present. By changing religious traditions he, as well as each individual, could change society. Thus, he waged a polemical and rhetorical war against Hinduism. Declaring Hinduism the root cause of dalit suffering Ambedkar challenged the orthodox beliefs of Indian culture head on, and was either reviled or loved for this audacity. These acts created support, criticism and fierce debate. Gandhi, upon hearing Ambedkar speak, was once said to have remarked, "religion is not like a horse or a cloak, which can be changed at will. It is a more integral part of one's self than one's own body".

Yet, while Gandhi criticized the idea of a choice in religion, Ambedkar studied all the world's faiths in order to find the one, which would best fit his 'untouchable' communities' needs. The act of choosing his religion was, for Ambedkar, the cement of a repositioned identity which was both personal and collective. As the answer to many of the needs of his 'untouchable' community, it was an act of social protest and self-help rolled into one. If his more outwardly social protests brought spite from Brahmins, his repositioned identity as a Buddhist would bring him deification among his own 'untouchable' community—something he himself was said to be uncomfortable with. On October 14th, 1956, on the 2500th anniversary of the Buddha's Nirvana, Ambedkar led a mass conversion of 'untouchable' Hindus to Buddhism. This was the culminating act of his now repositioned identity and in writing his own vows upon taking refuge Ambedkar ensured that he had created what some religious scholars have since called "neo-Buddhism". Through this repositioned identity he legitimated a new social perspective and Buddhism happened to be a means to the end of creating a new worldview and social discourse. As the ultimate *upaya* (skilful means), Buddhism itself was to give new hope and confidence to thousands of dalits. However, as Ambedkar died only six months after his controversial conversion, it is not completely clear what form of institutionalization his Buddhism would have taken. He nonetheless ignited a revitalization of Buddhism on the Indian subcontinent, inspiring many a social activist, and living up to his promise to not die a Hindu.

The above leadership narrative provides a common grounding for both secular and religiously inclined dalit rights activists. Yet, depending on the specifics of the story that is emphasized, one can see divergences in social movement organization. Two thousand plus years of caste discrimination has left a void in dalits' collective cultural identity, which Ambedkar attempted to fill. At the same time, future activists will continue to argue as to which void Ambedkar's narrative fills—a clarion call for secular rights or a human need for ultimate meaning? As Taylor, Bougie, and Caouette have argued, lack of a collective cultural identity is the most socially damaging and difficult to overcome aspect of a group's identity. It seems that Ambedkar's emphasis on the role of religion in society is an implicit acknowledgement of this argument and an attempt to reconstruct a new version of this collective cultural identity. The role of cultural collective identity is not merely for group members to have a shared cultural history. It is a stable reference group against which the individual engages positioning processes on an ongoing basis in order to develop a healthy personal identity.

Ambedkar was a pragmatist, studying under John Dewey at Columbia University, eager to develop a healthy collective cultural identity for those he considered his people the downtrodden of society. Religious narrative structures were used as a vehicle to attempt to redeploy a self-aware collective cultural identity. But his use of both secular and religious narrative structure as a means is telling. Ambedkar had a modern understanding of religion, which emphasized that belief was not only about ends, but also a means of social interpretation. He saw the wisdom of approaching social conflict from a position, which privileges neither simply religious nor secular explanations. Unfortunately, Ambedkar's Buddhist followers have failed to openly and fully explore the social and political resources of both the secular and religious narratives they have at their disposal. Despite the fact that Ambedkar dalit activists' discourse seems to strategically use one or the other these narrative structure religious or secular to support their cause and build support, an analysis of the social positions that each creates has been lacking. Secular attempts to focus on Ambedkar's injunction to "educate, organize, agitate" have failed to see the added value that creating a new religious identity can bring to oppressed groups' aspirations, not to mention the added value religious institutions bring to attempts at mass mobilization. Similarly, religiously inclined converts to Buddhism have failed to realize that their religious rhetoric can be exclusionary. Though preaching an inclusive and voluntary belief system, converted dalits often fail to realize their emphasis on religious-based explanation sidelines broad-based rights-based opportunities for mobilization. Further, each side of this spectrum of activism has seen the other side as problematic for maintaining their own base of support within the dalit community. In other words, followers of Ambedkar's religious narrative see secular rights talk as problematic since it relies too much on outside notions of liberty, democracy, fraternity, and agency while followers of Ambedkar's secular narrative see religious rhetoric as backward and pre-modern. In order to bridge these two narratives within the dalit rights movement their foundation, structures, and expressions have to be further explored and dissected, as both narratives provide important resources, which have the reach and impact all dalit activists desire.

Narrative of Dalit Activism

The religious narratives of dalit assertion focus on leaving the Hindu-fold, which is seen as the root cause of the dalit social condition. In doing so, the individual reasserts him/her self and repositions their identity as coming from a religiously converted worldview, as opposed to coming from a certain caste which is seen as a partitioning of society that has been too long sanctified by the hierarchical system now called Hinduism. As such, the religious framework of conversion as a means to social justice fosters a sort of dualistic identity among dalits by empowering dalits not only as newly self-reliant through the experience of conversion, but also as one that has been victimized in an all too recent past. The adversity of exclusion can be made to go hand in hand with the gifts of inclusion, but this fact should not deter us from seeing that the complexity of identity highlights the difficulty inherent in mobilizing people around "identity justice. In particular, the combination of liberation and victimization is problematic for mobilizing widespread international support. Conversion as the living out of theology's connection to praxis does not have the same universal appeal as a narrative structure which equates dalit rights with human rights. Despite a new identity as Buddhist—or Sikh or Christian—the converted dalit cannot completely divorce him/her self from the psychological legacy and mobilizing power of past experiences of injustice. This dual identity has both advantages and disadvantages for newly converted dalits as they attempt to achieve social justice. Ever cognizant of which identity to engage when, Dalit Buddhist followers of Dr. Ambedkar must navigate an array of dalit aspirations by balancing secular pragmatism with the desire to create a religious community based on Buddhist values.

The secular frame of social justice, by comparison, presents a more unified conception of dalit identity as first and foremost human. While this more materialist perspective on social justice places Dr. B.R. Ambedkar near the end of a long line of important low-caste social thinkers, it also downplays any religious proclivities as subordinate to secular humanism. Simultaneously, this secular frame presents a belief that the problems of dalits can only be cured with the help of the unified action of outside intervention, advocacy, and political agitation, taking the onus for change off the individual and placing it on the collective. From this view, the root causes of a lack of social justice, as contextual and unchangeable by any one individual, are confused by any attempt to focus attention on any sacred ultimate. It is as if religious commitments appear as anathema to those strict adherents of the secular rights frame. It is therefore, assumed from this secular perspective that the root causes of a lack of social justice must be approached from a religiously neutral position of secular re-humanization of the oppressed. As a consequence the concepts of reconciliation and healing are often overlooked by these secular humanists in a rush to realize the equitable society. In addition, the secular activists adherents' post-enlightenment aversion to religious discourse seems to run counter to the local cultural norms and history. Religion as a constituent part of the South Asian historical and cultural milieu is de-emphasized in favour of a perspective of global interdependence.

The secular narrative and social position of dalits as oppressed victim predominates among dalit social actors partly because of the slow, but steady, success of this narrative structure's ability to build transnational support and advocacy networks. Bob argues convincingly that "organizing" and "rhetorical" changes among dalit activists led to increased success of a dalit rights as human rights frame of contention in the late 1990s. But what has this increased reliance on a narrative structure of victimization cost the dalit rights cause? As Polletta explicitly argues: while "personal stories chip away at the public indifference" and "elicit sympathy on the part of the powerful," it is also evident that "narrative comes with risks as well as benefits". While the secular narrative structure has allowed activists to conflate dalit rights with human rights, it has also disempowered many religiously inclined dalits through its aversion to religious language and frames. Further, since transnational advocacy often does not respond effectively to local needs, many disenfranchised dalits are turned off by a secular approach to organizing that sees personal belief systems as irrelevant to mobilization success. In short, there is a cultural divide between Western post-enlightenment rights thinking and traditional thoughts rooted in local contexts that value ritualistic and institutional expressions of culture.

This is not to say that the dialectic between secular versus religious narratives can be explained simply by arguing that a postcolonial clash of civilizations or cultures is either the genesis of the divergence, or the solution to unifying these different worldviews. Rather, noticing this cultural divide does signal the risky footing one stands on if advocating either a strongly secular narrative structure to combat caste or a strongly religious one. As Ganguly concisely puts it: "The modernizing desire to first reify caste as a relic of times past, and then to annihilate it, is truly alive and well". This secular bias away from the traditional is neither the best nor most effective way to create social change. Instead, it often leads to sensational excitement outside of India, while faltering in the local context. The bias among secular dalit rights organizations, which disregard the conversion perspective so prevalent among Indian Ambedkarite Buddhists, serves as a case in point. During the recent, and first ever in the Unites States, Dalit Studies conference, an academic panel on the "Paradox of Religion" failed to raise this issue of religion's relation to traditional manners of thought, much less address the dalit rights movement from a perspective that privileges religious conversion as a crucial factor in the identity of low-caste groups. Beyond the academic community, however, a secular rights-based focus also creates a number of limitations and paradoxes for activists.

DANRIA, the organization portrayed in the second short vignette that began this piece provides a prime example of the dialectical problems that secular activists face in approaching their religiously-grounded counterparts. The DANRIA leaders desire to engage Ambedkar Buddhists, but within a frame of the strictly secular. At a DANRIA planning meeting in May 2007 Ambedkar Buddhist representatives from the TBMSG attempted to develop linkages with the work and resources of DANRIA members, and DANRIA members continually made it clear that their work was to support secular dalit education and empowerment. Partly due to how religion is understood in a post-reformation West, such interactions revolve around a judgment that equates support for religious-based organizations as support for the propagation of that religion. It is the old stigma of religious proselytisation; no matter what good work an organization may be doing it must always be scrutinized upon the backdrop of its religious commitments and the assumed privileged priority of those commitments. In this dance of assumptions and commitments, Ambedkar Buddhists try to re-frame their contention to fit the desires of secular activists, while secular activists assume religious organizations' exclusive goals and underestimate their ability and opportunities to mobilize.

Secular narrative structures of dalit contention present benefits to go along with the limitations, which they pose. They bring pragmatism to an often-disorganized array of activist decisions and goals. Through an unequivocal support for humanity and secular humanism these narrative structures provide grounding for international mobilization which bridges religious and cultural difference. The International Commission for Dalit Rights' (ICRD's) mission statement demonstrates this tendency to both symbolically and pragmatically bridge these aspects of difference within the dalit movement: "Eliminating rights-based human need and fulfilling freedom and democracy is necessary to achieve effective national and global development policies and programs, and to alleviate discrimination and extreme poverty." Sufficiently secular such a statement allows for the possibility of religious responses to lack of freedom, discrimination and poverty. In place of a strong religious commitment, the secular narratives that such organizations profess, are often founded on an enduring faith in ideology. In interviewing

Chadra Bhan Prasad, the only dalit writer for a major Indian weekly and a dalit rights activist who tends towards the secular end of the dalit movement's narrative structure, it was immediately evident that he was not even familiar with TBMSG, one of the major purveyors of the religious narrative of Ambedkar and dalit rights in Maharashtra. Though at first surprising, this observation seems more understandable given that Prasad, a native of Uttar Pradesh who is based in Delhi, is a strictly secular Ambedkarite who sees Ambedkar upon the backdrop of a Marxist analytical ideology of change. Now arguing that capitalism is the only thing that will save the dalit, Prasad draws an interesting comparison to the Ambedkar Buddhist activists of the TBMSG who see the solution for dalits as coming through the dharma.

This secular narrative structure implies that religious commitment can be sidelined in favour of an underlying, and more basic, commitment to humanism—an assumption, which runs deep in the dalit rights movement. One ICRD dalit activist even stated: "Despite the fact that many different dalit groups employ different strategies, our goal is the same." The idea that dalit activists' deploy diverging strategies despite common goals posits not only that dalit activists have one collective identity, but also that this collective's social justice concerns are all the same. Such broad assumptions, however, limit the effectiveness of dalit organizations by disempowering the potential to reflect on real difference.

Advocacy on Caste-based Discrimination

The current cooperation between Dalits and other caste-affected groups at the international level is predated by a long development at the domestic level of political awareness and self-organisation. The roots of this mobilisation are varied, stemming from endogenous resistance to the hierarchical structure of Hinduism, to the influence of external actors in shaping social relations. A long line of important activists that have influenced the contemporary movement. The anti-Brahmins were the first to conceive of 'rights' for Dalits, drawing from the liberal enlightenment thinkers and anti-slavery movements. They forged early forms of social organisation built upon by Dr. Ambedkar. Dr. Ambedkar's vision of Dalit emancipation and political rights, revealed in his extensive writings, continues to shape the goals of contemporary Dalit activists. His experimentation with political party mobilisation, his efforts to forge horizontal alliances with similar groups and his use of external powers to influence domestic political processes have been lessons for national Dalit NGOs. Likewise, the unsuccessful attempts at more militant tactics by the Dalit Panthers have likely dissuaded current civil society actors from using this approach. These experiences have pushed the mainstream of Dalit activism in a particular direction, combining grassroots civil society empowerment with international advocacy within a rights-based frame.

Transnational Advocacy Network

The contemporary Dalit movement is a web of organisations at the national and international level joined in "insider-outsider coalitions" of advocacy, research and/or funding relationships. Some of these actors have forged a transnational advocacy network (TAN) that is constituted by both vertical and horizontal relationships: horizontally, between domestic Dalit/caste NGOs within and (to a lesser extent) across borders; and vertically, by interactions of domestic NGOs with international NGOs and other IOs, such as UN institutions. The hub of the international caste TAN is the International Dalit Solidarity Network (IDSN), established in March 2000 as a focal point for transnational advocacy on caste-based discrimination. It brings together national Dalit and caste platforms and NGOs (e.g. the National Campaign on Dalit Human Rights (NCDHR); Dalit NGO Federation—Nepal (DNF); Buraku Liberation League), Dalit Solidarity Networks (e.g. DSN-UK) and key INGOs (e.g. IMADR, Lutheran World Federation, Human Rights Watch). The caste TAN is aided greatly by international donors, which serve both as targets and enablers of norm entrepreneurship. For example, governmental and inter-governmental donors (e.g. EU, DFID and DANIDA) have been persuaded to make Dalits a priority focus of their development work as one means of exerting pressure on governments of caste-affected states.

With the exception of appeals to the British authorities during decolonization and Dr. Ambedkar's overtures to the new UN, until the

1970s the focus and sphere of Dalit advocacy was strictly domestic. It took another twenty years before Dalits were making more sustained interventions at the international level, primarily within UN fora. These initial efforts at international advocacy were not well coordinated but they did manage to concentrate attention on international *human rights* institutions of the UN. This work forged early pathways within these institutions that had a strong influence on subsequent norm entrepreneurship by the caste TAN and helped to shape their normative agenda within a human rights – and specifically non-discrimination—frame.

The internationalization of advocacy on caste-based discrimination was enabled initially through the diaspora of Dalits that had migrated to Western states. A handful of organisations were established in the early 1970s and 1980s both inside and outside India that engaged in some transnational cooperation. These included the Federation of Ambedkarites and Buddhist Council established in the UK in 1970 and the Ambedkar Mission of Canada, located in Toront. Bob also names the Chennai-based Dalit Liberation Education Trust (DLET) and the Volunteers in Service to India's Oppressed and Neglected (VISION) based in Washington, D.C. as pioneering Dalit NGOs (176).

The first UN space in which the Dalit identity was asserted by civil society was the UN Sub-Commission on Human Rights. VISION first participated in the Sub-Commission in 1982, where its president, Dr. Laxmi Berwa, presented an intervention retelling the egregious issues faced by Dalits in India. After his intervention there is a long period of unexplained Dalit silence in the UN until the early 1990s. The only evidence of international action in the intervening period was an international meeting on 'Minority Strategies: Comparative Perspectives on Racism and Untouchability' organised by Minority Rights Group

(MRG) and held in New York in 1983; the Ambedkar Mission and VISION were among the participants. In 1991, Yogesh Varhade of the ACJP attended the UN Working Group on Indigenous Peoples (WGIP). It is not clear if the members of the WGIP readily accepted the Dalits as an 'indigenous people'. Two more domestic Dalit NGOs were present at the 1993 session of the WGIP (Dalit Youth Movement,

Dalit Solidarity Programme). The Working Group was a good entry point for Dalit NGOs because, unlike the Sub-Commission, participation in the WGIP did not require NGOs to have ECOSOC status with the UN. In 1994, many Dalit NGOs shifted from the WGIP to the UN Working Group on Minorities (WGM) for their advocacy. The DLET made its first appearance at the WGM in 1997, the NCDHR in 1999 and several other Dalit NGOs have followed since. The DLET and the ACJP participated in the 1993 World Conference on Human Rights in Vienna.

In the mid-1990s, several Dalit NGOs and INGOs tried to secure a UN investigation into caste, with a particular focus on India. For example, in 1996, the DLET, ACJP and the World Council of Churches submitted communications regarding the situation of Dalits in India to the UN Special Rapporteur on contemporary forms of racism urging him to conduct a country visit. The Special Rapporteur of this period, Mr. Gélé-Ahanhanzo, did manage some preliminary examination of the issue but made no concrete assertions as to whether caste should be considered under his mandate, concluding only that "specific attention should be given to the situation of the untouchables in India" and that a country visit was needed. The country visit to India never materialised but the exchange increased international attention on caste.

The queries of the Special Rapporteur were compounded by those made by CERD to India during the review of its periodic report on ICERD in 1996. The ACJP and the South Asian Human Rights Documentation Centre (SAHRDC) provided shadow reports/ information to CERD for its examination of India's periodic report urging them to raise the issue of discrimination on the basis of caste. This is reportedly the first time any NGO had submitted a shadow report on caste-based discrimination to a UN treaty body. It was an auspicious move for subsequent norm entrepreneurship on caste because it pushed CERD into taking a juridical position on whether caste fell within the remit of the committee.

By the late 1990s, Dalit NGOs and INGOs were exploring new institutions and approaches in their continued efforts to get international attention on caste. The DLET focused its efforts on interventions at the WGM in May 1997 and May 1998. In 1998, the

World Council of Churches urged the Sub-Commission "to undertake a study on caste-based discrimination and its manifestations in contemporary forms of slavery in the south Asian region". The intervention was made under the agenda item 'contemporary forms of slavery' marking a shift away from earlier interventions emphasizing racial discrimination or under the 'prevention of discrimination and protection of minorities' agenda item in the Sub-Commission.

These early representations of Dalit issues within international institutions were sporadic and lacked significant impact at the time. There did not appear to be a sustained effort to work with any one institution within the UN but a hopeful effort to raise the issue in as many fora as possible. The Dalit concerns did not fit easily into any identity frame either – indigenous rights, minority rights and racial discrimination were all attempted. Moreover, the normative agenda was only nascent – at most, activists sought to hold governments to account for existing domestic commitments on caste-based discrimination rather than creating new normative standards. Some points were made, however: Dalit concerns should be considered a human rights issue and caste-based discrimination was within the remit of ICERD. These advocates also put the Government of India on the defensive, prompting the Indian delegations to forge a position from the first Dalit intervention in 1982 at the Sub-Commission that caste-based discrimination was a matter of internal concern.

Formulating a Normative Agenda on Caste

Norm entrepreneurship by Dalits in the international sphere only started to solidify in the late 1990s when they began to build stronger horizontal relationships between Dalit groups and vertical relationships with INGOs and experts within IOs. From this organisational platform a second wave of transnational Dalit activism began and a normative agenda evolved.

The beginning of this second wave can be marked by the foundation of the NCDHR in October 1998 and by the *First World Dalit Convention* held in Kuala Lumpur the same month, organised primarily by Dalit NGOs from the diaspora in the US, UK and Canada under the name of the Dalit International Organisation. Both India and the UN human rights machinery are mentioned in their recommendations, which include a call for "the implementation of fundamental 'Human Rights' instrument for Dalits in India and other parts of the world" [sic]. A related follow-up event was held in London in September 2000, the *International Dalit Human Rights Conference,* organised by the Voice of Dalits International. These initiatives were important steps in consolidating transnational cooperation on Dalit advocacy but the norm emergence agenda was mostly absent, the cooperation serving primarily to put pressure on India.

Norm entrepreneurship on caste became more evident when Dalit activists forged stronger alliances with key human rights INGOs. The most important early international actor was Human Rights Watch (HRW). Bob reports that for many years Dalit activists had struggled unsuccessfully to get major human rights NGOs interested in caste-based discrimination until 1997 when HRW appointed Smita Narula to oversee a major research project on the situation of Dalits in India following increasing reports of violence against them. The report, *Broken People: Caste Violence Against India's "Untouchables"*, was published in 1999 and aimed to expose the issue to the international community. HRW was aided in its research by several Dalit activists, including Paul Divakar, Aloysius Irudayam, Henri Tiphagne, Ruth Manorama and Martin Macwan, who came together to reflect on the emerging report. Through a trio of meetings in Bangalore and Delhi it was agreed that to make the HRW report effective, a campaign was needed. The result was the creation of the NCDHR as a focal point. It was the first national coalition promoting Dalit human rights issues *qua* human rights, adopting the epithet "Dalit rights are human rights" as its rallying call. They undertook important domestic lobbying, using the golden jubilee of India's independence and the 50th anniversary of the UDHR to frame a major campaign that gathered 2.5 million signatures against caste-based discrimination. They also undertook a major project of documenting violations of human rights of Dalits, including publishing in 1999 a *Black Paper* on caste.

Although the campaign was visible, their leverage against the government was still weak. This work was supplemented with efforts to get the UN to take action in support of Dalits. Activists witnessed the impact of the Beijing and Vienna world conferences on domestic reforms and understood that India valued its reputation within the UN. By framing Dalit issues as human rights issues, they strategically situated their concerns within the (international) human rights discourse, enabling access to related political opportunity structures. It was hoped that international pressure would boost national advocacy and catalyse domestic reforms in an "insider-outsider" coalition effort.

NCDHR began to enlist further allies in the international sphere. One of the earliest stimulants was a meeting on contemporary forms of racism convened by the Geneva-based INGO the International Council on Human Rights Policy in December 1999. The meeting was organised to feed into the WCAR processes and brought together a select few actors from around the world to examine key issues of relevance. Among these was the issue of caste-based discrimination, represented by a working paper by Smita Narula of HRW. Martin Macwan of the Navsarjan Trust and then co-convener of the NCDHR and Atsuko Tanaka of IMADR were also present at the discussion. The meeting provided an important space to build up a nascent cooperation on a shared issue: HRW was engaged in India with the NCDHR and IMADR was long-linked to caste-issues through the Buraku Liberation League and had conducted some advocacy work on discrimination against Dalits.

In March 2000, a meeting was convened in London by the NCDHR and attended by HRW, IMADR, other Dalit NGOs, the few existing Dalit Solidarity Networks and interested INGOs, including Anti-Slavery International and the LWF. Together they established the International Dalit Solidarity Network as a vehicle for collective action on caste. The initial focus was on Dalits and the WCAR was one of the political opportunity structures in their sights. Peter Prove of the LWF reports that he raised the possibility at that meeting of securing a UN Sub-Commission resolution and report on caste-based discrimination, using existing good relations with some key Sub-Commission members. This set the caste-TAN down a norm emergence path, one that would take them through the UN Sub-Commission, cooperation with CERD and embroiled in controversy at the WCAR.

Three important factors shaped the normative agenda of the caste TAN: the desire to work within the UN; the absence of "caste" or Dalits in the lexicon of international law; and the opposition of India. Dalit advocates had long used human rights language to frame their concerns. Given that South Asia lacks any regional human rights institution the UN was the only IO with relevant state membership that could offer political opportunity structures for human rights advocacy. Members of the IDSN recognised there was a good chance to embed their claims institutionally within this UN human rights regime.

The caste TAN also had a degree of freedom regarding where in this human rights regime to focus their attention. There is no mention of 'caste' in any international human rights treaty and the UN human rights mechanisms had only dealt with the issue sporadically. Dalits and their allies therefore invested in institutionalizing the concept of caste-based discrimination within international law. This has helped to set clear parameters on what state practice should be and establishes a role for human rights monitoring mechanisms to encourage and scrutinize this practice.

Previous advocacy by Dalits had moved in and out of various mechanisms within the UN but two figured more prominently: the Sub-Commission and CERD. The Sub-Commission was an obvious ally because of its mandate to explore new human rights issues. CERD had been supportive in the past in considering caste-based discrimination to fall within the scope of ICERD. Members of the IDSN, such as Peter Prove and Atsuko Tanaka, had good relations with key actors in both of these institutions and recognised the potential for collaboration on norm emergence.

In these efforts the caste TAN faced one major opposition: the Government of India. India rejects any call for caste to be considered at the international level, asserting that its own advanced domestic measures are more than adequate and provide the appropriate remedies. The government is especially opposed to caste being considered under the rubric of racial discrimination, thus undermining attempts to use ICERD for norm entrepreneurship. Dalit leaders recognize that "caste may not be race" but maintain that in effect the practices are similar, with some going so far as to claim that caste is the first and/or worst form of racism. Their position has been disputed by some in civil society. Several prominent Indian academics, including André Béteille, Dipankar Gupta, and Soli Sorabjee, argue that while caste-based discrimination should be addressed, Dalits are politically, legally and scientifically misguided in their attempts to assert that caste is a form of racism, and, moreover, to use the UN as the vehicle for verifying their claims. The government itself has argued that any attempts by the UN to assert normative standards for the prevention of caste-based discrimination have in fact been a thinly veiled attack on one state, namely India. Until recently, with the exception of some capitulations of Nepal to CERD, no other caste-affected state had openly supported the development of new norms on caste-based discrimination nor accepted it to be within the scope of ICERD. India's stance was more or less unchallenged at the time.

To counter India's objections and diffuse its influence as a "critical state", the caste TAN has taken two tacks. The first is to expand the number of communities—and thus the number of states—being considered in the caste discourse, focusing not exclusively on Dalits or India but on groups across Asia and parts of Africa, in addition to the diaspora. This process was both proactive and reactive. Members of the IDSN report that the more they examined the issue of caste the more communities they found to be affected by analogous systems. The second tack is to avoid the language of caste in the normative agenda and to use instead 'discrimination based on work and descent'. This process was reactive. The language was initially formulated within the Sub-Commission upon the insistence of the Sub-Commissioner from India, Soli Sorabjee. It was clear that he would not support Sub-Commission investigation on the issue if caste was the explicit focus. This language also fit well with 'descent' as viewed by CERD and the two institutions have converged over time in their consideration of caste discrimination.

The normative agenda of the caste TAN quickly came to focus on three primary goals: recognition, norms and mechanisms. They wanted to secure recognition of caste-affected groups and of caste-based discrimination as a violation of international human rights law. Recognition of caste-affected groups would raise their profile in international society and increase the ability of these groups to gain the support of international actors in pushing for change at the domestic level. The acceptance that caste-based discrimination was a violation of international law would provide a short-cut to norm emergence by drawing on existing standards to outline a normative profile for the prohibition of caste-based discrimination without having to create new standards from scratch. The studies of the Sub-Commission could provide authoritative research on the groups and applicable international law; the WCAR could name caste-affected groups and recognize the prohibition of caste-based discrimination, serving as a soft law standard; and CERD could reiterate its claims that caste-based discrimination came under 'descent' in ICERD, firmly entrenching it in international law. Activists admit that the rubrics of racial discrimination and descent are not a perfect fit with caste-based identities and structures but reason that it is closely related and constitutes a sound "adjacency" strategy for norm emergence. The propensity for CERD to argue in this way further persuaded advocates to use this as the foundation of their normative claims. States also would need guidance on appropriate behaviour for eradicating caste-based discrimination and the Sub-Commission, WCAR and CERD could elaborate this in their respective recommendations to states. Finally, monitoring mechanisms to investigate state compliance with these emerging norms were also needed; the WCAR follow-up mechanisms and CERD could assist in this regard but the creation of a UN Special Rapporteur with specific responsibility to investigate caste-based discrimination would be even better.

Creating Opportunities for Socialisation

Post-Durban mobilisation by the caste TAN has aimed to socialise international actors and states to the concerns of caste-affected communities and to persuade them to exert pressure on caste-affected states. After Durban, the caste TAN focused on bringing new actors into a dialogue on caste. In late 2004, the IDSN co-convened the *International Consultation on Caste-Based Discrimination: Establishing Dalit Rights in the Contemporary World; the Role of Governments, the United Nations and the Private Sector* in Kathmandu. The output was the *Kathmandu Dalit Declaration,* providing nearly 100 paragraphs of recommendations. This was an important contribution to norm elaboration, drafted with direct participation of caste-affected groups. Among the most prominent national events was the India-wide *Bhopal Conference: Charting A New Course For Dalits For The 21st Century,* held in January 2002, which issued the Bhopal Declaration of detailed recommendations to the Indian government and the private sector. This meeting was followed up with an International Dalit Conference in Vancouver in

May 2003. The caste-based mobilisation around the 2004 World Social Forum held in India is also noteworthy. At the World Social Forum Polycentric held in Karachi in 2006, the South Asian national Dalit platforms consolidated to form an umbrella organisation, the South Asia Dalit Rights Forum (later renamed the Asian Dalit Rights Movement (ADRM)). At the People's SAARC Summit in Kathmandu in 2007, they issued a 'Charter of demands' asking, *inter alia,* that South Asian governments "Declare 2007- 2017, the SAARC (South Asian Association for Regional Cooperation) Dalit Rights Decade with concrete Acts, Policies, Programmes and Action Plan". The socialisation of SAARC to caste-based discrimination is an important innovation given that Dalit activists have previously focused almost exclusively on national or UN (and some EU) institutions in their advocacy. The scope for SAARC to include human rights in its mandate is unclear but the issue of caste could be an important catalyst for change in this direction and more attractive to India, diffusing unilateral scrutiny given the presence of Dalits in most SAARC member states.

The caste TAN increasingly has targeted influential states, aiming to change their discursive position on caste and to bring external pressure to bear on governments of countries with caste-affected groups. They have focused on EU institutions and on the governments in countries where Dalit solidarity networks are based. The IDSN has worked with the European Parliament to secure a number of statements and resolutions in favour of Dalits in India. The US Congress has also issued several statements encouraging the government of India to do more for Dalits. The UK Parliament has had debates on the issue of caste-based discrimination, with a focus on India. A hearing on caste discrimination was held in September 2008 in the Danish Parliament under the auspices of the Foreign Affairs Committee. All of these initiatives have fallen short of proposing economic or other sanctions against India, despite calls for such action from Dalit activists engaged in dialogue with these institutions. They have, however, socialised new actors to their cause and institutionalised discursive positions in a handful of declaratory statements.

In April 2009, the UN convened a Durban Review Conference (DRC) to assess progress in implementation of the DDPA. Dalit advocates were active in the DRC processes. This engagement was tempered by the absence of any reference to caste or to 'discrimination based on work and descent' in the WCAR documents but activists focused on references to 'descent' in lieu. India raised objections to the accreditation of several Dalit-focused NGOs, including the IDSN, the National Federation of Dalit Women and People's Watch Tamil Nadu. At the preparatory sessions the delegations of both India and Nepal underscored their objections to consideration of caste within the DRC. In contrast, the interventions of the EU Member States referenced the CERD General Recommendation XXIX to support discussion of caste in the DRC and the accreditation of caste-focused NGOs. Several states referred to caste-based discrimination in their high-level DRC interventions, including Nepal, Bangladesh, Pakistan, Mauritius and Slovenia, evidence of a change in discursive positions. Caste-focused advocates held a series of successful side-events and organised an effective media strategy, thus keeping their issues on the agenda. Given the preeminence of Durban in the transnational mobilisation of caste-affected groups their absence in the DRC outcome document was noted by several news reports and NGO interventions.

State and international actors may be more socialised to the realities of caste-based discrimination but still unwilling to persuade India into reforms. No state actively pushed for inclusion of discrimination based on work and descent in the DRC. Members of the caste TAN report that some British MEPs have been obstructive in their efforts to pass the European Parliament resolutions on Dalits. At the end of 2007, the caste TAN had an initial commitment from the European Commission to adopt a specific line of work on Dalits but witnessed a retreat by the Commission following country consultations (including with India) on their proposals. While individual staff members of the Commission remained supportive of the work, the official line was that such actions could be mainstreamed under work on minorities and vulnerable groups.

The Role of UN Human Rights Institutions

The caste TAN targeted the WCAR because the discourse and outcome of the WCAR processes would have been an effective stepping-stone to future (hard law) norms for the prohibition of caste-based discrimination. In the end, Durban could not deliver but it was never the only focus of their international advocacy. Two other bodies stand out: the UN Sub-Commission on Human Rights and the UN Committee on the Elimination of Racial Discrimination (CERD).

UN Sub-Commission on Human Rights

The UN Sub-Commission is an important forum for norm elaboration and institutionalization because it is mandated to examine emerging issues in the field of human rights. This has given the caste TAN a receptive environment for developing a broader understanding of caste-based discrimination and its prohibition in international law.

The first goal was to secure a Sub-Commission study on the issue, echoing earlier calls by Dalit advocates. The caste TAN was successful where past advocates were not because they had expertise on how to secure a report and strong relations with Sub-Commissioners willing to pursue this agenda. At the August 2000 session Paul Divakar of the NCDHR made an intervention urging the Sub-Commission to "commission a study of the situation of Dalits in South Asia and similar communities in Japan, Senegal and Nigeria". MRG, Pax Romana and the Lutheran World Federation also addressed caste in their interventions at the same session, the latter recommending a "study of discrimination based on caste or descent".

The Sub-Commission responded to these calls and passed Resolution 2000/4 on Discrimination Based on Work and Descent at the August 2000 session recommending, *inter alia,* a working paper on the subject. This was the first such resolution of the Sub-Commission on the issue of caste and came only after a heated debate among the Sub-Commission members. Notably, the language of caste is not used in the resolution, nor are terms such as 'Dalit' or 'Untouchable'. The principal objections came from Sub-Commissioner Soli Sorabjee (then Attorney-General of India) who was unable to accept the language of 'caste' given its strong association with India. He (informally) proposed instead the formulation 'discrimination based on occupation and descent', later morphed into 'work and descent' to secure a sound corresponding French translation of 'l'emploi et l'ascendance'. By keeping the frame broad, the Sub-Commission could proceed with the study without raising the alarm among concerned states that might have a pretext to object if caste-based discrimination were the explicit focus. The formulation of the 'work and descent' term created a new category of community in the international lexicon, namely those groups affected by discrimination based on work and descent. This was not the terminology initially sought by the caste TAN but it did enable further consideration of the issue at a critical juncture.

In August 2001, pursuant to Sub-Commission Resolution 2000/4, Sub-Commission expert Rajendra K.W. Goonesekere, a Sri Lankan national, presented his working paper on discrimination based on work and descent. He provided a preliminary analysis of the relationship between ascribed occupation and discrimination and attempted to outline the legal framework for its prohibition, referring firstly to the inclusion of 'descent' in ICERD and CERD's interpretation thereof "to mean not solely race but tribal or caste distinctions as well". Goonesekere limited the paper's focus to India, Sri Lanka, Nepal, Japan and Pakistan but stated that further study of African countries in particular was warranted.

Goonesekere was not re-elected to the Sub-Commission in 2002 with the effect that no further report on discrimination based on work and descent was presented at the August 2002 session of the Sub-Commission. In June 2003, Sub-Commissioners Asbjørn Eide and Yozo Yokota submitted an expanded working paper. They included a wider focus on several African countries. They also proposed an analytical framework of commonalities across cultures on this kind of discrimination, drawing the conclusion that "This form of discrimination is distinct, in its combination of causal factors and expressions, from other forms of discrimination examined in the history of the Sub-Commission". This statement suggests the need to recognise a discrete category of inquiry within the Sub-Commission, separate from existing categories like minorities or racial discrimination long common to the agenda of the Sub-Commission.

Eide and Yokota submitted a second expanded working paper in July 2004. This paper provides an analysis of the legal provisions on work and descent-based discrimination in several countries along with a review of CERD and CRC comments on state periodic reports relevant to the issue. Further research is also provided on diaspora communities where descent-based discrimination exists, in particular among the South Asian and Somali diaspora. The paper concludes with a proposed framework for a draft set of principles and guidelines for the elimination of discrimination based on work and descent and a recommendation to appoint a Special Rapporteur to prepare a finalized version. The authors demonstrate a clear desire to see this discrimination asserted within the framework of international human rights law, giving a helpful endorsement to norm emergence on caste. The report recommends that:

The principles expounded in the [principles and guidelines] document should, at a minimum, include the following:

> (a) Discrimination based on work and descent is a form of discrimination prohibited by international human rights law, including the International Convention on the Elimination of All Forms of Racial Discrimination. The basis of this prohibition in international human rights law could be further explicated.

The suggestion for "explication" provides an important norm emergence platform for reinterpreting existing standards and for perhaps creating new standards specifically on discrimination based on work and descent.

The Government of India was not satisfied with the Sub-Commission's persistence in making discrimination based on work and descent a major focus of its work and argued at the presentation of the August 2004 expanded working paper, that "it would be counterproductive for the Sub-Commission to develop a set of principles and guidelines on the question". It is therefore significant that in April 2005 when the UN Commission on Human Rights had before it the proposal for a Special Rapporteur to prepare a set of principles and guidelines on discrimination based on work and descent, India did not block the appointment. This was enabled by a *modus vivendi* between the caste TAN and India to focus on 'work and descent' instead of caste explicitly. Moreover, the caste TAN made clear to the Indian delegation that being obstructive as India had been in Durban would only serve to increase attention to the issue.

Yozo Yokota and Chin-Sung Chung were appointed as the Special Rapporteurs to prepare a comprehensive study and to finalise a "draft set of principles and guidelines for the effective elimination of discrimination based on work and descent". The mandate was operationally weak, offering no provisions for country visits or regional meetings. The process of consultation and research on the report was facilitated greatly by the IDSN and its domestic NGO partners. They organised a series of 'informal' (i.e. not by government invitation) visits to Bangladesh, Pakistan and India to meet with Dalit representatives. Plans to hold additional consultations in Africa never materialised. They engaged international institutions through a consultation organised by IDSN in Geneva in March 2006, attended by representatives of caste-affected groups, INGOs, and UN agencies including the World Bank and the ILO. A specific meeting on Dalit women's rights was held in The Hague in November 2006. Finally, an informal consultation on the draft principles and guidelines was convened in Kathmandu in April 2007 by IDSN and OHCHR, attended also by two other UN Special Rapporteurs (on racism and on indigenous peoples).

The Special Rapporteurs submitted their proposed principles and guidelines in June 2007 but the adoption was forestalled by institutional changes in the UN, namely transfer of mandates to the new Human Rights Council. With India as a member of the Council and the caste TAN struggled to get any state to expend the political capital necessary to push for the adoption of the principles and guidelines. The principles and guidelines were finally made public in May 2009, submitted only as a working paper of the Council and therefore not formally endorsed.

The final report prepared by the Special Rapporteurs provides an overview of their activities, state submissions and the "Draft Principles and Guidelines for the Effective Elimination of Discrimination Based on Work and Descent". Only five states officially submitted information: Japan, Colombia, the Republic of Croatia, the Federal Republic of Germany and Mauritius. Many of the recommendations are drawn from consultations with caste-affected communities (primarily Dalits) and international actors, including the UN Special Rapporteurs on racism and on the human rights of indigenous people. The Draft Principles and Guidelines make clear that "Discrimination based on work and descent is a form of discrimination prohibited by international human rights law". A definition of discrimination based on work and descent also is offered:

> Discrimination based on work and descent is any distinction, exclusion, restriction, or preference based on inherited status such as caste, including present or ancestral occupation, family, community or social origin, name, birth place, place of residence, dialect and accent that has the purpose or effect of nullifying or impairing the recognition, enjoyment, or exercise, on an equal footing, of human rights and fundamental freedoms in the political, economic, social, cultural, or any other field of public life. This type of discrimination is typically associated with the notion of purity and pollution and practices of untouchability, and is deeply rooted in societies and cultures where this discrimination is practiced.

The definition is notable for two reasons. First, it is modelled on Article 1.1 of ICERD make note that the definition "accordingly supports and encourages consistency with existing international law on the subject of discrimination, and should be read as such." This is important for "adjacency" in developing new norms on caste discrimination. Second, it does not subsume caste-based discrimination within ICERD *per se* but appears to establish this as a distinct form of discrimination. This could allay objections like those of India because it does not frame caste-based discrimination specifically as *racial* discrimination. This also opens up the possibility of a completely new international instrument, what some advocates have termed an International Convention Against the Elimination of all Forms of Caste-based Discrimination. The report concludes by acknowledging that "the issue of discrimination based on work and descent is regarded as a *specific* and important human rights issue to be properly addressed by the international community" (emphasis added), one that is found not only in South Asia but also in "parts of Africa, Latin America, and the Middle East and some countries of Western Europe".

The achievement of securing two Special Rapporteurs on discrimination based on work and descent was vital for the continuation of norm emergence and marked the realisation of a goal articulated at Durban in the NGO Forum outcome document. The reports, meetings and country visits of the Special Rapporteurs have kept the issue at the forefront of UN human rights dialogue and pushed states to engage in this dialogue. It has reinforced caste-based discrimination as a global concern necessitating intervention from the (global) UN level. The principles and guidelines developed by the

Special Rapporteurs will mark stronger institutionalisation of the norms, an important step in norm emergence.

Committee on the Elimination of Racial Discrimination

The fact that descent-based discrimination has not been well explored juridically in the past means that norm entrepreneurs have a greater scope for shaping new understandings of that norm and its implementation. Rather than trying to secure an entirely new international standard specifically on caste in the short term, the caste TAN has sought instead to 'reuse' an existing standard by expanding the normative interpretation of Article 1.1 of ICERD defining racial discrimination for the purposes of the treaty application. Article 1.1 includes 'descent' among the categories upon which racial discrimination can be based. CERD has interpreted this to cover caste-based discrimination, understanding caste as a system based on status at birth. Using ICERD also serves to frame Dalit concerns within an area of international law, i.e. racial discrimination, that is a deeply entrenched norm and widely considered part of the 'obligations *erga omnes*' of states making it a matter of international concern.

CERD is in a strategic position for norm emergence and socialisation, legitimated by its authority to review and comment on state practice and to establish jurisprudence on themes pertaining to the interpretation of ICERD in practice. CERD has prompted caste-affected states to consider their obligations towards caste-affected groups in light of their ICERD commitments and thereby to see the prohibition and prevention of caste-based discrimination as part of international human rights law.

States that might not otherwise recognise that caste-affected groups exist within their territory may be publicly called to account for obligations towards these communities by CERD. In this regard, the Committee also relies heavily on information from civil society actors in the form of shadow/alternative reports. These reports help to secure recognition of caste-affected groups and their concerns at the international level. CERD also has the mandate to produce General Recommendations to help states understand better the scope and application of the ICERD and undertook to elaborate a General Recommendation on Article 1, paragraph 1 of the Convention

(Descent). This has proven to be an important instrument of norm emergence and institutionalisation.

CERD has reviewed state reports of several countries where caste-based discrimination exists, including Nepal, Bangladesh, India, Japan, Mali, Nigeria, Pakistan, Senegal and Yemen. The earliest and the most important interactions have been with India. India ratified ICERD in December 1968. In 1986, it submitted its eighth and ninth periodic reports to CERD and after a gap of ten years submitted a consolidated report of its tenth to fourteenth periodic reports in 1996. In the 1986 session, CERD asked several questions about scheduled castes and untouchability, to which the Indian delegation responded without hesitation, making no apparent objections to the queries. By 1996, the government's tone had changed, following a more pointed approach by CERD in expressing its opinion that caste came under 'descent' in ICERD. The periodic report submitted in 1996 presents the following explanation of the government's view:

> Article 1 of the Convention includes in the definition of racial discrimination the term "descent". Both castes and tribes are systems based on "descent" since people are normally born into a particular caste or a particular tribe. It is obvious, however, that the use of the term "descent" in the Convention clearly refers to "race". Communities which fall under the definition of Scheduled Castes and Scheduled Tribes are unique to Indian society and its historical process. As conveyed to the Committee during the presentation of India's last periodic report, it is, therefore, submitted that the policies of the Indian Government relating to Scheduled Castes and Scheduled Tribes do not come under the purview of Article 1 of the Convention. As a matter of courtesy to the members of the Committee, the Government is, however, happy to provide any information that they may require on this subject.

India submitted its next (consolidated) periodic report in 2006. The position on caste within ICERD is maintained. The delegates detail their objections to considering caste within ICERD, arguing, "Caste was an institution unique to India, and had not entered into the considerations of those who drafted the Convention". This includes India, which had originally proposed the category of 'descent' under Article 1.1 in the treaty drafting process, reportedly not to address caste but "based on concerns regarding discriminatory treatment against

Indians in their own land while under colonial rule, and to persons of Indian descent in countries where they had settled in large numbers". The Indian delegation also noted with some criticism that "The Committee had first raised the issue of caste-based discrimination within the concept of discrimination based on descent over 30 years after its establishment", implying that the current views of CERD were *ex post facto* and motivated by something other than impartial juridical analysis.

CERD nevertheless has asserted its interpretative authority: in the Concluding Observations on India's report in 2007, CERD "maintains its position expressed in general recommendation No. 29 "that discrimination based on 'descent' includes discrimination against members of communities based on forms of social stratification such as caste and analogous systems of inherited status which nullify or impair their equal enjoyment of human rights". As a point of law, both the position of CERD and India are arguable. David Keane's (2007) in-depth analysis of caste-based discrimination in international law sums up the dialectic well, finding "descent was unrelated to caste when it was introduced into article 1(1) of the ICERD. Nevertheless, CERD is entitled to interpret the provisions of the Convention in a manner that allows the treaty to engage with all forms of racial discrimination".

Despite India's obstinacy, the February 2007 review of the state report provided an important platform for renewed Dalit mobilisation at the international level. Dalit NGOs cooperated with the Center for Human Rights and Global Justice and HRW to produce an extensive shadow report, *Hidden Apartheid: Caste Discrimination Against India's Untouchable*). This was complemented by several other NGO submissions, including a coalition-based submission by the NCDHR.

The NGO actors and the CERD Country Rapporteur for India, Linos-Alexander Sicilianos, were keen to capitalize on what they regarded as a marginal shift in the Indian position: the Indian Prime Minister Manmohan Singh at a national meeting on minorities and Dalits in December 2006 acknowledged:

> Dalits have faced a unique discrimination in our society that is fundamentally different from the problems of minority groups in general. The only parallel to the practice of untouchability was apartheid in South Africa.

The reference to apartheid is highly significant in the context of ICERD. Article 3 of the convention reads:

> States Parties particularly condemn racial segregation and apartheid and undertake to prevent, prohibit and eradicate all practices of this nature in territories under their jurisdiction.

CERD has been active in raising the issue of descent-based discrimination with an increasing number of countries. In this dialogue, states have taken a range of responses, from openly accepting that ICERD includes caste (Nepal), to adopting the Indian interpretation and rejecting that ICERD includes caste (Japan), to denying that caste-affected communities exist within their territory (Nigeria). CERD has also raised the issue in its review of diaspora states, such as the UK: in the Concluding Observations issued in 2003, CERD implies that the UK should consider adopting legislation for the prohibition of descent-based discrimination. This had the effect of introducing a completely new issue into the scope of the UK's reporting on ICERD, which has never previously mentioned caste.

Although the interpretations by CERD hold weight in international law, it is state practice that ultimately determines the scope of Article 1.1. Given that India is the "critical state" in this issue because it has the largest caste-affected population, so long as the Government of India refuses to accept this interpretation of ICERD, the scope of Article 1.1 remains in question. It is worth noting here that other UN treaty bodies, including the Human Rights Committee, the Committee on Economic, Social and Cultural Rights, the Committee on the Rights of the Child and the Committee on the Elimination of Discrimination Against Women, have also raised issues pertaining to caste-based discrimination in their dialogues with states. The more CERD and other treaty bodies can socialise states to their views, the greater the likelihood that changes in state practice will occur and a new norm could emerge regardless of India's objections.

CERD General Recommendation on Descent

CERD's efforts to see states give more attention to the issue of caste and analogous systems have been facilitated by the adoption in 2002 of General Recommendation XXIX on Article 1.1 of ICERD (Descent).

The General Recommendation was an important step in the institutionalization of new norms prohibiting caste-based discrimination. It has given CERD a concrete reference point for its critique of state practice and gives states a standard of achievement against which to measure their own implementation of ICERD vis-à-vis caste-affected communities. CERD also has facilitated an "adjacency" claim by situating caste in an existing normative framework to hasten and increase the likelihood of its acceptance.

The thematic discussion format brought together several NGOs, experts and the state delegations of India and Nepal in a quasi-formal dialogue. The NGOs present were primarily INGOs or domestic NGOs from Africa and Asia. Some 23 NGOs made statements to the thematic discussion, including one joint statement undersigned by 26 NGOs such as the NCDHR and other South Asian national Dalit platforms, IDSN, IMADR, Lutheran World Federation and five African NGOs from Nigeria, Senegal, Kenya, Niger and Somalia.

The proposal for a thematic discussion on 'descent' came in August 2001, following recommendations from members of the IDSN for such a session. According to Paul Divakar, a visit of CERD member Patrick Thornberry to India earlier in 2001 as part of an MRG workshop on advocacy training for Dalits was also an important catalyst. The timing was crucial, picking up the ball from the Sub-Commission after Goonesekere's absence threatened to derail the momentum on examining caste. Four members of the Sub-Commission also participated, providing a direct link between their discourse on discrimination based on work and descent with that of CERD.

The substantive scope of the thematic discussion was the source of some controversy. Not all CERD members were convinced that discrimination based on work and descent should be the main focus and were more inclined to using the rubric of 'descent' for a discussion on people of African descent, particularly post-WCAR where the group figured so prominently. Given the absence of 'work and descent' in the WCAR outcome documents, however, the focus on caste came to be privileged, evidence of the drive of some members of CERD to ensure caste would get an international hearing post-Durban. The Recommendation is not *limited* to caste-based discrimination; indeed it explicitly notes "discrimination based on 'descent' includes discrimination [...] based on forms of social stratification such as caste and analogous systems of inherited status" and gives reference to "persons of Asian and African descent and indigenous and other forms of descent in the Durban Declaration and Programme of Action" (preamble). Furthermore, several CERD members, and in particular Raghavan Pillai from India, took pains to stress that caste-based discrimination should not be the only focus of discussion. His caution was prudent, given that the Indian delegate, Rajesh Prasad, stated his concern that "the thematic discussion has been transformed into a debate of the situation allegedly (pertaining) to a particular country". In this regard, efforts to bring non-Indian and non-Asian NGOs to the discussion was equally prudent.

The Committee decided not to attempt a definition of 'descent'. This has kept the self-identification of groups affected by descent-based discrimination more open. The content of the Recommendation is broad, focusing on practical measures in several areas such as education, women's rights, the media and civil, economic, political and social rights. One of the first suggestions is that states "Consider the incorporation of an explicit prohibition of descent-based discrimination in the national constitution". Securing such a measure would be another key step for achieving norm emergence, designating a *distinct* category for this kind of discrimination and necessitating new action on the part of states.

In both its review of state reports and its elaboration of General Recommendations, CERD has proven to be a key elaborator and socialisation agent for new norms on the prohibition of caste-based discrimination. It has established a broad-based understanding of 'descent' in order to address the experiences of a wide range of affected groups. In so doing it has also avoided accusations of targeting individual states. As CERD increases the number of states to whom it addresses its concerns on 'descent'-based discrimination, it is directly contributing to norm emergence. As Thornberry points out, "Not all governments have objected to CERD activity [on caste], and even where objections have been lodged, the objecting governments have striven to emphasise the positive and ongoing nature of their efforts to combat this form of discrimination". This presents a dilemma for the caste TAN: in the short-term, use of CERD is helpful for norm entrepreneurship in the absence of other mechanisms but in the long-term, creation of a distinct mechanism might overcome the objections of states to the 'race' frame that CERD conveys. CERD can influence the discursive position of states, enable the norms to strengthen and to stimulate new "logics of appropriateness" for states either within ICERD or (ultimately) adjacent to it.

UN Special Rapporteur on Racism

Although the first Special Rapporteur on racism made some preliminary investigations into caste, the second Special Rapporteur, Doudou Diène, made caste a key theme in his work. Activists credit Diène for making a personal commitment to this issue but the shift can be attributed also to the work of members of the IDSN in raising the profile of the issue within the UN, evidenced in part by an increasing number of communications on caste issues to the Special Rapporteur, including from African countries. In his 2003 report to the UN General Assembly Diène recommended "The question of castes [...] should be given priority in the follow-up to the Durban Conference, the fight against all forms of discrimination and the promotion of human rights worldwide". Furthermore, in a 2007 report, he noted the relevance of caste-based discrimination to his mandate and announced his intention to focus on this issue in several activities in 2007. A country visit by the Special Rapporteur to Japan in 2005 was important for bringing attention to the Buraku community, an effort facilitated in large part by IMADR. Diène has also reiterated his interest to visit India as part of a regional visit including also Pakistan and Nepal to examine, *inter alia,* caste-based discrimination.

The Government of India has maintained its view that caste should not be seen within the purview of 'racial discrimination', criticizing Diène for undertaking this in his mandate. Diène for his part emphasizes the 'related forms of intolerance' aspect of his mandate to accommodate attention to caste without entering directly into debates on the normative aspects of this issue. His impact is nonetheless normative, because through his work caste-based discrimination is being kept on the international agenda. A small number of other Special Rapporteurs, like that on adequate housing and on violence against women, have also mentioned Dalits or other caste-affected groups in their regular reports and country visits. The cumulative effect is that attention to caste-affected groups becomes more and more a 'mainstreamed' consideration of Special Rapporteurs' thematic reports and country visits, thereby contributing to the norm emergence and socialisation processes.

Assessing the Impact of UN institutional Allies

The human rights institutions given attention in this section, the Sub-Commission on Human Rights, CERD and the Special Rapporteurs on racism and on discrimination based on work and descent, have each been important for enabling the emergence of a new set of norms pertaining to caste-based discrimination. They have been both leaders and followers in this process, at once dependent on NGO input and pressure whilst also taking the lead in asserting their own interpretations.

The (quasi-) permanent status of these institutions has meant that the issue of caste could be considered in a longer-term process than that afforded by the WCAR. Indeed, each of these institutions was considering caste well before and after the WCAR. Moreover, given that the WCAR outcome documents failed to mention caste-based discrimination, the caste TAN has been excluded formally from benefiting from the WCAR follow-up mechanisms. These human rights bodies have therefore served as an important alternative space. The regularised meetings of the Sub-Commission and CERD have given caste-advocates stable and predictable fora against which to plan long-term joint advocacy strategies. The fact that states are engaged directly in dialogue with each of these institutions has also made them important socialisation agents for states; CERD and the Special Rapporteur on racism in particular are able to engage in detailed country-specific recommendations on adhering to emergent norms on the prohibition of caste-based discrimination. Both have demonstrated their willingness to raise these issues even in the face of state opposition.

Certain members of CERD, the Sub-Commission and the Special Rapporteur on racism have also become socialised themselves to the issue of caste and have taken personal initiatives to see that the issue is considered further within their operational mandates. The epistemic community of human rights experts has proven a good pool from which to draw allies. These actors, conscious of the vagaries of international diplomacy from years of experience, have also successfully manoeuvred the discussions on caste through the rocky waters of state obstruction. Despite their insistence they are not acting according to a political agenda in their investigations of caste, the actors understood the sensitivity of the issue to many states.

The collective outputs of the Sub-Commission in its working papers on work and descent, CERD in its General Recommendation and Concluding Observations, and the Special Rapporteur in his annual/country reports have begun to shape norms on caste-based discrimination. States now have a body of recommendations that spell out clearly their responsibilities vis-à-vis caste-affected communities. The principles and guidelines prepared by the Special Rapporteurs on work and descent solidify this further. The more the norms are institutionalised, the less free will states be to deny knowledge and application of them.

These actors have been aware of the factors that can enable new norms to emerge. The adjacency principle is well understood by international lawyers and the experts have been careful to link their understanding of caste-based discrimination to the existing framework of international human rights law. This is most obvious in the case of CERD that has used a widely ratified treaty, ICERD, and a vague concept, 'descent', in which to embed the caste issue. By framing the protection of caste-affected groups under an existing norm – i.e. non-discrimination based on descent – the caste TAN has taken a short-cut to norm emergence, accessing an existing legally-binding standard and review structure. The trade-off has been the reluctance of states – particularly India – to accept the 'racial' rubric conferred by ICERD. The long-term development of a distinct standard and mechanism not associated with race *per se* may alleviate some of these state objections.

The frames used to construct this normative discourse have not come solely from the caste TAN but have been shaped in tandem with (and certified by) these international actors: the Sub-Commission created the frame of 'work and descent'; CERD has placed the emphasis on 'descent'; and the Special Rapporteur on racism has asserted that caste-based discrimination is a 'form of intolerance' within his mandate. Activists and IOs have used alternatives to 'caste-based discrimination' strategically to advance the normative agenda despite state opposition. In doing so they have not made recognition of the Dalit identity *per se* a priority, substituting this identity for more generic formulations.

This expansion of the identity frame is one way in which the outputs of CERD, the Sub-Commission and the Special Rapporteurs have helped to frame the issue as global. Being UN actors, their attention to the issue already suggests a global, as opposed to regional, relevance of this issue. In their commentaries they have consistently maintained that the issue of discrimination based on work and descent extends far beyond South Asia, not only to other Asian and African states but to diaspora countries as well.

Dalits, Caste, and Work and Descent

'Framing' of issues and identities is a crucial part of norm entrepreneurship. Through effective framing, Dalits have forged transnational links with other caste-affected groups, found useful allies in human rights institutions, challenged the assumptions of caste hierarchy and justified the need for caste-specific mechanisms in international law. This section will examine the framing process, starting with framing in the domestic sphere and then moving to the international discourse. Given that Dalits and other caste-affected groups have been pushed to the margins on the basis of socially constructed notions of privilege and 'pollution', it seems only fitting that these groups should use new social constructions of their own design for emancipation.

Creating New Identity Frames

Dalits have had to contend with many identity frames imposed on them from above. The British introduced 'depressed classes' and 'scheduled castes', Gandhi termed them *harijans* (children of God), upper castes termed them 'Untouchables' and even the term 'caste' is said to be a European import, derived from the Portuguese 'casta' (or Latin *castus*, meaning 'purity of breed'). The term 'Dalit' is not endogenous to the Hindu caste system but was created as a tool for mobilisation and empowerment. The term originally means 'broken people' in the Indic language Marathi. It was introduced by Dr. Ambedkar into the anti-caste discourse and has been used to denote the status of Dalits as a *people* rather than a social category, supporting as well their claims to be the original inhabitants of the Indian sub-continent. Dr. Ambedkar, and his predecessor Phule, shared the view that 'Untouchables' were the pre-Aryan inhabitants of India, subjugated by the invaders into positions of low status. He went further to argue that Dalits were originally Buddhist peoples and the Hindu religion was imposed upon them, a view designed to unite Dalits across India that were embedded in highly fragmented sub-castes and regional cultures.

The Dalit identity frame has over time taken on cultural markers as well, to unify and to build esteem for the identity. The manipulation of the identity frame in this way has aimed to consolidate the social and political mobilisation of Dalits at the same time as emancipating Dalits from the caste structure of Hinduism. This frame also potentially positions the Dalits for ethnogenesis. Many Dalit leaders no longer regard Dalits as mere 'outgroups' but as distinct communities with a shared social and cultural history portrayed as indigenous to the territory of modern India. The contemporary Dravidian movement in southern India has predicated its bids for secession on similar grounds, staking its claim in the liberation of a 'people' classified as backward classes by the Aryan invaders from the North.

The construction of the Dalit identity frame has important parallels with the construction of the 'indigenous peoples' identity frame: in both cases, the frame contends they are original inhabitants who retain certain (moral and material) entitlements having been unjustly denied equality by external 'colonising' forces. Dalits are unlikely candidates for secession but the Dravidian movement sets an interesting precedence and at least one Dalit leader admits that the armed mobilisation tactics of the Naxalites (or Nepalese Maoists) have benefited all Dalits by pushing actors to take their claims more seriously.

The term 'Dalit' did not take on political significance in India until the early 1970s when the Dalit Panthers used it in their discourse , gaining currency from the Dalit cultural movement's use of the term in the 1960s. The frame is clearly seen as empowering for domestic actors, building esteem of community members. This continues to be the preferred term of Dalits in India, on the international stage, and in other states.

The Dalit frame has not been transposed to other caste-systems, however, and the transnational coalition of caste-affected groups assert a number of different identity frames locally. In Japan, 'buraku' refers to a village where 'outcastes' live and Buraku people are the (outcaste) people from that village. Such communities were originally designated as Eta (extreme filth) and Hinin (non-human) classes. The government now uses instead the term 'Dowa' to describe these 'buraku'. In other caste-systems, the names given to caste-affected group usually translate as 'slaves and slave descendants' or 'caste peoples' in local languages. It is easy to understand why leaders within these communities would wish to articulate new identity frames that provide constituents with a greater sense of empowerment and which can become a vehicle for mobilisation.

Creating a Global Identity

Bringing these diverse communities into the common 'caste' frame is a recent innovation. Dr. Ambedkar himself said, "Untouchability among the Hindus is a unique phenomenon, unknown to humanity in other parts of the world". By finding a frame broad enough in which to situate very diverse experiences, however, advocates on caste have been able to swell their numbers and thus their leverage. The leverage is further enhanced by the fact that the groups using the caste frame extend well beyond one sub-region (i.e. South Asia) and across continents. This means that more states are implicated in the issue, increasing the justification for caste to be considered at the international level and in international law.

The global 'work and descent-based discrimination' frame is primarily a construction of INGOs, international experts and a small cadre of Dalit activists rather than of domestic caste-advocates writ large. Advocates were savvy to the constraints of the international system regarding norm elaboration, understanding that targeting a new norm at a single state or sub-region would be difficult. They accepted the need to steer the discussion away from spotlighting India and the

Hindu caste system and towards the elaboration of broad-based concepts applicable to multiple (even all) states. The use of the 'work and descent' and 'descent' frames are evidence in point – neither use the language of 'caste' directly—and the alternative possible frame of 'casteism' has not been widely incorporated in the international discourse. The expanded 'work and descent' identity frame enabled a greater focus on non-Dalit groups. For example, while the first report of HRW on caste (*Broken People*) examined only Dalits in India, its second report on caste was transnational, *Caste-Discrimination: A Global Concern*. The report was issued in conjunction with the WCAR and included discussion of caste-analogous systems in Japan, Africa and in diaspora communities. By expanding the community of caste-affected groups, they could better use the WCAR as a political opportunity structure for their norm entrepreneurship goals.

Because of this broader frame, however, the pressure on India/Hinduism has diffused with the effect that Dalits have to share the spotlight with other groups. Given that Dalits are the overwhelming majority of the caste-affected populations (some 240 million of the estimated 250 million so-affected), they have made a calculated trade off of direct attention to Dalit identities for the chance to establish a new (global) norm on caste-based discrimination. There is a tension between transnational advocacy targeting individual state practice and transnational advocacy for norm elaboration. In the short-term, a conventional 'campaigning' approach to pressuring individual states can offer important gains, while in the long-term the prospect of norm emergence and internalization can mark an arguably more permanent and thus stable change in state practice. The former wouldn't necessitate a new transnational identity frame, but the latter has.

The two approaches are not mutually exclusive, however, and work in tandem to affect normative change. The transnational identity frame offers greater leverage to the individual groups sharing the frame and is a tool to open space for dialogue on individual groups' concerns within the blocked domestic sphere. All of the caste TAN actors interviewed for this project reported that they felt both the country focus and the normative focus were important. The timing of the WCAR propelled the normative agenda, prompting both the Sub-Commission and CERD also to respond. The caste TAN has secured a recognition within the UN that work and descent-based discrimination exists, that it is prohibited in international law and they have developed a set of draft UN principles and guidelines on this discrimination. This would not have materialised if the only focus had been country-specific campaigning. In recent years there has been a shift back to country-focused advocacy: for example, India's submission of its periodic report to CERD in 2007 prompted a surge of domestic and INGO activity (e.g. in the form of preparing shadow reports). Members of the IDSN report that the major current of activity within UN fora now is to submit shadow reports to UN Treaty Bodies and also to the new Universal Periodic Review (UPR) system of the Human Rights Council. In both cases the efforts are state specific, although the focus on groups across Asia and Africa remains. Creating the global identity frame facilitated the norm emergence process, now providing a wide variety of caste-affected groups with new international standards to press for country specific change.

Transnational Social Mobilisation

The global advocacy strategy of the caste TAN has been to use international institutions to emphasise norms that would spotlight state failures and set a minimum basic standard of achievement for the eradication of caste-based discrimination. They reasoned that external actors would be better equipped to recognise the need for reform than states bound internally by caste-based discrimination norms. The initial stages of their norm entrepreneurship focused on three primary goals: recognition of their identities and concerns; norm elaboration; and the creation of new mechanisms on caste. In each they have achieved some success thanks to the creation of an effective organisational platform, strategic framing of their identities and rights, good use of political opportunity structures and constructive cooperation with IOs. These gains have been made in spite of the continuous opposition of the Government of India and weak support from other states.

Their success was aided by the establishment of strong forms of transnational social mobilisation. While earlier cooperation between domestic and international NGOs on caste had raised some awareness of the issues at the international level, it failed to build any organisational platform. The establishment of the IDSN was a crucial development that helped to bind nascent national platforms on caste and existing INGOs. Other caste-affected communities were soon incorporated into the mobilisation, creating a transcontinental network that increased the leverage of all participating identity groups. The caste TAN was born: caste-focused NGOs benefited from the expertise, information and resources of each other and INGOs to build a norm emergence campaign; and INGOs increased their credibility on caste issues through partnerships with caste-focused NGOs. This campaign profited from one timely political opportunity structure: the WCAR. The caste TAN did not achieve their main goal at Durban but caste became a *cause célèbre*, affording a newfound recognition for caste-affected communities on the international stage. This expedited norm elaboration: although international human rights institutions had tentatively addressed caste prior to Durban, the failure to secure specific mention of caste within the WCAR appears to have galvanised interest in advancing the normative agenda. Individuals like Patrick Thornberry of CERD and Asbjørn Eide and Yozo Yokota of the Sub-Commission took a personal interest in keeping the issue alive. They helped produce interpretive texts detailing the normative scope and content of the prohibition of caste-based discrimination and secured a specific mechanism on work and descent in the form of the two Special Rapporteurs.

This normative discourse has been facilitated by strategic use of identity frames. Dalits and other caste-affected groups have asserted a distinct identity based on the common experience of caste and analogous structures. They argued successfully that this identity warranted a particular focus in international society, aided by the "certification" of this identity by IOs. When it became clear that India would not accept overt references to caste, the identity frame was adapted to 'work and descent'. This had the dual effect of side-stepping India's objections whilst also embedding caste in an existing normative frame of 'descent' under ICERD. CERD was prepared to endorse this interpretation regardless of state objections and the caste TAN gained a legally binding norm without protracted inter-state negotiations. The Sub-Commission further legitimated the frame by elaborating on discrimination based on 'work and descent', which they confirmed is prohibited in international law. The caste TAN experience also supports Keck and Sikkink's assertion that emergent norms pertaining to 'bodily harm' or 'legal inequality' are more likely to be accepted. By emphasizing the structural inequality element of caste-based discrimination and the terrible effects on individual community members (such as extensive murder, rape, manual scavenging and the practices of 'untouchability') in the various reports and communications, the caste TAN has utilised these frames successfully.

Even with these successes, the caste TAN faces several obstacles in its ongoing efforts to achieve norm adherence. The first is its own fractured mobilisation in the domestic sphere. Dalit activists in India, for example, are split by region, religion, political allegiance, class and language. Those participating in the international sphere are few and can have divergent views on advocacy priorities and strategies to the majority of domestic activists who may not share their norm entrepreneurship goals. Leaders also express deep frustration with the so-called 'victim narrative' used by Dalits to justify their lamentable position in society. As 'victims' they are not empowered for mobilisation and fail to seek justice reasoning that their status is preordained (and dissuaded by the failures of the state justice system for Dalits). Even where they are mobilised, they have weak social capital to influence decision-makers. They face a still deeply-entrenched "caste culture" that makes internally driven social reform a poor prospect. Many domestic commentators in India view the actions of caste leaders as a betrayal of national loyalty, either sharing Gandhi's view that these actions are divisive or regarding solicitation of external interest as a return to colonialism. Activists struggle with the fine line between the benefits of mobilisation as a distinct Dalit community and the ultimate goal of eradication of the structure that created their distinction.

There is no strong evidence in the international sphere that states have firmly accepted emerging norms on caste-based discrimination. Only five countries had replied to the requests for information on caste as part of the Special Rapporteurs' study on work and descent. India is still reluctant to make caste an issue of international concern and continues to decline requests by Special Rapporteurs (on work and descent and on racial discrimination) to conduct country visits. Japan has not changed its principled stance on caste issues (in line with India's) but did capitulate to invite the Special Rapporteur on racism to visit, giving domestic Buraku-focused NGOs a vital opportunity for advocacy. Nepal is an important exception and has been the most open of the caste-affected states to domestic reforms vis-à-vis Dalits. This appears to be a consequence both of emerging norms and of domestic factors. The elaboration of norms in the international sphere has socialised state and resident IO actors to these concerns and strengthened the leverage of domestic Dalit actors to press for change. The post-conflict transition has created space for emergent norms to take root. Nepal has a smaller civil society of Dalit activists than India but a much more open dialogue with government. Although Dalits remain a weak constituency, the championing of Dalit rights in the Maoist movement's manifesto has given rationalist motivations for the new government to respond in earnest. At the international level, Nepal has accepted CERD's view that caste is within the scope of the ICERD but it has not been highly vocal on its views given India's position. Other caste-affected states similarly have been reticent on the issue, in part because domestic caste-NGOs are relatively weak in all but India, Nepal and Japan. A notable change was in evidence at the DRC, however: for example, both Pakistan and Nepal in their interventions noted the need for the outcome document to focus on caste-based discrimination, suggesting that India's neighbours are increasingly socialised to international attention to the issue. They did not openly criticise India but their statements represent an important discursive shift that could be utilized for future norm emergence. Diaspora states are only beginning to understand the implications of caste-based discrimination within their populations and Dalit solidarity networks have usually focused their attention on countries of origin rather than locally affected individuals.

In achieving wider norm recognition, the position of India as a "critical state" was always clear. India has the largest population of caste-affected groups and its acceptance of the norm would be instrumental to broader norm internalisation. Its persistent criticisms of the Sub-Commission, CERD and the Special Rapporteurs have attempted to undermine the process of norm emergence. India's obstinacy is influenced by both internal and external factors. Internally, caste-affected groups are an important constituency, one that is courted by all political parties. The expressed interest in Dalit issues, however, is often motivated by vote seeking: for example, the

Bhopal meeting in 2002 was convened by the state of Madhya Pradesh, where the Congress government relies on low caste support. The government across India has been able to placate Dalits with promises of a better future and a reservation system that is elusive to many. The balance of power in government institutions belongs to upper caste groups. They have limited motivation to relinquish this power and enforce laws that would protect the lower castes. Those parties focused on Hindu nationalism particularly would be loath to denigrate Hinduism by emphasising its structural injustices. The association of some Dalits with armed movements like the Naxalites, however, suggests that the government cannot rely on social hierarchy for stability. Dalit NGO leaders may not represent a security threat but with the support of the international community, they can bring pressure to bear on the government.

It is this external pressure that India has strived to avoid, pressure that threatens to undermine India's preferred identity in international society. Successive Indian governments have rejected the framing of caste as a racial discrimination issue at the same time as proclaiming firm commitment to the eradication of caste-based discrimination. It is the *racism* aspect that is offensive to them. Racial discrimination as a norm in international society holds great weight; it also has played an important role in post-colonial inter-state discourse. India's desire to present itself as a racism-free society is consistent with similar claims made by other post- colonial states. It cannot deny that caste discrimination persists but it can insist that the practice is not racist. This helps to portray India as a modern liberal and democratic state, projecting an image that intends to be more estimable than Western democracies that historically and currently grapple with racism.

Moreover, by presenting caste-based discrimination as a particular phenomenon and a domestic concern, India sidesteps calls for international scrutiny of the issue. India has been able to use its position in international society to dissuade other states from actively supporting the caste TAN. The caste TAN members report they have the moral sympathy of many states, but none are willing to expend the political capital necessary to meet their ideational concerns. India is among the most economically powerful post-colonial states and a regional hegemon, holding important positions in the UN Security Council, as a trade partner and also on the UN Human Rights Council.

It has made itself a bridge between the North and the South. Britain probably has the largest number of Dalits in the diaspora but is reluctant to take a hard line on caste no doubt because of its status as former coloniser and its desire to maintain a privileged position with the Government of India. The EU at large is dependent on India as a trade partner, making it similarly reluctant to harm relations. The discussion of caste at the DRC by Pakistan and Nepal can be interpreted from a rationalist perspective, these states aiming to undermine India's regional and international status by elevating caste as a focus of international attention. The EU support to Dalit NGO accreditation at the DRC, Slovenia's intervention at the DRC, Denmark's interventions on caste in the UPR and Guatemala's support during and after the WCAR, are evidence of shifting discursive positions that are not so easily tied to rational interests and could signal an increasing willingness to act in accordance with ideational commitments on caste-based discrimination.

Despite the weak support of states, the caste TAN has managed to institutionalise new norms for caste-affected groups but the important processes of state socialisation and persuasion have taken a back seat. Typically in norm entrepreneurship, socialisation and persuasion precede norm emergence. The caste TAN has done things in the reverse order for three key reasons. The first is the availability of political opportunity structures conducive to norm elaboration, such as the WCAR and the UN Sub-Commission. The second is the willingness of international actors to draft normative standards even in the face of state opposition. They have put the norms to paper and added the UN stamp of authority. States have been largely unable to stop these processes because they have taken place within independent expert (rather than inter-state) mechanisms like CERD and the Sub-Commission. The third factor has been the power of India to persuade states against openly accepting new norms focused on caste-based discrimination. Had the caste TAN relied solely on state persuasion, the norm elaboration was unlikely to occur, as was the case in Durban.

The availability and support of political opportunity structures for norm emergence has meant the caste-TAN has juggled both norm-focused and country-specific advocacy. These two objectives can be mutually beneficial but also compete for the time and resources of activists. It is not always clear whether this balance has fit the will, objectives or interests of caste-affected communities themselves. For example, the efforts to draw in other Asian and African communities under the rubric of 'discrimination based on work and decent', may have benefited Dalits much less than other groups. For Dalit leaders, specific attention to the experience of Dalits and states in which Dalits reside might have conferred greater immediate gains than focusing energy and resources on norm development. The problem is that constructive dialogue on norm adherence has been blocked in most states and the political opportunities offered by norm entrepreneurship have been more effective than domestic advocacy in generating media and government attention. Moreover, the geographical, religious and cultural divides among Dalits undermines efforts to forge an effective horizontal alliance for country-specific (or Dalit-specific) advocacy. Cooperation with each other in norm entrepreneurship has in some ways been more productive than domestic mobilisation. The success in norm emergence has helped to open space domestically for better adherence to existing and/or emerging norms on caste-based discrimination.

With the norm elaboration well advanced, the caste TAN is focusing more attention now on socialisation, country specific work and use of new international fora with stronger sanctioning power. Greater efforts are being made to strengthen domestic Dalit platforms in other parts of Asia to exert pressure from below. Bilateral advocacy by the caste TAN targeting Western states and institutions (such as the EU) continues to bring pressure from above on caste-affected countries and keeps caste-affected groups a funding priority for donors (at least in South Asia). Treaty bodies are being supplied with relevant information on caste. The caste TAN is working more with the private sector and labour rights issues and beginning engagement with the ILO's monitoring mechanisms. The UPR of the Human Rights Council has also proved a useful forum in which states have been willing to raise the issue of caste-based discrimination. The elaboration of norms has not been altogether abandoned and members of the caste TAN maintain a long-term vision of a legally binding instrument focused specifically on caste, such as an International Convention on the Elimination of All Forms of Caste-based Discrimination. The Special Rapporteur Chung has expressed her commitment to Dalit leaders to taking forward this proposal within the new UN Advisory Committee. In March 2009, on her first official visit to India and Nepal, the UN High Commissioner on Human Rights, Navanethem Pillay, made strong statements condemning caste-based discrimination and encouraged the Indian Government "to show leadership in combating caste-based discrimination globally". Whether they heed this call remains to be seen; the Government of India no doubt will consider the comparative material and identity costs of being an international crusader on caste versus maintaining its moral authority as a racism-free society *contra* the Western (colonial) experience.

References

Bob, Clifford. (2007). "Dalit Rights are Human Rights": Caste Discrimination, International Activism and the Construction of a New Human Rights Issue. *Human Rights Quarterly* 29 (1):167-193.

Divakar, Paul N. (2004). Post-Durban Reflections: Color Line-Caste Line. In *Caste, Race and Discrimination: Discourses in International Context*, edited by S. Thorat and Umakant. New Delhi: Indian Institute of Dalit Studies and Rowat Publications.

Finnemore, Martha, and Kathryn Sikkink. (1998). International Norm Dynamics and Political Change. *International Organization* 52 (4):887-917.

Gupta, Dipankar. (2004). Caste, Race, Politics. In *Caste, Race and Discrimination: Discourses in International Context*, edited by S. Thorat and Umakant. New Delhi: Indian Institute of Dalit Studies and Rawat Publications.

Human Rights Watch.(2001). *Caste-Based Discrimination: A Global Concern.* New York:

Keck, M., & Sikkink, K. (1998). *Activists Beyond Borders: Advocacy Networks in International Politics.* Ithaca, NY: Cornell University Press.

Khagram, Sanjeev, et.al. (2002). *Restructuring world politics : transnational social movements, networks, and norms, Social movements, protest, and contention; v. 14.* Minneapolis: University of Minnesota Press.

Smith, Peter Jay. (2007). The Dalit Movement: Going Global Against Casteism and in Defence of Dalit Human Rights. In *International Studies Association 48th Annual Convention.* Chicago, USA.

Thorat, Sukadeo, and Umakant, eds. (2004). *Caste, Race and Discrimination: Discourses in International Context.* New Delhi: Indian Institute of Dalit Studies and Rawat Publications.

10

The Protection of Human Rights Act, 1993

[As amended by the Protection of Human Rights (Amendment) Act, 2006–No. 43 of 2006]

PRELIMINARY

1. Short title, extent and commencement

(1) This Act may be called the Protection of Human Rights Act, 1993.

(2) It extends to the whole of India.

Provided that it shall apply to the State of Jammu and Kashmir only in so far as it pertains to the matters relatable to any of the entries enumerated in List I or List III in the Seventh Schedule to the Constitution as applicable to that State.

(3) It shall be deemed to have come into force on the 28th day of September, 1993.

2. Definitions

(1) In this Act, unless the context otherwise requires:

(a) "armed forces" means the naval, military and air forces and includes any other armed forces of the Union;

(b) "Chairperson" means the Chairperson of the Commission or of the State Commission, as the case may be;

(c) "Commission" means the National Human Rights Commission under section 3;

(d) "human rights" means the rights relating to life, liberty, equality and dignity of the individual guaranteed by the Constitution or embodied in the International Covenants and enforceable by courts in India.

(e) "Human Rights Court" means the Human Rights Court specified under section 30;

(f) "International Covenants" means the International Covenant on Civil and Political Rights and the International Covenant on Economic, Social and Cultural rights adopted by the General Assembly of the United Nations on the 16th December, 1966 [and such other Covenant or Convention adopted by the General Assembly of the United Nations as the Central Government may, by notification, specify"] ;

(g) "Member" means a Member of the Commission or of the State Commission, as the case may be;

(h) "National Commission for Minorities" means the National Commission for Minorities constituted under section 3 of the National Commission for Minorities Act, 1992;

(i) "National Commission for the Scheduled Castes" means the National Commission for the Scheduled Castes referred to in Article 338 of the Constitution;

(ia) "National Commission for the Scheduled Tribes" means the National Commission for the Scheduled Tribes referred to in Article 338A of the Constitution;

(j) "National Commission for Women" means the National Commission for Women constituted under section 3 of the National Commission for Women Act, 1990;

(k) "Notification" means a notification published in the official Gazette;

(l) "Prescribed" means prescribed by rules made under this Act;

(m) "Public servant" shall have the meaning assigned to it in section 21 of the Indian Penal Code;

(n) "State Commission" means a State Human Rights Commission constituted under section 21.

(2) Any reference in this Act to a law, which is not in force in the State of Jammu and Kashmir, shall, in relation to that State, be construed as a reference to a corresponding law, if any, in force in that State.

Chapter II. The National Human Rights Commission

3. Constitution of a National Human Rights Commission

(1) The Central Government shall constitute a body to be known as the National Human Rights Commission to exercise the powers conferred upon, and to perform the functions assigned to it, under this Act.

(2) The Commission shall consist of:

(a) a Chairperson who has been a Chief Justice of the Supreme Court;

(b) one Member who is or has been, a Judge of the Supreme Court;

(c) one Member who is, or has been, the Chief Justice of a High Court;

(d) two Members to be appointed from amongst persons having knowledge of, or practical experience in, matters relating to human rights.

(3) The Chairperson of the National Commission for Minorities, [the National Commission for the Scheduled Castes, the National Commission for the Scheduled Tribes] and the National Commission for Women shall be deemed to be Members of the Commission for the discharge of functions specified in clauses (b) to (j) of section 12.

(4) There shall be a Secretary-General who shall be the Chief Executive Officer of the Commission and shall exercise such powers and discharge such functions of the Commission [except judicial functions and the power to make regulations under section 40 B], as may be delegated to him by the Commission or the Chairperson as the case may be.

(5) The headquarters of the Commission shall be at Delhi and the Commission may, with the previous approval of the Central Government, establish offices at other places in India.

4. Appointment of Chairperson and other Members

(1) The Chairperson and [the Members]shall be appointed by the President by warrant under his hand and seal;

Provided that every appointment under this sub-section shall be made after obtaining the recommendations of a Committee consisting of–

(a) The Prime Minister — Chairperson

(b) Speaker of the House of the People — Member

(c) Minister in-charge of the Ministry of Home Affairs in the Government of India — Member

(d) Leader of the Opposition in the House of the People — Member

(e) Leader of the Opposition in the Council of States — Member

(f) Deputy Chairman of the Council of States — Member

Provided further that no sitting Judge of the Supreme Court or sitting Chief Justice of a High Court shall be appointed except after consultation with the Chief Justice of India.

(2) No appointment of a Chairperson or a Member shall be invalid merely by reason of any [vacancy of any member in the Committee referred to in the first proviso to sub-section (1)].

5. Resignation and removal of Chairperson and Members

(1) The Chairperson or any Member may, by notice in writing under his hand addressed to the President of India, resign his office.

(2) Subject to the provisions of sub-section (3), the Chairperson or any Member shall only be removed from his office by order of the President of India on the ground of proved misbehaviour or incapacity after the Supreme Court, on reference being made to it by the President, has, on inquiry held in accordance with the procedure prescribed in that behalf by the Supreme Court, reported that the Chairperson or the Member, as the case may be, ought on any such ground to be removed.

(3) Notwithstanding anything in sub-section (2), the President may, by order, remove from office the Chairperson or any Member if the Chairperson or such Member, as the case may be–

(a) is adjudged an insolvent; or

(b) engages during his term of office in any paid employment outside the duties of his office; or

(c) is unfit to continue in office by reason of infirmity of mind or body; or

(d) is of unsound mind and stands so declared by a competent court; or

(e) is convicted and sentenced to imprisonment for an offence which in the opinion of the President involves moral turpitude.

6. Term of office of Chairperson and Members

(1) A person appointed as Chairperson shall hold office for a term of five years from the date on which he enters upon his office or until he attains the age of seventy years, whichever is earlier.

(2) A person appointed as a Member shall hold office for a term of five years from the date on which he enters upon his office and shall be eligible for re-appointment for another term of five years.

Provided that no Member shall hold office after he has attained the age of seventy years.

(3) On ceasing to hold office, a Chairperson or a Member shall be ineligible for further employment under the Government of India or under the Government of any State.

7. Member to act as Chairperson or to discharge his functions in certain circumstances

(1) In the event of the occurrence of any vacancy in the office of the Chairperson by reason of his death, resignation or otherwise, the President may, by notification, authorise one of the Members to act as the Chairperson until the appointment of a new Chairperson to fill such vacancy.

(2) When the Chairperson is unable to discharge his functions owing to absence on leave or otherwise, such one of the Members as the President may, by notification, authorise in this behalf, shall discharge the functions of the Chairperson until the date on which the Chairperson resumes his duties.

8. Terms and conditions of service of Chairperson and Members

The salaries and allowances payable to, and other terms and conditions of service of, the [Chairperson and] Members shall be such as may be prescribed.

Provided that neither the salary and allowances nor the other terms and conditions of service of [the Chairperson or] a Member shall be varied to his disadvantage after his appointment.]

9. Vacancies, etc., not to invalidate the proceedings of the Commission

No act or proceedings of the Commission shall be questioned or shall be invalidated merely on the ground of existence of any vacancy or defect in the constitution of the Commission.

10. Procedure to be regulated by the Commission

(1) The Commission shall meet at such time and place as the Chairperson may think fit.

(2) Subject to the provisions of this Act and the rules made thereunder, the Commission shall have the power to lay down by regulations its own procedure.

(3) All orders and decisions of the Commission shall be authenticated by the Secretary-General or any other officer of the Commission duly authorised by the Chairperson in this behalf.

11. Officers and other staff of the Commission

(1) The Central Government shall make available to the Commission:

   (a) an officer of the rank of the Secretary to the Government of India who shall be the Secretary-General of the Commission; and

   (b) such police and investigative staff under an officer not below the rank of a Director General of Police and such other officers and staff as may be necessary for the efficient performance of the functions of the Commission.

(2) Subject to such rules as may be made by the Central Government in this behalf, the Commission may appoint such other administrative, technical and scientific staff as it may consider necessary.

(3) The salaries, allowances and conditions of service of the officers and other staff appointed under sub-section (2) shall be such as may be prescribed.

CHAPTER III. FUNCTIONS AND POWERS OF THE COMMISSION

12. Functions of the Commission

The Commission shall perform all or any of the following functions, namely:

(a) inquire, suo motu or on a petition presented to it by a victim or any person on his behalf [or on a direction or order of any court], into complaint of

   (i) violation of human rights or abetment thereof; or

   (ii) negligence in the prevention of such violation, by a public servant;

(b) intervene in any proceeding involving any allegation of violation of human rights pending before a court with the approval of such court;

(c) visit, notwithstanding anything contained in any other law for the time being in force, any jail or other institution under the control of the State Government, where persons are detained or lodged for purposes of treatment, reformation or protection, for the study of the living conditions of the inmates thereof and make recommendations thereon to the Government;

(d) review the safeguards provided by or under the Constitution or any law for the time being in force for the protection of human rights and recommend measures for their effective implementation;

(e) review the factors, including acts of terrorism that inhibit the enjoyment of human rights and recommend appropriate remedial measures;

(f) study treaties and other international instruments on human rights and make recommendations for their effective implementation;

(g) undertake and promote research in the field of human rights;

(h) spread human rights literacy among various sections of society and promote awareness of the safeguards available for the protection of these rights through publications, the media, seminars and other available means;

(i) encourage the efforts of non-governmental organisations and institutions working in the field of human rights;

(j) such other functions as it may consider necessary for the protection of human rights.

13. Powers relating to inquiries

(1) The Commission shall, while inquiring into complaints under this Act, have all the powers of a civil court trying a suit under the Code of Civil Procedure, 1908, and in particular in respect of the following matters, namely :

  (a) summoning and enforcing the attendance of witnesses and examining them on oath;

  (b) discovery and production of any document;

  (c) receiving evidence on affidavits;

  (d) requisitioning any public record or copy thereof from any court or office;

  (e) issuing commissions for the examination of witnesses or documents;

  (f) any other matter which may be prescribed.

(2) The Commission shall have power to require any person, subject to any privilege which may be claimed by that person under any law for the time being in force, to furnish information on such points or matters as, in the opinion of the Commission, may be useful for, or relevant to, the subject matter of the inquiry and any person so required shall be deemed to be legally bound to furnish such information within the meaning of section 176 and section 177 of the Indian Penal Code.

(3) The Commission or any other officer, not below the rank of a Gazetted Officer, specially authorised in this behalf by the Commission may enter any building or place where the Commission has reason to believe that any document relating to the subject matter of the inquiry may be found, and may seize any such document or take extracts or copies therefrom subject to the provisions of section 100 of the Code of Criminal Procedure, 1973, in so far as it may be applicable.

(4) The Commission shall be deemed to be a civil court and when any offence as is described in section 175, section 178, section 179, section 180 or section 228 of the Indian Penal Code is committed in the view or presence of the Commission, the Commission may, after recording the facts constituting the offence and the statement of the accused as provided for in the Code of Criminal Procedure, 1973, forward the case to a Magistrate having jurisdiction to try the same and the Magistrate to whom any such case is forwarded shall proceed to hear the complaint against the accused as if the case has been forwarded to him under section 346 of the Code of Criminal Procedure, 1973.

(5) Every proceeding before the Commission shall be deemed to be a judicial proceeding within the meaning of sections 193 and 228, and for the purposes of section 196, of the Indian Penal Code, and the Commission shall be deemed to be a civil court for all the purposes of section 195 and Chapter XXVI of the Code of Criminal Procedure, 1973.

(6) Where the Commission considers it necessary or expedient so to do, it may, by order, transfer any complaint filed or pending before it to the State Commission of the State from which the complaint arises, for disposal in accordance with the provisions of this Act;

Provided that no such complaint shall be transferred unless the same is one respecting which the State Commission has jurisdiction to entertain the same.

(7) Every complaint transferred under sub-section(6) shall be dealt with and disposed of by the State Commission as if it were a complaint initially filed before it.

14. Investigation

(1) The Commission may, for the purpose of conducting any investigation pertaining to the inquiry, utilise the services of any officer or investigation agency of the Central Government or any State Government with the concurrence of the Central Government or the State Government, as the case may be.

(2) For the purpose of investigating into any matter pertaining to the inquiry, any officer or agency whose services are utilised under sub-section (1) may, subject to the direction and control of the Commission:

  (a) summon and enforce the attendance of any person and examine him;

  (b) require the discovery and production of any document; and

  (c) requisition any public record or copy thereof from any office.

(3) The provisions of section 15 shall apply in relation to any statement made by a person before any officer or agency whose services are utilised under sub-section (1) as they apply in relation to any statement made by a person in the course of giving evidence before the Commission.

(4) The officer or agency whose services are utilised under sub-section (1) shall investigate into any matter pertaining to the inquiry and submit a report thereon to the Commission within such period as may be specified by the Commission in this behalf.

(5) The Commission shall satisfy itself about the correctness of the facts stated and the conclusion, if any, arrived at in the report submitted to it under sub-section (4) and for this purpose the Commission may make such inquiry (including the examination of the person or persons who conducted or assisted in the investigation) as it thinks fit.

15. Statement made by persons to the Commission

No statement made by a person in the course of giving evidence before the Commission shall subject him to, or be used against him in, any civil or criminal proceeding except a prosecution for giving false evidence by such statement:

Provided that the statement:

(a) is made in reply to the question which he is required by the Commission to answer; or

(b) is relevant to the subject matter of the inquiry.

16. Persons likely to be prejudicially affected to be heard

If, at any stage of the inquiry, the Commission:

(a) considers it necessary to inquire into the conduct of any person; or

(b) is of the opinion that the reputation of any person is likely to be prejudicially affected by the inquiry; it shall give to that person a reasonable opportunity of being heard in the inquiry and to produce evidence in his defence:

Provided that nothing in this section shall apply where the credit of a witness is being impeached.

CHAPTER IV. PROCEDURE

17. Inquiry into complaints

The Commission while inquiring into the complaints of violations of human rights may–

(i) call for information or report from the Central Government or any State Government or any other authority or organisation subordinate thereto within such time as may be specified by it:- Provided that–

  (a) if the information or report is not received within the time stipulated by the Commission, it may proceed to inquire into the complaint on its own;

  (b) if, on receipt of information or report, the Commission is satisfied either that no further inquiry is required or that the required action has been initiated or taken by the concerned Government or authority, it may not proceed with the complaint and inform the complainant accordingly;

(ii) without prejudice to anything contained in clause (i), if it considers necessary, having regard to the nature of the complaint, initiate an inquiry.

18. Steps during and after inquiry

[The Commission may take any of the following steps during or upon the completion of an inquiry held under this Act, namely:

(a) where the inquiry discloses the commission of violation of human rights or negligence in the prevention of violation of human rights or abetment thereof by a public servant, it may recommend to the concerned Government or authority –

  (i) to make payment of compensation or damages to the complainant or to the victim or the members of his family as the Commission may consider necessary;

  (ii) to initiate proceedings for prosecution or such other suitable action as the Commission may deem fit against the concerned person or persons;

  (iii) to take such further action as it may think fit;

(b) approach the Supreme Court or the High Court concerned for such directions, orders or writs as that Court may deem necessary;

(c) recommend to the concerned Government or authority at any stage of the inquiry for the grant of such immediate interim relief to the victim or the members of his family as the Commission may consider necessary;

(d) subject to the provisions of clause (e), provide a copy of the inquiry report to the petitioner or his representative;

(e) the Commission shall send a copy of its inquiry report together with its recommendations to the concerned Government or authority and the concerned Government or authority shall, within a period of one month, or such further time as the Commission may allow, forward its comments on the report, including the action taken or proposed to be taken thereon, to the Commission;

(f) the Commission shall publish its inquiry report together with the comments of the concerned Government or authority, if any, and the action taken or proposed to be taken by the concerned Government or authority on the recommendations of the Commission.]

19. Procedure with Respect to Armed Forces

(1) Notwithstanding anything contained in this Act, while dealing with complaints of violation of human rights by members of the armed forces, the Commission shall adopt the following procedure, namely :-

(a) it may, either on its own motion or on receipt of a petition, seek a report from the Central Government;

(b) after the receipt of the report, it may, either not proceed with the complaint or, as the case may be, make its recommendations to that Government.

(2) The Central Government shall inform the Commission of the action taken on the recommendations within three months or such further time as the Commission may allow.

(3) The Commission shall publish its report together with its recommendations made to the Central Government and the action taken by that Government on such recommendations.

(4) The Commission shall provide a copy of the report published under sub-section (3) to the petitioner or his representative.

20. Annual and special reports of the Commission

(1) The Commission shall submit an annual report to the Central Government and to the State Government concerned and may at any time submit special reports on any matter which, in its opinion, is of such urgency or importance that it should not be deferred till submission of the annual report.

(2) The Central Government and the State Government, as the case may be, shall cause the annual and special reports of the Commission to be laid before each House of Parliament or the State Legislature respectively, as the case may be, along with a memorandum of action taken or proposed to be taken on the recommendations of the Commission and the reasons for non-acceptance of the recommendations, if any.

CHAPTER V. STATE HUMAN RIGHTS COMMISSIONS

21. Constitution of State Human Rights Commissions

(1) A State Government may constitute a body to be known as the

(name of the State) Human Rights Commission to exercise the powers conferred upon, and to perform the functions assigned to, a State Commission under this chapter.

(2) [The State Commission shall, with effect from such date as the State Government may by notification specify, consist of—

(a) a Chairperson who has been a Chief Justice of a High Court;

(b) one Member who is, or has been, a Judge of a High Court or District Judge in the State with a minimum of seven years experience as District Judge;

(c) one Member to be appointed from amongst persons having knowledge of, or practical experience in, matters relating to human rights.]

(3) There shall be a Secretary who shall be the Chief Executive Officer of the State Commission and shall exercise such powers and discharge such functions of the State Commission as it may delegate to him.

(4) The headquarters of the State Commission shall be at such place as the State Government may, by notification, specify.

(5) A State Commission may inquire into violation of human rights only in respect of matters relatable to any of the entries enumerated in List II and List III in the Seventh Schedule to the Constitution:

Provided that if any such matter is already being inquired into by the Commission or any other Commission duly constituted under any law for the time being in force, the State Commission shall not inquire into the said matter:

Provided further that in relation to the Jammu and Kashmir Human Rights Commission, this sub-section shall have effect as if for the words and figures "List II and List III in the Seventh Schedule to the Constitution", the words and figures "List III in the Seventh Schedule to the Constitution as applicable to the State of Jammu and Kashmir and in respect of matters in relation to which the Legislature of that State has power to make laws" had been substituted.

(6) [Two or more State Governments may, with the consent of a Chairperson or Member of a State Commission, appoint such

Chairperson or, as the case may be, such Member of another State Commission simultaneously if such Chairperson or Member consents to such appointment:

Provided that every appointment made under this sub-section shall be made after obtaining the recommendations of the Committee referred to in sub-section(1) of section 22 in respect of the State for which a common Chairperson or Member, or both, as the case may be, is to be appointed.]

22. Appointment of Chairperson and [Members] of State Commission

(1) The Chairperson and [Members] shall be appointed by the Governor by warrant under his hand and seal:

Provided that every appointment under this sub-section shall be made after obtaining the recommendation of a Committee consisting of

(a) the Chief Minister — Chairperson

(b) Speaker of the Legislative Assembly — Member

(c) Minister in-charge of the Department of Home, in that State — Member

(d) Leader of the Opposition in the Legislative Assembly — Member

Provided further that where there is a Legislative Council in a State, the Chairman of that Council and the Leader of the Opposition in that Council shall also be members of the Committee.

Provided also that no sitting Judge of a High Court or a sitting District Judge shall be appointed except after consultation with the Chief Justice of the High Court of the concerned State.

(2) No appointment of a Chairperson or a Member of the State Commission shall be invalid merely by reason of [any vacancy of any Member in the Committee referred to in sub-section(1)].

23. [Resignation and Removal of Chairperson or a Member of the State Commission]

[(1) The Chairperson or a Member of a State Commission may, by notice in writing under his hand addressed to the Governor, resign his office

(1A) Subject to the provisions of sub-section (2), the Chairperson or any Member of the State Commission shall only be removed from his office by order of the President on the ground of proved misbehaviour or incapacity after the Supreme Court, on a reference being made to it by the President, has, on inquiry held in accordance with the procedure prescribed in that behalf by the Supreme Court, reported that the Chairperson or such Member, as the case may be, ought on any such ground to be removed.]

(2) Notwithstanding anything in sub-section (1A), the President may by order remove from office the Chairperson or any [Member] if the Chairperson or such [Member], as the case may be –

(a) is adjudged an insolvent; or

(b) engages during his term of office in any paid employment outside the duties of his office; or

(c) is unfit to continue in office by reason of infirmity of mind or body; or

(d) is of unsound mind and stands so declared by a competent court; or

(e) is convicted and sentenced to imprisonment for an offence which in the opinion of the President involves moral turpitude.

24. Term of office of [Chairperson and] Members of the State Commission

(1) A person appointed as Chairperson shall hold office for a term of five years from the date on which he enters upon his office or until he attains the age of seventy years, whichever is earlier;

(2) A person appointed as a Member shall hold office for a term of five years from the date on which he enters upon his office and shall be eligible for re-appointment for another term of five years;

Provided that no Member shall hold office after he has attained the age of seventy years.

(3) On ceasing to hold office, a Chairperson or a Member shall be ineligible for further employment under the Government of a State or under the Government of India.

25. Member to act as Chairperson or to discharge his functions in certain circumstances

(1) In the event of the occurrence of any vacancy in the office of the Chairperson by reason of his death, resignation or otherwise, the Governor may, by notification, authorise one of the Members to act as the Chairperson until the appointment of a new Chairperson to fill such vacancy.

(2) When the Chairperson is unable to discharge his functions owing to absence on leave or otherwise, such one of the Members as the Governor may, by notification, authorise in this behalf, shall discharge the functions of the Chairperson until the date on which the Chairperson resumes his duties.

26. [Terms and conditions of service of Chairperson and Members of the State Commissions

The salaries and allowances payable to, and other terms and conditions of service of, the Chairperson and Members shall be such as may be prescribed by the State Government;

Provided that neither the salary and allowances nor the other terms and conditions of service of the Chairperson or a Member shall be varied to his disadvantage after his appointment.]

27. Officers and other staff of the State Commission

(1) The State Government shall make available to the Commission

(a) an officer not below the rank of a Secretary to the State Government who shall be the Secretary of the State Commission; and

(b) such police and investigative staff under an officer not below the rank of an Inspector General of Police and such other officers and staff as may be necessary for the efficient performance of the functions of the State Commission.

(2) subject to such rules as may be made by the State Government in this behalf, the State Commission may appoint such other addministrative, technical and scientific staff as it may consider necessary.

(3) The salaries, allowances and conditions of service of the officers and other staff appointed under sub-section (2) shall be such as may be prescribed by the State Government.

28. Annual and special reports of State Commission

(1) The State Commission shall submit an annual report to the State Government and may at any time submit special reports on any matter which, in its opinion, is of such urgency or importance that it should not be deferred till submission of the annual report.

(2) The State Government shall cause the annual and special reports of the State Commission to be laid before each House of State Legislature where it consists of two Houses, or where such Legislature consists of one House, before that House along with a memorandum of action taken or proposed to be taken on the recommendations of the State Commission and the reasons for non-acceptance of the recommendations, if any.

29. Application of certain provisions relating to National Human Rights Commission to State Commissions

The provisions of sections 9, 10, 12, 13, 14, 15, 16, 17 and 18 shall apply to a State Commission and shall have effect, subject to the following modifications, namely:

(a) references to "Commission" shall be construed as references to "State Commission";

(b) in section 10, in sub-section (3), for the word "Secretary General", the word "Secretary" shall be substituted;

(c) in section 12, clause (f) shall be omitted;

(d) in section 17, in clause (i), the words "Central Government or any" shall be omitted;

Chapter VI. Human Rights Courts

30. For the purpose of providing speedy trial of offences arising out of violation of human rights, the State Government may, with the concurrence of the Chief Justice of the High Court, by notification, specify for each district a Court of Session to be a Human Rights Court to try the said offences.

Provided that nothing in this section shall apply if

(a) a Court of Session is already specified as a special court; or

(b) a special court is already constituted, for such offences under any other law for the time being in force.

31. Special Public Prosecutor

For every Human Rights Court, the State Government shall, by notification, specify a Public Prosecutor or appoint an advocate who has been in practice as an advocate for not less than seven years, as a Special Public Prosecutor for the purpose of conducting cases in that Court.

Chapter VII. Finance, Accounts And Audit

32. Grants by the Central Government

(1) The Central Government shall after due appropriation made by Parliament by law in this behalf, pay to the Commission by way of grants such sums of money as the Central Government may think fit for being utilised for the purposes of this Act.

(2) The Commission may spend such sums as it thinks fit for performing the functions under this Act, and such sums shall be treated as expenditure payable out of the grants referred to in sub-section (1).

33. Grants by the State Government

(1) The State Government shall, after due appropriation made by Legislature by law in this behalf, pay to the State Commission by way of grants such sums of money as the State Government may think fit for being utilised for the purposes of this Act.

(2) The State Commission may spend such sums as it thinks fit for performing the functions under Chapter V, and such sums shall be treated as expenditure payable out of the grants referred to in sub-section (1).

34. Accounts and Audit

(1) The Commission shall maintain proper accounts and other relevant records and prepare an annual statement of accounts in such form

as may be prescribed by the Central Government in consultation with the Comptroller and Auditor-General of India.

(2) The Accounts of the Commission shall be audited by the Comptroller and Auditor-General at such intervals as may be specified by him and any expenditure incurred in connection with such audit shall be payable by the Commission to the Comptroller and Auditor-General.

(3) The Comptroller and Auditor-General or any person appointed by him in connection with the audit of the accounts of the Commision under this Act shall have the same rights and privileges and the authority in connection with such audit as the Comptroller and Auditor-General generally has in connection with the audit of Government accounts and, in particular, shall have the right to demand the production of books, accounts, connected vouchers and other documents and papers and to inspect any of the offices of the Commission.

(4) The accounts of the State Commission, as certified by the Comptroller and Auditor-General or any other person appointed by him in this behalf, together with the audit report thereon, shall be forwarded annually to the State Government by the State Commission and the State Government shall cause the audit report to be laid, as soon as may be after it is received, before the State Legislature.

(4) The accounts of the Commission as certified by the Comptroller and Auditor-General or any other person appointed by him in this behalf, together with the audit report thereon shall be forwarded annually to the Central Government by the Commission and the Central Government shall cause the audit report to be laid as soon as may be after it is received before each House of Parliament.

35. Accounts and Audit of State Commission

(1) The State Commission shall maintain proper accounts and other relevant records and prepare an annual statement of accounts in such form as may be prescribed by the State Government in consultation with the Comptroller and Auditor-General of India.

(2) The accounts of the State Commission shall be audited by the Comptroller and Auditor-General at such intervals as may be

specified by him and any expenditure incurred in connection with such audit shall be payable by the State Commission to the Comptroller and Auditor-General.

(3) The Comptroller and Auditor-General or any person appointed by him in connection with the audit of the accounts of the State Commission under this Act shall have the same rights and privileges and the authority in connection with such audit as the Comptroller and Auditor-General generally has in connection with the audit of Government accounts and, in particular, shall have the right to demand the production of books, accounts, connected vouchers and other documents and papers and to inspect any of the offices of the State Commission.

CHAPTER VIII. MISCELLANEOUS

36. Matters not subject to jurisdiction of the Commission

(1) The Commission shall not inquire into any matter which is pending before a State Commission or any other Commission duly constituted under any law for the time being in force.

(2) The Commission or the State Commission shall not inquire into any matter after the expiry of one year from the date on which the act constituting violation of human rights is alleged to have been commited.

37. Constitution of special investigation teams

Notwithstanding anything contained in any other law for the time being in force, where the Government considers it necessary so to do, it may constitute one or more special investigation teams, consisting of such police officers as it thinks necessary for purposes of investigation and prosecution of offences arising out of violations of human rights.

38. Protection of action taken in good faith

No suit or other legal proceeding shall lie against the Central Government, State Government, Commission, the State Commission or any Member thereof or any person acting under the direction either of the Central Government, State Government, Commission or the State Commission in respect of anything which is in good faith done or intended to be done in pursuance of this Act or of any rules or any order made thereunder or in respect of the publication by or under the authority of the Central Government, State Government, Commission or the State Commission of any report paper or proceedings.

39. Members and officers to be public servants

Every Member of the Commission, State Commission and every officer appointed or authorised by the Commission or the State Commission to exercise functions under this Act shall be deemed to be a public servant within the meaning of section 21 of the Indian Penal Code.

40. Power of Central Government to make rules

(1) The Central Government may, by notification, make rules to carry out the provisions of this Act.

(2) In particular and without prejudice to the generality of the foregoing power, such rules may provide for all or any of the following matters namely :-

(a) the salaries and allowances and other terms and conditions of service of the [Chairperson and Members] under section 8;

(b) the conditions subject to which other administrative, technical and scientific staff may be appointed by the Commission and the salaries and allowances of officers and other staff under sub-section (3) of section 11;

(c) any other power of a civil court required to be prescribed under clause (f) of sub-section (1) of section 13;

(d) the form in which the annual statement of accounts is to be prepared by the Commission under sub-section (1) of section 34; and

(e) any other matter which has to be, or may be, prescribed.

(3) Every rule made under this Act shall be laid, as soon as may be after it is made, before each House of Parliament, while it is in session, for a total period of thirty days which may be comprised in one session or in two or more successive sessions, and if, before the expiry of the session immediately following the session or the successive sessions aforesaid, both Houses agree in making any modification in the rule or both Houses agree that the rule should

not be made, the rule shall thereafter have effect only in such modified form or be of no effect, as the case may be; so however, that any such modification or annulment shall be without prejudice to the validity of anything previously done under that rule.

40 A. Power to make rules retrospectively

The power to make rules under clause (b) of sub-section (2) of section 40 shall include the power to make such rules or any of them retrospectively from a date not earlier than the date on which this Act received the assent of the President, but no such retrospective effect shall be given to any such rule so as to prejudicially affect the interests of any person to whom such rule may be applicable.

Power of Commission to make Regulations

[40(B) (1) Subject to the provisions of this Act and the rules made thereunder, the Commission may, with the previous approval of the Central Government, by notification, make regulations to carry out the provisions of this Act.

(2) In particular and without prejudice to the generality of the foregoing power, such regulations may provide for all or any of the following matters, namely:

(a) the procedure to be followed by the Commission under sub-section(2) of Section 10;

(b) the returns and statistics to be furnished by the State Commission;

(c) any other matter which has to be, or may be, specified by regulations.

(3) Every regulation made by the Commission under this Act shall be laid, as soon as may be after it is made, before each House of Parliament, while it is in session, for a total period of thirty days which may be comprised in one session or in two or more successive sessions, and if, before the expiry of the session or the successive sessions aforesaid, both Houses agree in making any modification in the regulations or both Houses agree that the regulation should not be made, the regulation shall thereafter have effect only in such modified form or be of no effect, as the case may be; so however, that any such modification or annulment shall be without prejudice to the validity of anything previously done under that regulation.]

41. Power of State Government to make rules

(1) The State Government may, by notification, make rules to carry out the provisions of this Act.

(2) In particular and without prejudice to the generality of the foregoing power, such rules may provide for all or any of the following matters, namely :

(a) the salaries and allowances and other terms and conditions of service of the Chairperson and Members under section 26;

(b) the conditions subject to which other administrative, technical and scientific staff may be appointed by the State Commission and the salaries and allowances of officers and other staff under sub-section (3) of section 27;

(c) the form in which the annual statement of accounts is to be prepared under sub-section (1) of section 35.

(3) Every rule made by the State Government under this section shall be laid, as soon as may be after it is made, before each House of the State Legislature where it consists of two Houses, or where such Legislature consists of one House, before that House.

42. Power to remove difficulties

(1) If any difficulty arises in giving effect to the provisions of this Act, the Central Government, may by order published in the Official Gazette, make such provisions, not inconsistent with the provisions of this Act as appear to it to be necessary or expedient for removing the difficulty.

Provided that no such order shall be made after the expiry of the period of two years from the date of commencement of this Act.

(2) Every order made under this section shall, as soon as may be after it is made, be laid before each house of Parliament.

43. Repeal and Savings

(1) The Protection of Human Rights Ordinance, 1993 is hereby repealed.

(2) Notwithstanding such repeal, anything done or any action taken under the said Ordinance, shall be deemed to have been done or taken under the corresponding provisions of this Act.

Bibliography

Abraham, T. (2007). *Introducing Postcolonial Theories: Issues and Debates*. DelhiMacmillan India, Ltd.

Ahuja, R. (1998). *Violence Against Women*, Rawat Publication, New Delhi.

Ajwad, Mohamed Ihsan (2006) "Anti-Poverty Programs in Uttar Pradesh", World Bank Staff Paper, World Bank, Washington.

Ambedkar, B.R. 1987. *Writings and Speeches*, vol. 3. Mumbai: government of Maharashtra.

Antony, P., H. Dayal, and A.K. Karan, eds. (2003). *Poverty and Deprivation Among Scheduled Tribes in India*. Delhi: Institute for Human Development.

Bailey, F.G. (1960). *Tribe, Caste, and Nation: A Study in Political Activity and Political Change in Highland Orissa*. Manchester University Press.

Bandhu, P. (2003). *Dalit Women's cry for Liberation*: *My Rights Are Rising like the Sun, will you deny this sunrise"?* Edited in Rao (2003) *Caste and Gender*, Kali For Women, New Delhi.

Barbara R. Joshi, (1986), *Untouchable!: Voices of the Dalit Liberation Movement*, Zed Books.

Bhowmik, K.L. (ed.) (1988). Development of Scheduled Communities. *Current Anthropological and Archaeological Perspectives*, Vol. 6. New Delhi: Inter-India Publications.

Bob, Clifford. (2007). "Dalit Rights are Human Rights": Caste Discrimination, International Activism and the Construction of a New Human Rights Issue. *Human Rights Quarterly* 29 (1):167-193.

Cassirer, E. (1946). *Language and Myth* (S. Langer, Trans.). New York: Dover Publications, Inc.

Centre for Human Rights and Global Justice (CHRGJ) and Human Rights Watch (HRW). 2007. *Caste Discrimination Against Dalits or So-Called Untouchables in India*, Report submitted to CERD, available at www.ohchr.org/english/bodies/cerd/docs/ngos/ chrgj_hrw.pdf

Cernea, M.M. (1998). Impoverishment or Social Justice? A Model for Planning Resettlement. In Mathur, H.M., and D. Marsden, eds. *Development Projects and Impoverishment Risks: Resettling Project-Affected People in India*. Delhi: Oxford University Press.

Corrie, B.D. (1995). A human development index for the Dalit child in India, *Social Indicators Research* 34: 395-409

Davis, S.H. (1993). Introduction. In Davis, S.H., ed. *Indigenous View of Land and the Environment*. Washington, DC: World Bank.

Department of Education (2006) *Sarva Shiksha Abhiyan: Fourth joint Review Mission*. Aide Memoire, New Delhi.

Derez, Jean and Haris Gazdar. 1996. "Uttar Pradesh: The burden of Inertia", in Derez Jean and Amartya Sen, editors, *India Development*. Delhi: Oxford university Press.

Desai, A.R. (1996), *Social Background of Indian Nationalism*, Popular Prakashan, Bombay.

Dietrich, G (2003). *Dalit Movement and Women's Movement*, Edited in Rao (2003) *Caste and Gender*, Kali for women, New Delhi.

Divakar, Paul N. (2004). Post-Durban Reflections: Color Line-Caste Line. In *Caste, Race and Discrimination: Discourses in International Context*, edited by S. Thorat and Umakant. New Delhi: Indian Institute of Dalit Studies and Rowat Publications.

Eleanor Zilliot. (2005), *From Untouchable to Dalit - Essays on the Ambedkar Movement*, Manohar Publications, New Delhi.

Elwin, V. (1963). *A New Deal for Tribal India*. Delhi: Government of India/ Ministry of Home Affairs.

Fabricius, C., and C. de Wet. (2002). In Chatty, D., and M. Colchester, ed. *Conservation and Mobile Indigenous Peoples: Displacement, Forced Settlement, and Sustainable Development*. New York and Oxford: Berghahn Books.

Fernando Franco, Jyotsna Macwan, Suguna Ramanathan. (2004), *Journeys to Freedom: Dalit Narratives*, Popular Prakashan.

Finnemore, Martha, and Kathryn Sikkink. (1998). International Norm Dynamics and Political Change. *International Organization* 52 (4):887-917.

Freeman, J.M. (1986).The consciousness of freedom amongst India's Untouchables. In D.K. Basu & R. Sisson (eds) *Social and Economic Development in India*. New Delhi: Sage.

Gail Omvedt. (1994), *Dalits and the Democratic Revolution - Dr. Ambedkar and the Dalit Movement in Colonial India*, Sage Publications, New Delhi.

Gail Omvedt. (2006), *Dalit Visions: The Anti-caste Movement and the Construction of an Indian Identity*, Orient Longman.

Galanter, M. (1986). Pursuing equality. An assessment of India's policy of compensatory discrimination for disadvantaged groups. In D.K. Basu & R. Sisson (eds) *Social and Economic Development in India*. New Delhi: Sage.

Ganguly, D. (2005). *Caste, Colonialism and Counter-Modernity: Notes on a Postcolonial Hermeneutics of Caste*. New York: Routledge.

Government of India (2003) *Tenth Five Year Plan 2003-2007*, Planning Commission, New Delhi.

Government of India. (1976). *Report of the National Commission on Agriculture* (vol. 9: *Forests*). Delhi: Ministry of Agriculture and Irrigation.

Gupta, Dipankar. (2004). Caste, Race, Politics. In *Caste, Race and Discrimination: Discourses in International Context*, edited by S. Thorat and Umakant. New Delhi: Indian Institute of Dalit Studies and Rawat Publications.

Human Rights Watch.(2001). *Caste-Based Discrimination: A Global Concern*. New York:

IIPS (International Institute for Population Sciences), 1999a, National Family Health Survey II, 1998/9, National Report, Mumbai.

Illaiah, Kancha. 1996. *Why I am not a Hindu*. Calcutta: Samya Publications.

Jabbi, Mona and C. Rajyalakshmi. 2001. "Education of Marginalised Social Groups in Bihar", in Vaidyanathan, A. and P.R.Gopinath Nair, editors, *Elementary Education in Rural India: A Grassroots View*. New Delhi: Sage Publications.

Jogdand, P (1995) *Dalit Women, Issues and Perspectives*, Gyan Publication, New Delhi.

Johnson, Glen, and Sipra Bose, *Social Mobility Among Untouchables*, in Gupta.

Jonsson, Urban (2003) *Human Rights Approach to Development Programming*, Eastern and Southern Africa Regional Office, UNICEF, Nairobi.

Joshi, B. (1987). Recent developments in inter-regional mobilization of Dalit protest in India, *South Asia Bulletin* 7, 86-96.

Kakade, S.R. (1990), *Scheduled Castes and National Integration*, Radiant publishers, New Delhi.

Kantowsky, D. (2003). *Buddhists in India Today: Descriptions, Pictures, and Documents* (H.-G. Tuerstig, Trans.). New Delhi: Manohar.

Keck, M., & Sikkink, K. (1998). *Activists Beyond Borders: Advocacy Networks in International Politics*. Ithaca, NY: Cornell University Press.

Khagram, Sanjeev, et.al. (2002). *Restructuring world politics : transnational social movements, networks, and norms, Social movements, protest, and contention; v. 14*. Minneapolis: University of Minnesota Press.

Ling, T. (1980). *Buddhist Revival In India: Aspects of the Sociology of Buddhism*. New York: St. Martin's Press.

MacIntyre, A. (1984). *After Virtue: A Study in Moral Theory* (Second ed.). Notre Dame, Indiana: University of Notre Dame Press.

Mahar, P. (1960). Changing religious practices of an Untouchable caste, *Economic Development and Cultural Change* 8.

Maurya, R.L. (1991). Changing status of the Scheduled Castes. In R.S. Tripathi & P.D. Tiwari (eds) *Dimensions of Scheduled Caste Development in India*. New Delhi: Uppal.

Michael, S M (2007), *Dalits in Modern India - Vision and Values*, , Sage Publications, New Delhi.

Mulk Raj Anand, (1992), *An Anthology of Dalit Literature*, Gyan Books, New Delhi.

Oliver Mendelsohn, Marika Vicziany, (1998), *The Untouchables: Subordination, Poverty and the State in Modern India*, Cambridge University Press.

Pradeep K. Sharma, (2006), *Dalit Politics and Literature*, Shipra Publications, New Delhi.

Rajshekhar, V.T. (2003), *Dalit: The Black Untouchables of India*, 2nd print, Clarity Press, Inc.

Ranabira Samaddara, Ghanshyam Shah, (2001), *Dalit Identity and Politics*, Sage Publications, New Delhi.

Sachchidanand, (1977), *The Harijan Elite, Thompson Press, Faridabad,* p. 162.

Sharankumar Limbale. (2004), *Towards an Aesthetic of Dalit Literature*, Orient Longman.

Smith, Peter Jay. (2007). The Dalit Movement: Going Global Against Casteism and in Defence of Dalit Human Rights. In *International Studies Association 48th Annual Convention*. Chicago, USA.

Thorat, Sukadeo, and Umakant, eds. (2004). *Caste, Race and Discrimination: Discourses in International Context*. New Delhi: Indian Institute of Dalit Studies and Rawat Publications.

Zelliot, E.(1992) *From Untouchable to Dalit: Essays on Ambedkar Movement*. Manohar Publications New Delhi.

Index